JUDAISM

Postbiblical and Talmudic Period

The Library of Liberal Arts

OSKAR PIEST, FOUNDER

JUDAISM

Postbiblical and Talmudic Period

Edited, with an introduction and notes, by

SALO W. BARON

and

JOSEPH L. BLAU

The Library of Liberal Arts

published by

THE BOBBS-MERRILL COMPANY, INC.

INDIANAPOLIS · NEW YORK

COPYRIGHT © 1954

THE LIBERAL ARTS PRESS, INC.

A Division of
THE BOBBS-MERRILL COMPANY, INC.

Printed in the United States of America

ISBN 0-672-60344-6 (pbk)

ISBN 0-672-51057-X

Library of Congress Catalog Card Number: 55-1342

Seventh Printing

PREFACE

The period with which this volume is concerned, from the Maccabean uprising in the second century B.C. to the completion of the Babylonian Talmud in the fifth century A.D., has long been considered by Jews and Christians alike as the second classical period of Judaism, bringing to new heights the religious developments out of the Hebrew Bible. The Jewish people believed in the unbroken continuity of its tradition from the days of Moses; it recognized no break between "Israelitic" and "Jewish" history, and modern scholarship is coming to accept this view and gradually discounting the hypothesis that there was such a break. The Jewish people regarded the Talmudic literature as simply the spelling out in detail of all the principles laid down with perfect finality in the Torah. Holding this conviction, the Jews were tempted to gloss over entirely the intervening period of Apocryphal writings and of Hellenistic Jewish literature, including Philo and Josephus. All of these owe their influence, even their very preservation, to the belief of the ancient Christian teachers that, together with the Old Testament, they offered the most extensive documentation for the *praeparatio evangelica*. Modern Jewry, however, even outside of scholarly circles, has long since come to appreciate the great independent value of these literary relics of Jewish life and thought at a most crucial period of the transformation of the ancestral Jewish culture from that of a nation centered around its own Commonwealth to that of a diaspora people, with vital contacts, hostile as well as friendly, with the western, Graeco-Roman world.

It is small wonder, then, that these developments have aroused the passionate curiosity of modern scholars. This curiosity has borne fruit in an enormous literature of commentary, some of it of great intrinsic value, that has been accumulating for centuries in the world's libraries. A complete listing of all books and articles pertaining to this period published during any single year of the twentieth century might easily become a multi-volume bibliography. Here, however, we need only refer the reader to such older classics, available in English, as Emil Schürer's *History of the Jewish People in the Time of Jesus Christ* (English translation from the second revised edition), 3 volumes, New York, 1890–91; George Foot Moore's *Judaism in the First Centuries of the Christian Era*, 3 volumes, Cambridge, Mass., 1927–30; Solomon Schechter's *Some Aspects of Rabbinic Theology*, New York, 1909; and Leo Baeck's *Essence of Judaism*, revised edition, New York, 1948. More recent literature is readily available in Robert H. Pfeiffer's *History of New Testament Times*, New York, 1949; and Salo W. Baron's *Social and Religious History of the Jews*, revised edition, volumes I-II, New York, 1952. In view of the ample documentation readily accessible in these works, the compilers of the present small collection were able to reduce their own bibliographical references and explanatory notes to bare essentials.

S.W.B.
J.L.B.

COLUMBIA UNIVERSITY
October, 1953

CONTENTS
. . . .

vii

ACKNOWLEDGMENTS

The editors wish to make special acknowledgment to the following publishers for their permission to quote copyrighted material in the present volume:

Selections from I Maccabees, edited and translated by Sidney Tedesche, and from IV Maccabees, edited and translated by Moses Hadas, both in the Dropsie College edition of Jewish Apocryphal Literature, have been used by the kind permission of The Dropsie College for Hebrew and Cognate Learning, Philadelphia, Pa., and its president, Abraham A. Neuman

Selections from R. H. Charles, The Apocrypha and Pseudepigrapha of the Old Testament are used with the permission of the Oxford University Press, Inc.

Selections from the Loeb Classical Library edition and translation of the works of Philo have been reprinted by permission of the Harvard University Press

Selections from A. Dupont-Sommer, The Dead Sea Scrolls, have been used by permission of The Macmillan Company

Selections from Herbert Danby, The Mishnah, have been used by the kind permission of The Clarendon Press of Oxford, England, and their American representative, the Oxford University Press, Inc.

Selections from the Mekhilta, translated by J. Z. Lauterbach, have been included by permission of The Jewish Publication Society of America

Selections from the Soncino editions of The Babylonian Talmud and The Midrash have been used by the kind permission of The Soncino Press, Ltd., of London. Where deletions in the text of the Soncino translations have been made by the editors, such deletions are indicated by the use of suspension points (...). The annotations which are an important feature of the Soncino editions, making them invaluable for scholarly use, have been omitted by the editors in order to make this volume of selections more easily read by the student who wishes an introduction to the literature of the postbiblical and talmudic periods of Judaism.

NOTE ON THE TEXT

The exact source of each of the selections included in this volume is given in the notes. Square brackets and parentheses appearing in this text are those of the translators, not of the editors. Square brackets indicate the translators' reconstructions of a fragmentary text; parentheses indicate words added by the translators in the interest of euphonious or idiomatic English. To avoid the multiplication of quotation marks, in the sections reproducing late Rabbinic materials Biblical quotations are set in italic type and quotations from the Mishnah are set in small capitals. Titles for the selections and footnotes have been supplied by the editors. While, in general, tampering with the text has been kept to a minimum, there has been an adaptation of both punctuation and spelling to contemporary American usage. Obvious typographical errors have been corrected, and in some few cases a minor slip in translation has been remedied.

INTRODUCTION

In the year 586 B.C., the Kingdom of Judah, home of the Temple of Jerusalem and of its priesthood, was captured by the Babylonians. Many of its inhabitants were driven into exile; the beautiful Temple that had been built during the reign of the great King Solomon was destroyed; the neighboring nomadic tribes rushed into the territory and absorbed the land. Undoubtedly some of the exiles assimilated themselves to the life of Babylonia and to the cosmopolitan delights of its chief city, the world-renowned city of Babylon. Other exiles, among them the prophet Ezekiel, devoted themselves to the task of keeping up the morale of the people, repeating to them the consoling words that the Lord had not abandoned them; that, although they were being punished for their offenses, the time would come when they would again be restored to their former place and the nations that had oppressed them would be punished in their turn. This morale-building task was aided by the work of the scribes, men of learning who devoted themselves to the preservation of the literary remains of the period of Jewish national independence. During the period of exile, too, some modifications of religious practices took place. It was no longer possible to maintain the sacrificial cult of the Temple at Jerusalem; but a memorial of these sacrificial occasions could be preserved by meeting together and repeating the ritual formulas, hymns, and possibly prayers that had been customary accompaniments of the sacrifices. Thus, perhaps for the first time in the history of the Jewish people, a form of congregational worship was developed.

Not quite half a century after the destruction of the Temple, part at least of the exilic community returned to the ancient homeland. The new-risen Persian Empire, under the leadership of Cyrus, King of the Medes and Persians, conquered the mighty Babylonians. Whatever the motivation may have been, one of the early acts of Cyrus was to grant permission to the Judean exiles to return, and to reëstablish their Temple and their cult. Carrying on the work in spite of many hardships and many obstacles, the returned portion of the community rebuilt the Temple, on a much smaller scale; although, because of interruptions, the work was not completed until 515 B.C. The sacrificial cult was reinstituted and carried on without further interruption for a period of about three hundred and fifty years. During this period, the group living in the homeland was only one of a number of Jewish groups living in various parts of the Persian Empire. From time to time, parties of Jews came from Babylonia to join the community in Palestine. One such party, in 458 B.C., was led by Ezra, a scribe who came of a priestly family. Another group came in the train of Nehemiah, cupbearer to the Persian emperor, when he arrived as royal governor in 445 B.C. Ezra's enthusiasm had not produced much of a "reformation" before the arrival of Nehemiah; but when this enthusiasm was coupled with Nehemiah's administrative ability, the religious revival came speedily. This revival was marked by the supplementing of the sacrificial cult, which had become something of a routine affair, with adherence to the "Law of Moses"—a compilation of the materials that had been collected or created by the scribes during the period of exile. The entire people—presumably of the area immediately surrounding Jerusalem, which long constituted the Second Commonwealth— gathered together into what has ever since been known as the Great Assembly; Ezra recited the "Law" to them, and the people in solemn covenant bound themselves to observe its provisions faithfully.

From this time until the conquest of the Persian Empire by Alexander the Great in 334 B.C., a veil of semi-obscurity descends upon the history of the Second Commonwealth of Judea. We know that during this period of obscurity the nominal rulers of the province were Persian satraps, while the actual day-to-day government of the people was in the hands of the High Priests, who merged religious and political functions. It was in describing this form of organization of the community that Josephus the historian used the term "theocracy." [1] Many of the meticulously detailed ritual laws that are preserved in the Biblical books of Leviticus and Numbers presuppose the existence of the sort of social organization characteristic of this period. Undoubtedly the scribes continued to flourish, to collect and edit both newer and older writings of religious value. The people remained largely agricultural. One major schismatic group—that of the Samaritans, with its shrine on Mount Gerizim—emerged during this period.[2]

The people of Judea accepted the conquest by Alexander with little difficulty. Actually, in the first instance, it made very little difference to their lives who chose the formal overlord or governor, as long as they were left undisturbed in their internal community organization. This Alexander the Great seems to have been willing to permit; indeed, he went beyond the Persian rulers who had preceded him in combining his favor to the Jews with hostility toward the Samaritans. This preference made the introduction of Greek culture into Palestine a comparatively easy and friendly process. Especially among the upper classes it became fashionable to ape Greek manners, without abandoning the Jewish religion.

When Alexander died in 323 B.C., there was an internecine struggle among his chief generals for the control of various fragments of the conqueror's empire. These "successors" (*diadochi*) waged furious war with each other; in the end Palestine fell under the sway of the Ptolemies, whose major realm was Egypt. The Seleucids, who ruled over Syria, had claimed Palestine too; and though the Ptolemies achieved rule there, the Seleucid claim was never abandoned. The Ptolemies continued the relatively tolerant policies of Alexander toward the Jews. During the period in which they held sway, the importance and the political influence of the High Priest seem to have increased, although a patrician opposition, spearheaded by the family of Tobias, the tax farmers, developed and threatened to split the community. It was during the period of domination by the Ptolemies that the trans-

[1] See pages 54–63.
[2] See pp. 67–71.

lation of the Bible into Greek was first undertaken.[3] The process of gradual Hellenization continued, with new Greek cities being founded in Palestine and Jewish emigrants settling throughout the Greek world.

Palestine remained under the rule of the Ptolemies for a little more than a century, but the struggle of the Ptolemies and Seleucids for control continued through the whole period, and in fact there were brief intervals during which the Seleucids had temporary domination over the land. In 198 B.C., however, the Seleucid Antiochus the Great overwhelmed the forces of the Ptolemies. Palestine passed into the hands of the Seleucid rulers. Antiochus IV, who became king in 175 B.C., had more missionary zeal for the propagation of Greek culture than his Ptolemaic or Seleucid predecessors. Despite the eager co-operation of the High Priest Jason in promoting Hellenization, Antiochus, who called himself "the manifest god" (*Epiphanes*), was dissatisfied. Complete control over Palestine had become more important to him because of the rise of Rome to power. Instigated by a small but influential party of Jewish "Hellenizers," he decided to attempt by force what he had been unable to do by persuasion or politics: to assimilate the Jews completely to Hellenistic ways of life and beliefs. His regulations, leading to the desecration of the Temple, were enforced with rigor. Jews who resisted were martyred. Finally, under the leadership of the priestly family of the Hasmoneans, Mattathias and his five sons, the people revolted. Judas, the third son of Mattathias, succeeded his father in the leadership of the rebellion. His stalwart efforts earned him the surname Maccabee, a word whose derivation is uncertain; from this surname the revolt is known in history as the Maccabean revolt. Fortunately, Antiochus was not able to muster his full force against the Jewish rebels; nor were his armies able to check the guerrilla tactics of the Judean bands. Finally, in 164 B.C., the Seleucid ruler had to capitulate, to rescind his harsh laws, to permit the forces of the Maccabees to reoccupy Jerusalem. There the successful rebels cleansed and purified the Temple and restored the Jewish worship. The anniversary of the rededication of the Temple, the

[3] See pages 45–48.

twenty-fifth day of Kislev, has been celebrated since that time under the name of *Hanukkah*.[4]

The period between the Maccabean revolt (165 B.C.) and the conclusion of the Babylonian Talmud (about 500 A.D.) has rightly been called the classical period of Judaism. The acceptance of this division must not be taken to mean that there was any sharp break in continuity between the pre-exilic Hebrew religion and the Jewish faith of the post-exilic period. This theory, long held by biblical scholars, has been undermined by more recent investigation. Neither the ancient Jews themselves nor their opponents among early Christian apologists ever claimed that there was such a break. The claim was based entirely upon the dating of the Pentateuch sources by the nineteenth- and twentieth-century school of biblical critics. These critics followed Wellhausen[5] in postulating a serious difference between the prophetic Israelitic religion before the first fall of Jerusalem and the emphasis upon law characteristic of Judaism as it developed in the Persian Empire. Today it is almost universally recognized that the prophetic and legalist strands run side by side throughout the history of the ancient Jewish religion, both before and after the Babylonian Exile. There were differences in the respective emphases at one time or another, but no fundamental divergencies in approach, belief, or ritual.

Nevertheless, the Hellenistic and Roman periods brought some of the older trends to a focus and modified them under the impact of an unprecedented situation. In the Persian Empire of the Achaemenids, the extent of which exceeded even that of the Roman Empire, the Jews had met a variety of civilizations. They had been stimulated by them and had injected, in return, significant ingredients of their own into the amalgam of races and beliefs that constituted Persian culture. Under Hellenism, how-

---

[4] See pages 4–6.

[5] Julius Wellhausen (1844–1918) was the systematizer of earlier "higher criticism" of the biblical text. The positions he espoused, especially in his *Geschichte Israels*, 1878 (English translation from the second edition, *Prolegomena to the History of Israel*, 1895), were extreme and have not been upheld by later textual analysis.

ever, which was in itself a mixture of Greek and Oriental elements, a new universal civilization had developed, pervading all walks of life in the vast area from Greece to India. Jews, too, both those living in Palestine and those in larger numbers inhabiting the lands of the diaspora, were profoundly influenced by Hellenism, the new civilization. Not only the Greek language, but also Greek modes of thinking, Greek legal and political institutions, and Greek economic as well as social ways of life had penetrated deeply into the Jewish outlook and mode of living. At the crucial moment, however, when the fate of the Jewish religion hung in the balance, the Maccabean revolt not only reasserted the Jewish tradition but also, in many ways, helped to set in motion an Oriental reaction which gathered momentum in later centuries, and brought about a new and preponderantly Oriental synthesis of East and West that ultimately culminated in the victorious expansion of Islam.

In this clash between East and West, Jewish leadership, both in the homeland and in the dispersion, had to keep on defending its own position against the overwhelmingly assimilatory forces in the new environment and to persuade principally its own adherents, but also some outsiders, of the righteousness of its cause. The Maccabean revolt itself in some ways brought significant new concepts into the world. Not only was it unprecedented as a war of religion—until that time wars were fought over political and economic issues, religion playing but a secondary role—but it also created a new form of religious martyrdom. Suffering death for one's religious conviction, even in the hope of earning thereby a reward in the hereafter, was essentially different from death on the battlefield or even self-sacrifice on behalf of one's individual conviction. It is small wonder that in the later, particularly Christian tradition the Maccabeans were remembered more as martyrs than as fighters for national independence.

In addition, the Jews developed an apologetic literature in the struggle to maintain their identity. Jewish apologists did not limit themselves to self-defense. In Egypt especially they went over to the offensive. In many writings that undoubtedly reflect the endless oral discussions between Jews and their neighbors on all levels of society, protagonists of the Jewish faith argued with great vigor and persuasiveness the superiority of Jewish religious and ethical values over those of the pagan majority. The ensuing debate was rather one-sided. Spokesmen for the pagan faith did not consider it necessary to reply in detail until after the rise of the Christian menace. Only occasionally did they attack the Jewish people and its religion, and then in general, rather vague terms that gave rise to an inferior brand of antisemitic literature. These writings of classical antisemitism ultimately produced even so-called "Acts of Heathen Martyrs." Nevertheless, a great many Gentiles who were dissatisfied with their ancestral faith joined Judaism either as full-fledged proselytes or as partially converted God-fearing non-Jews. Ultimately, it seems that, as a result of such conversions and, even more, of great natural growth and free migratory movements, the Jews amounted to some 10 per cent of the population of the Roman Empire and exceeded that ratio in many eastern provinces.

Such external challenges, combined with internal strains in the socially restless Palestinian homeland, generated conflicting forces of religious syncretism and sectarianism. In the two centuries before the second fall of Jerusalem, in 70 A.D., the Palestinian scene was filled with violent controversy, out of which emerged the sectarian movements of Pharisees, Sadducees, Essenes, and so-called New Covenanters, in addition to the older sect of Samaritans. These heteredox currents, often permeated by strong messianic expectation, finally gave rise to Christianity.

The crisis of 70 A.D. forced a far more rigorous reformulation of Judaism than any event in Jewish history since the Babylonian Exile. With the second destruction of the Temple and the utter destruction of all political possibilities for the ruling priestly and Sadducean aristocracy, dynamic leadership in the attempt to consolidate what was left of the Jewish people and their religion passed into the hands of the Pharisees. This group almost immediately suppressed all other sectarian movements except Samaritanism. A complete break between Pharisaic Judaism and the nascent Christian Church came about. From this time Pharisaism held undisputed sway over the Jewish people, both in Palestine and in the communities of the diaspora. Under the leadership of Rabbi Johanan ben Zakkai and his successors, Pharisaic Judaism reformulated the whole system of Jewish beliefs and practices. For about three centuries the intellectual and religious life of the Pharisaic and Rabbinic Jews in Palestine was intense and vigorous. During the third and fourth centuries A.D., however, the Palestinian center grew weaker. Leadership among the Rabbis shifted to Babylonian Jewry, living under the then relatively tolerant rule of Sassanian Persia. The Babylonian Jewish scholars, amplifying the basis provided by their predecessors in Palestine, continued the elaboration of the Jewish religious structure down to its minutest details. It is this elaboration that is preserved to us in the Talmud.

The new work of reformulation had an inward orientation that eschewed not only internal sectarian movements but also much of the external influence. Talmudic Judaism concentrated on the sources of its own tradition with little, if any, reference to those outside pressures. The rabbinic leadership, concentrated in the outstanding academies of Yabneh, Usha, Tiberias, and Sepphoris in Palestine, and Nehardea, Sura, and Pumbedita in Babylonia, pursued the policy of ignoring antagonistic forces rather than overtly combating them. The work of reconstruction was limited to making positive restatements of the religious and moral duties of each Jew and of every Jewish community. Judaism now halted the open missionary activity that it had carried on before the second fall of Jerusalem and pursued instead an ambivalent policy toward proselytism. As one ancient rabbi expressed it, "The right hand shall attract while the left hand repels." Without giving up its ultimate aspirations toward universal acceptance, and without relinquishing for a moment its belief in a universal God and the universal validity of the Torah ordained by him, Judaism in the period from 70 A.D. to about 500 A.D. concentrated on developing those particularistic features that were to safeguard the continued existence of the chosen people, deprived of its moorings in its state and, soon, in its own land.

These tragic vicissitudes of the people and its religious struggle found memorable expression in literature. The literary creativity of the biblical age continued without interruption. Palestinian Jewry and, to a lesser extent, Egyptian Jewry produced memorable works along the lines of the Old Testament literature during the period of Seleucid and Roman domination. While no new prophets arose to take their place alongside of the ancient *nebiim*, a large number of anonymous writers added significant works to the historical, poetic, and wisdom literature of the earlier post-exilic era. Going far beyond Ezekiel, a new apocalyptic literature produced visions of great emotional intensity which, in their very ambiguity, stirred the imagination of many generations of men and gave rise to a kaleidoscopic variety of theosophic and eschatological speculations. Some of the new works found their way into the Old Testament canon, which was laid down with finality soon after Jerusalem had fallen under Roman attacks. Among these Old Testament writings of the new era, the Book of Ecclesiastes stands out as an example of the interpenetration of Hellenistic and Jewish thought patterns; while the Book of Daniel, largely arising out of the Maccabean revolt, is a supreme example of the new apocalyptic visions and messianic expectations. Other works of this type were refused inclusion in the canon on dogmatic or esthetic grounds. Nevertheless some of these writings were of extraordinary beauty and bore a great religious message. Probably only a small number of those written have been salvaged for posterity and included in extracanonical collections, which have come to be known under the name of "Apocrypha and Pseudepigrapha."

Since the Jewish masses even in Palestine no longer spoke Hebrew, it also became necessary to make their literary heritage available to them in either Aramaic or Greek, the two regional languages of the period. According to tradition, the Aramaic version of the Pentateuch had already been produced in the days of Ezra in the fifth century B.C. Whether or not this tradition is reliable, Aramaic versions of individual books of the Old Testament seem to have been in existence long before the second fall of Jerusalem, although the Aramaic translations now going under the name of "Onkelos," Jonathan ben Uziel, and the "Palestinian

Targum" are all of a late talmudic and even posttalmudic vintage. Better preserved, though not necessarily in its original form, is the Greek translation accomplished largely by the Egyptian Jews in the third and second centuries B.C. Because it was regarded as a divinely inspired work of seventy translators (in accordance with a story narrated in the Letter of Aristeas and briefly summarized with variations in the talmudic literature[6]) it went under the name Septuagint. The Septuagint translation in our possession, however, as represented by ancient manuscripts and papyri, does not bear out the traditional story. It is the residuum of various translations made at different times, by different authors, almost all of whom were animated by specific apologetic and allegorical preconceptions of Egyptian Jewry. Since this version lent itself admirably to the allegorical interpretation of Christian missionaries, Palestinian Jewish leadership, after the fall of Jerusalem, encouraged Aquila ('Aqilas) to produce a more literal Greek version. With the decline of the Jewish communities in the Roman Empire, however, Aquila's translation, together with other Greek versions prepared by such Jews as Symmachus or Theodotion, and possibly also some Latin translations, almost totally vanished from use in the synagogue, while the Aramaic versions used in Babylonia and other eastern communities grew in importance and assumed virtually a semicanonical authority.

In addition to these translations of the Scriptures, there were other religious writings of Hellenistic Jewry. The Jews of Alexandria were participants in the broad stream of the new cultural diffusion, and some of them tried to reinterpret Judaism to the Greeks in Greek terms. Formally, their literature is Greek, not only in language but also in its general outlook and method. Whether they wrote Greek epics or drama, or composed histories or chronologies in the vein of the contemporary Greek and Roman historians, or even philosophical and theological treatises, these writers followed unquestioningly the accepted Greek models. In content, however, these works were all apologetic defenses of the Jewish faith and people. Rarely did they directly attack other religions. Only the Jewish and later Christian poets who wrote

[6] See pages 45–48.

under the guise of the ancient Sibylla mingled their prediction of the eventual victory of Jewish monotheism with deprecatory allusions to contemporary pagan creeds. The others, like Philo, were prepared to accept the essential greatness of Greek philosophy, but tried to point out that all its truths had already been communicated to the world by Moses and later Israelitic prophets, and that there was no essential distinction between the noblest insights of Greek thought and the beliefs formulated in the Old Testament. The Greeks had used allegorical methods to interpret the Homeric poems; Hellenistic Jewish writers applied these methods to the Bible, revealing hidden truths underlying its literal meaning. Stylistically, too, the Jewish writers followed Greek models; an ancient popular adage had it that one could not tell "whether Philo writes like Plato or Plato like Philo." In substance, on the other hand, they were unflinchingly Jewish, as patriotic and loyal as any Palestinian Jew. Philo especially extolled every detail of Jewish law, while the Egyptian author of the Third Book of Maccabees voiced what was almost the equivalent of a modern ultra-Zionist rejection of diaspora existence. Even Josephus, a Palestinian Pharisee who, by his own admission, played a very ambiguous role in the crucial war with Rome and who wrote his historical and apologetic work at the imperial court of Rome, made great concessions in the political and cultural domains, but staunchly adhered to his conviction of the religious superiority of Judaism.

Greek influence accounts for much of the literary creativity in still another sense. The very act of confiding one's thoughts to writing now became much more prevalent than it had been in the pre-Hellenistic period. Even after Alexander, the Oriental peoples, including the Jews, continued to cultivate and amplify their oral tradition in all forms. Only a small part of this oral tradition ultimately found its way into a written record. Of this record only a tiny fraction has been preserved in the biblical and postbiblical literature. It is almost impossible to estimate the number of oral traditions communicated from generation to generation and increased by new sayings, legal commandments or prohibitions, judicial precedents, tales, and moralistic apothegms by anonymous spokesmen in each new generation. Modern man often has difficulty in gauging the extent and faithfulness of such oral transmission. A part of the training of almost every student consisted in developing exactitude in memorizing and repeating statements heard from teachers. There also were professional memorizers at temples and schools of higher learning, whose duty it was to preserve for posterity such traditional lore without the slightest alteration. The rabbis were so firmly convinced of the superiority of oral over written transmission that they long discouraged the writing down of the oral law. They avowed their apprehension that the written copies might differ from one another, and thus cause dissension in Israel. They were prepared to rely rather on controlled oral transmission, in which relatively minor differences could more readily be ironed out through discussion in the academies.

In the end, however, the rabbis had to give up their resistance and themselves help to prepare written summaries of their centuries-old oral teachings. The compilation of selected traditions from the entire body of Jewish law was entirely a work of the second century A.D. It was begun by Rabbi Akiba, early in the century, continued by Rabbi Meir and concluded by R. Judah the Patriarch with the assistance of his academy, at the end of the century. The resulting product, called the *Mishnah,* a systematic code divided, as we shall presently see, into six orders and subdivided into sixty tractates, may or may not have been committed to writing during R. Judah's own lifetime. Before very long, however, written copies by rabbis of the third and fourth centuries began to circulate both in Palestine and Babylonia. These elicited a great many supplementary comments.

The *Mishnah* was but a small selection from the existing traditional material. Even before R. Judah, compilations had been made of similar sayings and interpretations, arranged in accordance with the sequence of the Books of Moses. These collections (Mekhilta, on Exodus; Sifra, on Leviticus; and Sifre, on Numbers and Deuteronomy) are known as the Halakhic [legal] Midrashim because they offer hermeneutic conclusions drawn from scriptural passages largely relating to Jewish law. Since the Book of Genesis contains but few laws, no compilation was prepared to follow its sequence. More in accordance with the systematic division of the Mishnah was the Tosefta, apparently prepared by disciples of R. Judah the Patriarch. Divided like the Mishnah in the same six orders of sixty tractates, this compilation contains, as its name indicates, additional material which for one reason or another was not included by R. Judah himself. Still other material, dating before the end of the second century, is available in the Baraitot, which are selections from such older sources quoted in either the Babylonian or the Palestinian Talmud. Many other sayings of rabbis came to light in still later sources. With all these, we have at our disposal what is evidently but a tiny fraction of the oral tradition handed down from generation to generation in ancient times.

With the compilation of the Mishnah, the age of the classic sages called Tannaim came to an end. They were followed by the Amoraim of the third to the fifth centuries, who considered themselves inferior in learning to their predecessors. These rabbis, some of them of the highest intellectual acumen and, from the historical standpoint, hardly less authoritative than the sages before 200 A.D., concentrated on explaining the ramifications of the laws included in the Mishnah. For this purpose they utilized the older Tannaitic materials now available, as well as much that has undoubtedly been lost. At the same time, they continued their independent intellectual creativity, particularly in the direct hermeneutic interpretation of Scripture. Like their predecessors, they lectured to students in academies, delivered sermons before public audiences, and established legal precedents by administering the law. The new learning thus produced served as a basis for new and ambitious compilations (Talmudim) in both Palestine and Babylonia. In both countries academies undertook to arrange this vast body of material, once again in a selective fashion, following the sequence of the Mishnah tractates. As a result of outward pressures, however, and of the growing anarchy of Jewish life in Palestine within a century after Constantine, the work on the Palestinian Talmud was never completely finished. That is why our text of that Talmud reveals many of the weaknesses of an editorially unfinished product. The Babylonian Talmud fared somewhat better. Beginning with R. Ashi (died 427 A.D.), several generations of Babylonian leaders participated in this work of redaction. Apparently not committed to writing for a long time thereafter, that compilation too lacks some of the finishing touches by the editor. This deficiency was made up only in part by the Saboraim, scholars and commentators of the sixth and seventh centuries.

The two Talmudim repeat the text of the Mishnah with some relatively minor variations and add the discussions and comments of the Amoraim. In them was embodied the main intellectual output of the Jewish people from 100 to 500 A.D. Some of the sources go back much further, in fact partly to immemorial antiquity. The rabbis themselves were convinced that their tradition represented an oral law revealed to Moses on Sinai together with the written Torah. Modern critical scholarship, too, increasingly realizes not only that the biblical law as now summarized in the Pentateuch is itself the outgrowth of old traditions extended over centuries, but also that it offers merely a small selection from the oral traditions current in biblical days. Such oral transmission and creativity, particularly through adjustments to changing conditions, continued throughout the second commonwealth. Much of that traditional lore, cherished and cultivated by the Pharisees,[7] ultimately found its way, together with later accretions and modifications, into the Talmud. This is also true of much of the nonlegal material, the so-called Aggaddah. In the latter were collected legends concerning the patriarchs, Moses, and other biblical heroes; tales of events, historical as well as apocryphal, of a later date; ethical epigrams, dialogues between Jews and non-Jews, and hermeneutic lessons derived from Scripture, concerning almost any phase of human life. While the Mishnah steers rather clear of this Aggaddic material, some of it is included in the Halakhic Midrashim and the Tosefta. Both Talmudim are replete with it. The bulk of this ancient lore, however, orally transmitted for many generations, ultimately found its way into the Aggaddic Midrashim. Some of these were compiled

[7] See the chain of tradition cited on pages 102–107.

before the end of the talmudic period. For the most part, however, they date from the later centuries almost to the end of the Middle Ages. But even the younger midrashim contain indubitably authentic material going back even to the Tannaitic age. In any case we must remember that—

the Talmud is primarily *law*. This truism needs special emphasis, in view of tendencies in recent generations to elevate the aggadic or legendary part of it to a position of prominence which it certainly does not deserve in the perspective of talmudic doctrine. To the Talmudist, law really mattered, while the Aggadah represented an accession of often irresponsible, private and uncontrolled tales and opinions which, even if incorporated in the Talmud or Midrash, did not by any means become representative of the whole of Judaism. Even the reiterated saying, "One must not question an Aggadah," merely intended to convey the idea of the latter's irrationality, not of its indisputable authority.[8]

On the other hand, law itself far transcended the boundaries of what in modern civilization is considered its legitimate domain. To civil and criminal law, both the Mishnah and Talmud devoted only one of the six orders, namely the fourth. Family law, including marriage and divorce, is treated in the bulk of the third order. The first two orders are entirely devoted to agricultural laws, including the various benedictions to be pronounced before the consumption of food and other occasions, and to those governing the observance of Jewish Sabbaths and holidays. The last two orders are even more ritualistic. They are largely devoted to the problems connected with Temple sacrifices and other rituals, and with the laws of purity. After the fall of Jerusalem in 70 A.D., and particularly in the Jewish communities of the dispersion, the agricultural laws and those ritual laws dealt with in the last two sections progressively lost their importance in Jewish life. These changes are reflected in the differences between the Palestinian and Babylonian Talmudim. The Palestinian Talmud still comments at great length on the entire first section of the Mishnah, whereas the Babylonian Talmud limits its remarks and extensions

[8] Salo W. Baron, *A Social and Religious History of the Jews*, revised edition (New York, Columbia University Press, 1952), Vol. II, p. 298.

on the first order solely to the tractate dealing with benedictions. Both Talmudim limit very greatly their discussions of regulations concerning the menstruating woman, as found in the last two orders of the Mishnah. Among both Palestinian and Babylonian rabbis, comment was made only on regulations that continued to be observed after the destruction of the Temple. In neither Talmud is there any comment on regulations that could not be observed in the changed circumstances of Jewish life. Again, the Babylonian Talmud alone has much to say on the tractate concerning nonsacrificial food (*hullin*) included in the fifth order.

In all these respects, the talmudic and extratalmudic literature of ancient Jewry reflects the all-embracing realities of Jewish life of the period. Judaism itself was not merely a religion, according to our modern terminology, but also a national culture of Palestinian Jewry and a slightly modified ethnic-religious culture of the Jewish community in the dispersion. As such, it embraced all domains of individual and group life, and placed the entire behavior of each individual and the community at large under the sanction of a divinely ordained law. Compelled by outside pressures increasingly to withdraw into its inner self, but at the same time protected in the exercise of its ethnic-religious self-determination by the laws of both the pagan and the Christian Roman Empire, the Jewish people weathered all storms, cultivating and enlarging upon its already millennial heritage.

SALO W. BARON

COLUMBIA UNIVERSITY   JOSEPH L. BLAU
March, 1953

PART ONE

APOCRYPHAL MATERIALS

I

THE MACCABEAN BOOKS

The four books of Maccabees are connected chiefly by their common name and by the persistent themes of religious persecution, the staunch loyalty of martyrs, and the special concern of God for the Jews. The First and Second Books of Maccabees contain a historical account of the Maccabean revolt, some of the tales of devotion and heroism associated with this revolt, and its victorious culmination in the rededication of the Temple, the occasion for the establishment of the feast of Hanukkah. While the First Book covers a period of some forty years, to the death of the High Priest and King Simon (175–135 B.C.), the Second Book, an epitome of a five-book narrative by Jason of Cyrene, deals only with the early years of the revolt (to 161 B.C.). The Third Book details another example of the well-nigh miraculous preservation of the Jews in a time of persecution under the Egyptian King Ptolemy IV, Philopator (about 217 B.C.). The Fourth Book is basically a homiletic expansion of one of the tales of heroism in II Maccabees, and includes the discourse on reason and the passions (a typical Stoic theme) which is reproduced below.

Various theories have been advanced as to the dates of these four books. These critical theories are summarized, and full bibliographical references given, in the works referred to in the Preface. In the light of the variety of theories, it is still safe to assume that the first two books originated soon after the events narrated in them and, even in their present form, date from the late second or early first century B.C. The Third Book, revealing keen resentment of Jewish Diaspora existence, was probably written shortly before or after the beginning of the Christian era, while the composition of the Fourth Book, too, preceded the fall of Jerusalem in 70 A.D.

THE REDEDICATION OF THE TEMPLE [1]

JUDAH AND HIS BROTHERS SAID: "Now that our enemies are crushed, let us go up to purify and dedicate the sanctuary."

The entire army gathered together and went up to Mount Zion. They saw the sanctuary desolated and the altar profaned, the gates burned up, and weeds growing in the courts as in a forest or as on one of the mountains, and the priests' chambers torn down. They tore their garments and made great lamentation, and put ashes on their heads, and fell on their faces on the ground, blew solemn blasts upon the trumpets, and cried out to Heaven. Judah appointed certain men to fight against the garrison in the citadel, until he could cleanse the sanctuary. He selected priests without blemish, whose delight was in the Law, and they purified the sanctuary, carrying out the stones that had defiled it into an unclean place. They took counsel as to what they should do about the altar of burnt offering, which had been defiled. A good plan occurred to them, namely, to tear it down, lest it become a reproach to them, because the heathen had defiled it. So they pulled down the altar, and put away the stones in the Temple mount, in a suitable place, until a prophet should come to decide what to do with them. They took whole stones, according to the Law, and constructed a new altar like the former one. They built the sanctuary and the interior of the Temple, and hallowed the courts, and made new holy vessels, and brought the candlestick, the altar of incense and the table into the Temple. They burned incense on the altar, and lit the lights on the candlestick so that they would shed light in the Temple. They put loaves of bread upon the table, hung up the curtains, and finished all the work which they had undertaken to do.

On the twenty-fifth day of the ninth month, that is the month of Kislev, in the one hundred and forty-ninth year,[2] they arose early and offered sacrifice according to the Law upon the new altar of burnt offering which they had made. At the same time and on the same day on which the heathen had profaned it, on that very day it was consecrated with songs and harps and lutes and cymbals. All the people fell on their faces and prostrated themselves, and uttered praises to Heaven who had caused them to prosper. They celebrated the dedication of the altar for eight days, brought burnt offerings with joy, and offered a sacrifice of deliverance and praise. They also adorned the front of the Temple with golden crowns and small shields, and rededicated the gates and the priests' chambers, and fitted them with doors. Thus there was great joy among the people, and the reproach caused by the heathen was removed. Judah and his brothers and the entire congregation of Israel decreed that the days of the dedication of the altar should be kept with gladness and joy at their due season, year after year, for eight days from the twenty-fifth of the month of Kislev. At that time they built high walls and strong 'owers around Mount Zion, so that the heathen could never again come and destroy them, as they had done before. He especially assigned a garrison there, to guard it, and fortified Beth Zur,[3] so that the people might have a fortification facing Idumaea.

THE ORIGIN OF HANUKKAH[4]

To the brethren, the Jews in Egypt, greeting. The brethren, the Jews in Jerusalem and throughout the land of Judaea, wish you perfect peace; yea, may God do good unto you, and remember his covenant with Abraham and Isaac and Jacob, his faithful servants; may he give you all a heart to worship him and do his pleasure with hearty courage and a willing soul; may he give you an open heart for his law and for his statutes, and make peace, and hearken to your supplications; may he be reconciled to you, and .1ot forsake you in time of evil. Such, then, are our prayers for you in this place. In the reign of Demetrius, in the hundred threescore and ninth year,[5] we the Jews have already written unto you in the extreme tribulation that came upon us during these years, from the time that Jason and his company revolted from the holy land and the kingdom, setting the porch on fire and shedding innocent blood; but we besought the Lord and were heard; we offered sacrifice and made the meal offering, we lighted the lamps and set forth the showbread. See that ye keep the days of the feast of tabernacles in the month Kislev. Written in the hundred fourscore and eighth year.[6]

THE SEVEN BROTHERS [7]

It also came to pass that seven brothers and their mother were arrested and shamefully lashed with whips and scourges, by the King's orders, that they might be forced to taste the abominable swine's flesh. But one of them spoke up for the others and said, "Why question us? What wouldst thou learn from us? We are prepared to die sooner than transgress the laws of our fathers." Then the King, in his exasperation, ordered pans and caldrons to be heated, and, when they were heated immediately, ordered the tongue of the speaker to be torn out, had him scalped and mutilated before the eyes of his brothers and mother, and then had him put on the fire, all maimed and crippled as he was, but still alive, and set to fry in the pan. And as the vapor from the pan spread abroad, they and their mother exhorted one another to die nobly, uttering these words: "The Lord God beholdeth this, and truly hath compassion on us, even as Moses declared in his Song which testifieth against them to their face, saying, 'And he shall have compassion on his servants.'"

And when the first had died after this manner, they brought the second to the shameful torture, tearing off the skin of his head with the hair and asking him, "Wilt thou eat, before we punish thy body limb by limb?" But he answered in the language of his fathers and said to them, "No." So he too underwent the rest of the torture, as the first had done. And when he was at the last gasp, he said, "Thou cursed miscreant! Thou dost dispatch us from this life, but the King of the world shall raise us up, who have died for his laws, and revive us to life everlasting." And after him the third was made a mockingstock. And when he was told to put out his tongue, he did so at once, stretching forth his hands courageously, with the noble words, "These I had from Heaven; for his name's sake I count them naught; from him I hope to get them back again." So much so that the King himself and his company were astounded at the spirit of the youth, for he thought nothing of his sufferings. And when he too was dead, they tortured the fourth in the same shameful fashion. And when he was near his end, he said: "'Tis meet for those who perish at men's hands to cherish hope divine that they shall be raised up by God again, but thou—thou shalt have no resurrection to life." Next they brought the fifth and handled him shamefully. But he looked at the King and said, "Holding authority among men, thou doest what thou wilt, poor mortal; but dream not that God hath forsaken our race. Go on, and thou shalt find how his sovereign power will torture thee and thy seed!" And after him they brought the sixth. And when he was at the point of death, he said, "Deceive not thyself in vain! We are suffering this on our own account, for sins against our own God. That is why these awful horrors have befallen us. But think not thou shalt go unpunished for daring to fight against God!" The mother, however, was a perfect wonder; she deserves to be held in glorious memory, for, thanks to her hope in God, she bravely bore the sight of seven sons dying in a single day. Full of noble spirit and nerving her weak woman's heart with the courage of a man, she exhorted each of them in the language of their fathers, saying, "How you were ever conceived in my womb, I cannot tell! 'Twas not I who gave you the breath of life or fashioned the elements of each! 'Twas the Creator of the world who fashioneth men and deviseth the generating of all things, and he it is who in mercy will restore to you the breath of life even as you now count yourselves naught for his laws' sake." Now Antiochus felt that he was being humiliated, but, overlooking the taunt of her words, he made an appeal to the youngest brother, who still survived, and even promised on oath to make him rich and happy, and a friend and a trusted official of state, if he would give up his fathers' laws. As the young man paid no attention to him, he summoned his mother and exhorted her to counsel the lad to save himself. So, after he had exhorted her at length, she agreed to persuade her son. She leaned over to him and, befooling the cruel tyrant, spoke thus in her fathers' tongue, "My son, have pity on me. Nine months I carried thee in my womb, three years I suckled thee; I reared thee and brought thee up to this age of thy life. Child, I beseech thee, lift thine eyes to heaven and earth, look at all that is therein, and know that God did not make them out of the things that existed. So is the race of men created. Fear not this butcher, but show thyself worthy of thy brothers and accept thy death, that by God's mercy I may receive thee again together with thy brothers." Ere she had finished, the young man cried, "What are you waiting for? I will not obey the King's command, I will obey the command of the law given by Moses to our fathers. But thou, who hast devised all manner of evil against the Hebrews, thou shalt not escape the hands of God. We are suffering for our own sins, and though our living Lord is angry for a little, in order to rebuke and chasten us, he will again be reconciled to his own servants. But thou, thou impious wretch, vilest of all men, be not vainly uplifted with thy proud, uncertain hopes, raising thy hand against the heavenly children; thou hast not yet escaped the judgment of the Almighty God who seeth all. These our brothers, after enduring a brief pain, have now drunk of ever-flowing life, in terms of God's covenant, but thou shalt receive by God's judgment the just penalty of thine arrogance. I, like my brothers, give up body and soul for our fathers' laws, calling on God to show favor to our nation soon, and to make thee acknowledge, in torment and plagues, that he alone is God, and to let the Almighty's wrath, justly fallen on the whole of our nation, end in me and in my brothers." Then the King fell into a passion and had him handled worse than the others, so exasperated was he at being mocked. Thus he also died unpolluted, trusting absolutely in the Lord. Finally after her sons the mother also perished.

Let this suffice for the enforced sacrifices and the excesses of barbarity.

THE PRAYER OF SIMON THE HIGH PRIEST [8]

Then the High Priest Simon,[9] bowing his knees before the holy place, and spreading out his hands in calm reverence, prayed after this manner: "Lord, Lord, King of the heavens, and sovereign of all creation, holy among the holy ones, only ruler, almighty, give ear to us who are grievously troubled by one wicked and profane, made wanton in insolence and might. For thou who has created all things and governest the whole world are a righteous ruler, and judgest those who do aught in violence and arrogance. Thou didst destroy those who aforetime did iniquity, among whom were giants trusting in their strength and boldness, bringing upon them a boundless flood of water. Thou didst burn up with fire and brimstone the men of Sodom, workers of arrogance, who had become known of all for their crimes, and didst make them an example to those who should come after. Thou didst try with manifold and grievous punishments the insolent Pharaoh when he enslaved thy holy people Israel, and didst make known thy mighty power. And when he pursued with chariots and a multitude of peoples thou didst overwhelm him in the depth of the sea, but those who trusted in thee, the ruler of all creation, thou didst bring safely through. And they, seeing the works of thy hands, did praise thee, the almighty. Thou, O King, when thou didst create the boundless and measureless earth, didst choose this city and sanctify this place for thy name for thyself, who hast need of nothing, and didst glorify it by a splendid manifestation, establishing it to the glory of thy great and honorable name. And loving the house of Israel, thou didst promise that if there should be a falling away, and distress should overtake us, and we should come to this place and make our supplication, thou wouldst hear our prayer. And indeed thou art faithful and true. And seeing that oftentimes when our fathers were afflicted thou didst succor them in their humiliation, and didst deliver them from great evils, behold now, O holy King, for our many great sins we are grievously troubled and put into subjection to our foes, and faint in weakness. In our low estate this insolent and profane man seeketh to do violence to the holy place which is consecrated upon earth to the name of thy glory. For man cannot reach thy dwelling place, the heaven of heavens. But since thy good pleasure was in thy glory amongst thy people Israel, thou didst hallow this place. Punish us not by the uncleanness of these men, neither chastise us by their profane doings, lest the transgressors boast in their wrath or exult in the insolence of their tongue, saying, 'We have trodden down the house of the sanctuary as the houses of the abominations are trodden down.' Blot out our sins and scatter abroad our offenses and manifest thy mercy at this hour. Let thy compassion speedily overtake us, and put praises in the mouth of the fallen and broken in heart, granting us peace."

REASON AND THE PASSIONS [10]

Our inquiry, then, is whether reason is sovereign over the emotions. We must determine what reason is, and what emotion is, how many types of emotion there are, and whether reason holds the mastery over all of them. Reason, then, is the intellect choosing with correct judgment the life of wisdom; and wisdom is knowledge of things human and divine, and of their causes. Such wisdom is education in the Law, through which we learn things divine reverently and things human advantageously. The types comprised in wisdom are prudence, justice, courage, and temperance. Of these prudence has the greatest authority of all, for it is through it that reason rules over the emotions. Of the emotions the two most comprehensive classes are pleasure and pain, and of these each involves both the body and the soul. A numerous suite of emotions attends upon both pleasure and pain: desire precedes pleasure, and joy follows after pleasure; fear precedes pain, and sorrow follows after pain. Anger is an emotion common to both pleasure and pain, if one considers how it affects him. Under pleasure, too, is included malicious temper, which presents the most varied aspects of all the emotions: those of the soul are braggadocio and avarice and publicity seeking and quarrelsomeness and backbiting; those of the body are indiscriminate voracity and gluttony and secret gormandizing. Pleasure and pain thus being as it were two branches burgeoning from body and soul, there are many offshoots of these emotions. Each of these, reason, the universal gardener, purges and prunes and binds up and waters and irrigates by diverse devices, and so tames the wild growth of inclinations and emotions. For reason is the guide of virtues, and of emotions the sovereign.

Observe in the first place how, in the case of deeds which hamper temperance, reason is sovereign over the emotions. Temperance is in fact mastery over desires, of which some pertain to the soul and others to the body; over both of these reason manifestly exercises mastery. How is it that when we are drawn to forbidden foods we turn away from the pleasures they afford? Is it not because reason possesses the power to master the appetites? I think it is. When we crave seafood or fowl or quadrupeds or any sort of food which is forbidden to us according to the Law, it is due to the mastery of reason that we abstain. For the emotions of the appetites are reduced and checked by the temperate intellect, and all the motions of the body are muzzled by reason.

What wonder then if the desires of the soul for union with beauty lose their force? It is for this reason that the praise of the temperate Joseph is merited: rationality gave him the upper hand over voluptuousness; though a young man and at the prime of sexual appetite, he frustrated the goad of passion by the force of reason. And not only over the goadings of voluptuousness is reason seen to possess mastery, but over all desire, for the Law says, "Thou shalt not covet thy neighbor's wife nor anything that is his." Well then, if the Law has bidden us not to covet, it becomes easier for me to persuade you that reason is able to exercise rule over the desires.

And so it does over the emotions which hamper justice; for how could a man whose character is that of a secret gormandizer or glutton, or even a drunkard, be reformed by education unless it were evident that reason is lord over the emotions? As soon as a man subjects his conduct to the Law, then even if he be covetous he constrains his own inclination and lends to the needy without interest, canceling the debt at the approach of the seven-year period. And if a man be niggardly he rules himself through reason to obey the Law, and neither to glean over his harvested fields nor to garner the last grapes on his vines.

And so in other instances also we are enabled to perceive that reason holds mastery over the emotions. For the Law prevails even over benevolence to parents, and will not for their sake betray virtue; it maintains the upper hand over love for a wife, and chides her for transgression; it takes precedence over love for children, and punishes their wickedness; and it bears sway over the attachment of friends, and rebukes them for evil. Nor must you regard it as a paradox that reason is able to bear rule even over enmity; the fruit trees of the enemy must not be cut down, one must save cattle of a personal enemy and help raise his beast up if it has fallen.

Reason manifestly holds mastery over the more violent emotions also—love of authority, vain self-esteem, braggadocio, arrogance, backbiting; all these malicious emotions the temperate intellect thrusts out, as it does anger, for over anger too it holds sway. Moses was indeed angry at Dathan and Abiram,[11] yet he took no measure against them in anger, but regulated his anger by reason. For the temperate intellect, as I have said, is able to triumph over the emotions and to transform some of them and render others impotent. Why else did our eminently wise father Jacob inculpate Simeon and Levi and their friends for massacring, without employing reason, the whole tribe of Shechemites,[12] and exclaim, "Cursed be their anger?" Unless reason were able to master anger, he would not have so spoken. When God fashioned man He implanted in him emotions and inclinations, but at the same time He enthroned intellect, through the agency of the senses, as the sacred guide over all. To the intellect He gave the Law, and he who lives subject to it shall reign over a realm of temperance, and justice, and goodness, and courage.

How is it then, someone may object, if reason is lord of the emotions that it has no mastery over forgetfulness and ignorance? Such logic is altogether laughable, for reason is manifestly master not of its own emotions but of those [contrary to justice, courage, temperance, and prudence; and of these it is master, not in order to destroy them, but in order not to yield to them]. None of you, for example, can extirpate desire, but reason can secure that you be not enslaved to desire. Anger none of you can extirpate from his soul, but reason is able to assuage anger. Malice none of you can extirpate, but reason may be your ally in not submitting to malice. For reason is not the uprooter of emotions but their antagonist.

This can be explained quite clearly by the story of King David's thirst. David had been fighting against the Philistines for a whole day, and with the soldiers of his own people had slain many of them; and then when evening fell he went to the royal pavilion around which the entire army of our forebears was bivouacked. All of the others addressed themselves to their supper, but the King, intensely parched as he was, though he had abundant springs of water, was not able to allay his thirst from them. An irrational desire for the water which was in the enemy's sector tensed the King and inflamed him, loosed and consumed him. When his guards chafed at the King's desire, two stout young warriors who reverenced it attired themselves in full panoply and, carrying a pitcher, scaled the enemy's ramparts. They eluded the sentries at the gates, and in their search traversed the entire encampment of the enemy; and when they discovered the spring, they boldly drew from it and conveyed the drink to the King. But he, though feverish with thirst, reasoned that a drink reckoned of like value with blood was a very terrible danger to his soul; and so, setting reason against desire, he made libation of the drink to God; [13] for the temperate intellect is able to vanquish the compulsion of the emotions and quench their flaming goads, to surmount the sufferings of the body, however extreme, and through the nobility of reason to scorn and reject the tyranny of the emotions.

II

DIVINE WISDOM IN HISTORY [14]

The evidently Alexandrian-Jewish author of The Wisdom of
Solomon (most probably of the first pre-Christian century)
tried to build a bridge between Greek philosophy and the ancient Hebrew wisdom literature, as exemplified in the biblical
Proverbs and Job or in the postbiblical book of Ben Sira
(Ecclesiasticus). He therefore made the wise King Solomon
orate on the superiority of Jewish religious "wisdom" over the
various atheistic or idolatrous forms of wisdom current in contemporary pagan society. In the third and longest section of the
book (Chapters 9 to 19), the highest stress is laid on the history
of Israel as the ultimate test of the superiority of Judaism's
ethical-historical monotheism over the natural religions of the
pagan world.

O GOD OF THE FATHERS, and Lord who keepest thy
mercy,
Who madest all things by thy word;
And by thy wisdom formedst man,
That he should have dominion over the creatures that were
made by thee.
And rule the world in holiness and righteousness,
And execute judgment in uprightness of soul;
Give me wisdom, her that sitteth by thee on thy throne;
And reject me not from among thy servants;
Because I am thy bondman and the son of thy handmaid,
A man weak and short-lived.
And of small power to understand judgment and laws.
For even if a man be perfect among the sons of men,
[Yet] if the wisdom that cometh from thee be not with
him, he shall be held in no account.
Thou didst choose me before [my brethren] to be king of
thy people,
And to do judgment for thy sons and daughters.

14

Thou gavest command to build a sanctuary in thy holy
     mountain.
And an altar in the city of thy habitation,
A copy of the holy tabernacle which thou preparedst afore-
     hand from the beginning.
And with thee is wisdom, which knoweth thy works,
And was present when thou wast making the world,
And which understandeth what is pleasing in thine eyes,
And what is right according to thy commandments.
Send her forth out of the holy heavens,
And from the throne of thy glory bid her come,
That being present with me she may toil [with me],
And [that] I may learn what is well-pleasing before thee.
For she knoweth all things and hath understanding
     [thereof]
And in my doings she shall guide me in [ways of] soberness,
And she shall guard me in her glory.
And [so] shall my works be acceptable,
And I shall judge thy people righteously,
And I shall be worthy of my father's throne.
For what man shall know the counsel of God?
Or who shall conceive what the Lord willeth?
For the thoughts of mortals are timorous,
And our devices are prone to fail.
For a corruptible body weigheth down the soul,
And the earthy frame lieth heavy on the mind that is full
     of cares.
And hardly do we divine the things that are on earth,
And the things that are close at hand we find with labor;
But the things that are in the heavens who [ever yet] traced
     out?
And who [ever] gained knowledge of thy counsel, except
     thou gavest wisdom,
And sentest thy holy spirit from on high?
And it was thus that the ways of them which are on earth
     were corrected,
And men were taught the things that are pleasing unto thee;
And through wisdom were they saved.

She guarded to the end the first formed father of the
world,[15] that was created alone,
And delivered him out of his transgression,
And gave him strength to get dominion over all things.
But when an unrighteous man[16] fell away from her in his
anger,
He perished himself in the rage wherewith he slew his
brother.
And when for his cause the earth was drowning with a flood,
Wisdom again saved it,
Guiding the righteous man's[17] course by a poor piece of
wood.

Moreover, when nations consenting together in wickedness
had been confounded,
Wisdom knew the righteous man,[18] and preserved him
blameless unto God,
And kept him strong when his heart yearned toward his
child.
While the ungodly were perishing, wisdom delivered a
righteous man,[19]
When he fled from the fire that descended out of heaven on
Pentapolis.[20]
To whose wickedness a smoking waste still witnesseth,
And plants bearing fair fruit that cometh not to ripeness;
([Yea and] a disbelieving soul hath a memorial [there], a
pillar of salt [still] standing).[21]
For having passed wisdom by,
Not only were they disabled from recognizing the things
which are good,
But they also left behind them for [human] life a monument
of their folly;
So that wherein they had offended could not but be known;
But wisdom delivered out of troubles those that waited on
her.

When a righteous man[22] was a fugitive from a brother's
wrath, wisdom guided him in straight paths;

She showed him God's kingdom, and gave him knowledge
of holy things;
She prospered him in his toils, and multiplied the fruits of
his labor;
When in their covetousness men dealt hardly with him,
She stood by him and made him rich;
She guarded him from enemies,
And from those that lay in wait she kept him safe,
And in his sore conflict she guided him to victory,
That he might know that godliness is more powerful than
all.

When a righteous man[23] was sold, wisdom forsook him not,
But from sin she delivered him;
She went down with him into a dungeon,
And in bonds she left him not,
Till she brought him the scepter of a kingdom,
And authority over those that dealt tyrannously with him;
She showed them also to be false that had accused him,
And gave him eternal glory.
She delivered a holy people and a blameless seed from a
nation of oppressors.
She entered into the soul of a servant of the Lord,[24]
And withstood terrible kings in wonders and signs.
She rendered unto holy men a reward of their toils;
She guided them along a marvelous way,
And became unto them a covering in the daytime,
And a light of stars through the night.[25]
She brought them over the Red Sea,
And led them through much water;
But their enemies she drowned,
And out of the bottom of the deep she cast them up.[26]
Therefore the righteous spoiled the ungodly;
And they sang praise to thy holy name, O Lord,
And extolled with one accord thy hand that fought for
them;[27]
Because wisdom opened the mouth of the dumb,
And made the tongues of babes to speak clearly.

III

A MESSIANIC VISION 28

The Apocalypse of Baruch is typical of an extensive branch of ancient Jewish literature which, beginning with Ezekiel, served to buoy up the faith of the Jewish people in its great historical emergencies. Apparently written by a Palestinian author soon after the second fall of Jerusalem, the Book of Baruch turned the attention of many despairing contemporaries to the earlier catastrophe of the destruction of the first Temple. These comforting prophecies, addressed to his own and to succeeding generations, were attributed to a witness of the first destruction, Baruch ben Neriah, amanuensis of the great prophet Jeremiah. No wonder, then, that this consolatory apocalypse (now extant only in a Syriac version) seems to have been frequently recited in the synagogue services of the Ninth of Ab, the day of mourning for the loss of both Temples.

A<small>ND HE ANSWERED</small> and said unto me: "Into twelve parts is that time divided, and each one of them is reserved for that which is appointed for it. In the first part there shall be the beginning of commotions. And in the second part (there shall be) slayings of the great ones. And in the third part the fall of many by death. And in the fourth part the sending of the sword. And in the fifth part famine and the withholding of rain. And in the sixth part earthquakes and terrors. [Wanting.] And in the eighth part a multitude of specters and attacks of the Shedim. And in the ninth part the fall of fire. And in the tenth part rapine and much oppression. And in the eleventh part wickedness and unchastity. And in the twelfth part confusion from the mingling together of all those things aforesaid. For these parts of that time are reserved, and shall be mingled one with another and minister one to another. For some shall leave out some of their own and receive (in its stead) from others, and some complete their own and that of others, so that those may not understand who are upon the earth in those days that this is the consummation of the times. Nevertheless, whosoever understandeth shall then be wise. For the measure and reckoning of that time are two parts a week of seven weeks."

And I answered and said: "It is good for a man to come and behold, but it is better that he should not come lest he fall. [But I will say this also: 'Will he who is incorruptible despise those things which are corruptible, and whatever befalls in the case of those things which are corruptible, so that he might look only to those things which are not corruptible?'] But if, O Lord, those things shall assuredly come to pass which thou has foretold to me, so do thou show this also unto me if indeed I have found grace in thy sight. Is it in one place or in one of the parts of the earth that those things are come to pass, or will the whole earth experience (them)?"

And he answered and said unto me: "Whatever will then befall (will befall) the whole earth; therefore all who live will experience (them). For at that time I will protect only those who are found in those selfsame days in this land. And it shall come to pass, when all is accomplished that was to come to pass in those parts, that the Messiah shall then begin to be revealed. And Behemoth[29] shall be revealed from his place and Leviathan[30] shall ascend from the sea, those two great monsters which I created on the fifth day of creation and shall have kept until that time; and then they shall be for food for all that are left. The earth also shall yield its fruit ten thousandfold, and on each vine there shall be a thousand branches, and each branch shall produce a thousand clusters, and each cluster produce a thousand grapes, and each grape produce a cor[31] of wine. And those who have hungered shall rejoice; moreover, also, they shall behold marvels every day. For winds shall go forth from before me to bring every morning the fragrance of aromatic fruits, and at the close of the day clouds distilling the dew of health. And it shall come to pass at that selfsame time that the treasury of manna shall again descend from on high, and they will eat of it in those years, because these are they who have come to the consummation of time.

"And it shall come to pass after these things, when the time of the advent of the Messiah is fulfilled, that he shall return in glory.

"Then all who have fallen asleep in hope of him shall rise again. And it shall come to pass at that time that the treasuries will be opened in which is preserved the number of the souls of the righteous, and they shall come forth; and a multitude of souls shall be seen together in one assemblage of one thought, and the first shall rejoice and the last shall not be grieved. For they know that the time has come of which it is said that it is the consummation of the times. But the souls of the wicked, when they behold all these things, shall then waste away the more. For they shall know that their torment has come and their perdition has arrived."

IV

TOBIT

The story of Tobit, a literary biography, or rather a fictional account of Jewish families living in Nineveh and Ekbatana in Assyrian times, describes in picturesque detail the orthodox way of life in the Jewish communities of the dispersion. Probably written in Egypt during the Maccabean era, the story was intended to fortify the survivalist forces among the Jews of the diaspora. It constitutes a reply to the assimilationists by depicting the hero's staunch observance of the law and his charitable conduct, as well as the ultimate rewards he reaped thereby for himself and his family.

A JEWISH POLONIUS [3:]

IN THAT DAY Tobit remembered the money which he had left in trust with Gabael in Rages of Media, and he said in his heart, "Behold, I have asked for death. Why do I not call my son Tobias and show unto him concerning this money before I die?"

And he called Tobias his son, and he came unto him and he said unto him, "Bury me well, and honor thy mother; and forsake her not all the days of her life, and do that which is pleasing before her, and grieve not her spirit in any matter. Remember her, child, that she hath experienced many dangers for thee in her womb; and when she is dead, bury her by me in one grave. My child, be mindful of the Lord all thy days, and let not thy will be set to sin and to transgress his commandments; do acts of righteousness all the days of thy life, and walk not in the ways of unrighteousness. For if thou doest the truth, success shall be in thy works, and [so it shall be] unto all that do righteousness. Give alms of thy substance; turn not away thy face from any poor man, and the face of God shall not be turned away from thee. As thy substance is, give alms of it according to thine abundance; if thou have much, according to the abundance thereof, give alms; if thou have little, bestow it, and be not afraid to give alms according to that little, for thou layest up a good treasure for thyself against the day of necessity, because alms delivereth from death and suffereth not to come into darkness. Alms is a good offering in the sight of the Most High for all that give it. Beware, my child, of all whoredom, and take first a wife of the seed of thy fathers; take not a strange wife, which is not of thy father's tribe, for we are the sons of the prophets. Noah, Abraham, Isaac, Jacob, our fathers of old time, remember, my child, that they all took wives of their kinsmen and were blessed in their children, and their seed shall inherit the land. And now, my child, love thy brethren, and scorn not in thy heart thy brethren and the sons and daughters of thy people, so as not to take one of them; for in scornfulness is destruction and much trouble, and in idleness is decay and great want, for idleness is the mother of famine. Let not the wages of any man which shall work for thee tarry with thee, but render it unto him out of hand, and if thou serve God, recompense shall be made unto thee. Take heed to thyself, my child, in all thy works, and be discreet in all thy behavior. And what thou thyself hatest, do to no man. Drink not wine unto drunkenness, and let not drunkenness go with thee on thy way. Give of thy bread to the hungry and of thy garments to them that are naked; of all thine abundance give alms, and let not thine eye be grudging when thou givest alms. Pour out thy bread and thy wine on the tomb of the just, and give not to sinners. Ask counsel of every man that is wise, and despise not any counsel that is profitable. And bless the Lord thy God at all times, and ask of him that thy ways may be made straight and that all thy paths and counsels may prosper; for every nation hath not good counsel, but the Lord will give to them all good things; and whom he will the Lord humblest unto the nethermost Hades. And now, child, remember these commandments and let them not be blotted out of thy heart. And now, child, I show thee that I left ten talents of silver in trust with Gabael the brother of Gabri at Rages of Media. And fear not,

my child, because we have become poor; thou hast much wealth,
if thou fear God and avoid every kind of sin and do the things
which are good in the sight of the Lord thy God."

A PRAYER OF JOY [33]

B LESSED IS GOD that liveth forever, and his kingdom,
   For he chastiseth, and showeth mercy.
     He leadeth down to Hades below the earth,
And he bringeth up from the great destruction;
And there is nothing that shall escape his hand.

Give thanks unto him before the Gentiles, ye children of
    Israel,
   For he hath scattered you among them,
   And there he hath shown you his greatness;
   And extol ye him before all the living.

Because he is our Lord, and he our God, and he our Father,
   Yea, he is God to all the ages:
   He will chastise you for your iniquities,
   And will show mercy unto you all.

When ye turn unto him out of all the nations
   Whithersoever ye shall be scattered,
   With your whole heart and with your whole soul, to do
    truth before him,
   Then he will turn unto you, and will no longer hide his
    face from you.

And now see what he hath wrought with you,
   And give him thanks with your whole mouth,
   And bless the Lord of righteousness,
   And exalt the everlasting King.

I, in the land of my captivity, give him thanks,
   And show his strength and majesty unto nations of
    sinners.
   Turn, ye sinners, and do righteousness before him.
   Who can tell if he will accept you and have mercy on you?

I exalt my God, and my soul shall rejoice in the King of
    heaven;
    Of his greatness let all men tell,
    And let them give him thanks in Jerusalem.

O Jerusalem, thou holy city! He will chastise thee for the
    works of thy hands,
    And will again have mercy on the sons of the righteous.
    Give thanks to the Lord with goodness, and bless the ever-
    lasting King.

That thy tabernacle may be builded in thee again with joy,
    And that he may make glad in thee all that are captives,
    And love in thee all that are miserable and all the genera-
    tions of eternity.

A bright light shall shine unto all the ends of the earth;
    Many nations shall come from afar,
    And the inhabitants of the utmost ends of the earth unto
    thy holy name;

With their gifts also in their hands unto the King of heaven,
    Generations of generations shall utter rejoicing in thee,
    And thy name that is elect unto the generations of
    eternity.

Cursed shall be all they that shall speak a hard word;
    Cursed shall be all they that demolish thee,
    And throw down thy walls;

And all they that overthrow thy towers,
    And set on fire thy habitations;
    But blessed shall be all they that fear thee forever.

Then go and be exceeding glad for the sons of the righteous:
    For they shall all be gathered together,
    And bless the everlasting Lord.

Blessed [shall] they [be] that love thee;
    And blessed [shall] they [be]
    That shall rejoice for thy peace:

And blessed [shall be] all the men
   That shall sorrow for thee
   For all thy chastisements:

Because they shall rejoice in thee
   And shall see all thy joy forever.

My soul doth bless the Lord the great King;
   For Jerusalem shall be builded again as his house unto
      all the ages.

Happy shall I be if the remnant of my seed come to see thy
      glory
   And give thanks unto the King of heaven.

And the gates of Jerusalem shall be builded with sapphire
      and emerald,
   And all thy walls with precious stone.

The towers of Jerusalem shall be builded with gold,
   And their battlements with pure gold.
The streets of Jerusalem shall be paved
   With carbuncle and stones of Ophir.

And the gates of Jerusalem shall utter hymns of gladness
   And all her houses shall say, Halleluiah.

Blessed is the God of Israel.
   And the blessed shall bless the name
   That is holy forever and ever.

V

THE PRAYER OF MANASSES [34]

Among the apocryphal efforts to fill in gaps in the biblical narrative (we possess such additions to the Books of Ezra, Daniel, and Esther), there appears a prayer attributed to the repentant King Manasseh of seventh-century Judah. Supposedly this was the very prayer that the Chronicler had recorded as "written among the acts of the kings of Israel."[35] The date of the apocryphal Prayer of Manasses cannot be ascertained, although some scholars are inclined to associate the implied appeal to universal repentance with some such national emergency as the Maccabean revolt.

O Lord Almighty, which art in heaven,
   Thou God of our fathers,
   Of Abraham and Isaac and Jacob,
   And of their righteous seed;
Thou who hast made the heaven and the earth,
   With all the array thereof:
Who has bound the sea by the word of thy command;
   Who has shut up the deep, and sealed it
   With thy terrible and glorious name;
Whom all things do dread; yea, they tremble before thy
      power:
   For the majesty of thy glory cannot be borne,
   And the anger of thy threatening against sinners is un-
      endurable:
Infinite and unsearchable is thy merciful promise;
   For thou art the Lord Most High, of great compassion,
      long-suffering and abundant in mercy, and repentest
      thee for the evils of men.
Thou, O Lord, according to thy great goodness hast promised
   repentance and forgiveness to them that have sinned

against thee; and in the multitude of thy mercies hast
appointed repentance unto sinners, that they may be
saved.
Thou, therefore, O Lord, that art the God of the righteous,
hast not appointed repentance unto the righteous, unto
Abraham, and Isaac and Jacob, which have not sinned
against thee:
But thou hast appointed repentance unto me that am a
sinner;
For [the sins] I have sinned [are] more in number than the
sands of the sea.
For my transgressions were multiplied, O Lord:
My transgressions were multiplied,
And I am not worthy to behold and see the height of heaven
by reason of the multitude of mine iniquities.
And now, O Lord, I am justly punished and deservedly
afflicted;
For lo! I am in captivity,
Bowed down with many an iron chain,
So that I cannot lift up mine head by reason of my sins,
Neither have I any respite:
Because I provoked thy wrath, and did that which was evil
in thy sight.
I did not do thy will, neither kept I thy commandments:
I set up abominations, and multiplied detestable things.
And now I bow the knee of mine heart, beseeching thee of
thy gracious goodness.
I have sinned, O Lord, I have sinned,
And I acknowledge mine iniquities.
But, I humbly beseech thee,
Forgive me, O Lord, forgive me,
And destroy me not with mine iniquities.
Neither, in thy continual anger against me,
Lay up evil in store for me:
Nor pass thou sentence against me,
When I am in the lowest parts of the earth.
For thou, O Lord, art the God of them that repent;

And in me thou wilt show forth all thy goodness:
For thou wilt save me, unworthy that I am,
　According to thy great mercy.
And I will praise thee forever all the days of my life:
For all the host of heaven doth sing thy praise,
　And thine is the glory forever and ever. AMEN.

PART TWO

HELLENISTIC MATERIALS

I

PHILO OF ALEXANDRIA

Hellenism as an assimilatory force presented a major problem to the leaders of Palestinian Jewry. This threat, however, was faced under cultural conditions that favored Judaism; Hellenism was the invading culture and was carried chiefly by men of trade and of war, often the loudest but rarely the best spokesmen for a culture. In Egypt, on the other hand, and notably in Alexandria, which was the literary, scientific, and cultural center of the Hellenistic world, the Jewish community faced the challenge of Hellenism at its best and most vigorous. Spokesmen for Judaism had to use the forms of thought and expression of the Greek culture to defend their religion against attack and, more positively, to affirm the universal cultural values of Judaism. Of the Alexandrian Jewish writers, Philo Judaeus (about 20 B.C. to about 50 A.D.) assumed the role of chief philosophic exponent of the Jewish religion.

Philo did not compose systematic philosophic treatises, save for some minor pieces usually assigned to his apprentice years. Yet his adaptation of philosophic tendencies current in Alexandria in his day has been widely influential on Christian and Mohammedan as well as on Jewish religious philosophers. Philo's basic intention was to show that Judaism is a philosophic religion, consistent with the ideas of the Greek philosophers, especially in the Platonic tradition. The method by means of which he attempted to demonstrate this was an allegorical interpretation of the Pentateuch. His allegory was designed to explain away anthropomorphisms in the biblical text, to interpret particularistic passages in a universalistic sense, and to show the accord of biblical ethics and cosmology with that of the Greeks. The selections below illustrate various aspects of his philosophical allegorizing of Judaism; they illustrate, too, that Philo makes the initial, unphilosophic assumption that the Pentateuch is the absolute revealed truth.

It is interesting to note that, despite the wide influence of Philo's thought, it had so little relevance to the defense of Judaism in the Palestinian situation that a careful combing of Rabbinic literature has brought to light only a few very doubtful references to Philo. He was an interpreter of Judaism in and for the diaspora—a diaspora which has never long been free from the sort of anti-Jewish episode discussed in the last of the Philonic selections below. The interest in his work has been strongest where the problem faced has been Philo's problem, the justification of Judaism to an alien and non-Jewish culture in the language and the literary forms of that alien culture.

THE EXISTENCE AND NATURE OF GOD [1]

DOUBTLESS hard to unriddle and hard to apprehend is the Father and Ruler of all, but that is no reason why we should shrink from searching for him. Now in such searching, two principal questions arise which demand the consideration of the genuine philosopher. One is whether the Deity exists, a question necessitated by those who practice atheism, the worst form of wickedness, the other is what the Deity is in essence. Now to answer the first question does not need much labor, but the second is not only difficult but perhaps impossible to solve. Still, both must be examined. We see then that any piece of work always involves the knowledge of a workman. Who can look upon statues or painting without thinking at once of a sculptor or painter? Who can see clothes or ships or houses without getting the idea of a weaver and a shipwright and a housebuilder? And when one enters a well-ordered city in which the arrangements for civil life are very admirably managed, what else will he suppose but that this city is directed by good rulers? So then he who comes to the truly Great City, this world, and beholds hills and plains teeming with animals and plants, the rivers, spring-fed or winter torrents, streaming along, the seas with their expanses, the air with its happily tempered phases, the yearly seasons passing into each other, and then the sun and moon ruling the day and night, and the other heavenly bodies fixed or planetary, and the whole firmament revolving in rhythmic order, must he not naturally or rather necessarily gain the conception of the Maker and Father and Ruler also? For none of the works of human art is self-made, and the highest art and knowledge is shown in this universe, so that surely it has been wrought by one of excellent knowledge and absolute perfection. In this way we have gained the conception of the existence of God.

As for the divine essence, though in fact it is hard to track and hard to apprehend, it still calls for all the inquiry possible. For nothing is better than to search for the true God, even if the discovery of him eludes human capacity, since the very wish to learn, if earnestly entertained, produces untold joys and pleasures. We have the testimony of those who have not taken a mere sip of philosophy, but have feasted more abundantly on its reasonings and conclusions. For with them the reason soars away from earth into the heights, travels through the upper air, and accompanies the revolutions of the sun and moon and the whole heaven, and in its desire to see all that is there finds its powers of sight blurred, for so pure and vast is the radiance that pours therefrom that the soul's eye is dizzied by the flashing of the rays. Yet it does not therefore faintheartedly give up the task, but with purpose unsubdued presses onward to such contemplation as is possible, like the athlete who strives for the second prize since he has been disappointed of the first. Now second to the true vision stands conjecture and theorizing, and all that can be brought into the category of reasonable probability. So then just as, though we do not know and cannot with certainty determine what each of the stars is in the purity of its essence, we eagerly persist in the search because our natural love of learning makes us delight in what seems probable, so too, though the clear vision of God as he really is is denied us, we ought not to relinquish the quest. For the very seeking, even without finding, is felicity in itself; just as no one blames the eyes of the body because, when unable to see the sun itself, they see the emanation of its rays as it reaches the earth, which is but the extremity of the brightness which the beams of the sun give forth.

It was this which Moses, the sacred guide, most dearly beloved of God, had before his eyes when he besought God with the words, "Reveal thyself to me." In these words we may almost hear plainly the inspired cry, "This universe has been my teacher, to bring me to the knowledge that thou art and dost subsist. As thy son, it has told me of its Father, as thy work, of its contriver. But what thou art in thine essence I desire to understand, yet find in no part of the All any guide to guide me to this knowledge. Therefore I pray and beseech thee to accept the supplication of a suppliant, a lover of God, one whose mind is set to serve thee alone; for as knowledge of the light does not come by any other source but what itself supplies, so too thou alone canst tell me of thyself. Wherefore I crave pardon if, for lack of a teacher, I venture to appeal to thee in my desire to learn of thee." He replies, "Thy zeal I approve as praiseworthy, but the request cannot fitly be granted to any that are brought into being by creation. I freely bestow what is in accordance with the recipient; for not all that I can give is within man's power to take, and therefore to him that is worthy of my grace I extend all the boons which he is capable of receiving. But the apprehension of me is something more than human nature, yea even the whole heaven and universe will be able to contain. Know thyself,[2] then, and do not be led away by impulses and desires beyond thy capacity; nor let yearning for the unattainable uplift and carry thee off thy feet, for of the obtainable nothing shall be denied thee."

When Moses heard this, he addressed to him a second petition and said, "I bow before thine admonitions, that I never could have received the vision of thee clearly manifested, but I beseech thee that I may at least see the glory that surrounds thee; and by thy glory I understand the powers that keep guard around thee, of whom I would fain gain apprehension, for though hitherto that has escaped me, the thought of it creates in me a mighty longing to have knowledge of them." To this he answers, "The powers which thou seekest to know are discerned not by sight but by mind, even as I, whose they are, am discerned by mind, and not by sight; and when I say 'they are discerned by mind,' I speak not of those which are now usually apprehended by mind, but mean that if these other powers could be apprehended it would not be by sense but by mind at its purest. But while in their essence they are beyond your apprehension, they nevertheless present to your sight a sort of impress and copy of their active working. You men have for your use seals which, when brought into contact with wax or similar material, stamp on them any number of impressions, while they themselves are not docked in any part thereby but remain as they were. Such you must conceive my powers to be, supplying quality and shape to things which lack either, and yet changing or lessening nothing of their eternal nature. Some among you call them not inaptly 'forms' or 'ideas,' since they bring form into everything that is, giving order to the disordered, limit to the unlimited, bounds to the unbounded, shape to the shapeless, and in general changing the worse to something better.[3] Do not, then, hope to be ever able to apprehend me or any of my powers in our essence. But I readily and with right good will will admit you to a share of what is attainable. That means that I bid you come and contemplate the universe and its contents, a spectacle apprehended, not by the eye of the body, but by the unsleeping eyes of the mind. Only let there be the constant and profound longing for wisdom which fills its scholars and disciples with verities glorious in their exceeding loveliness." When Moses heard this, he did not cease from his desire, but kept the yearning for the invisible aflame in his heart.

ON THE CREATION OF THE WORLD [4]

The aforesaid numeral [4], then having been deemed worthy of such high privilege in nature, it was a matter of course that its Maker arrayed the heaven on the fourth day with a most divine adornment of perfect beauty, namely the light-giving heavenly bodies; and, knowing that of all things light is best, he made it the indispensable means of sight, the best of the senses; for what the intellect is in the soul, this the eye is in the body; for each of them sees, one the things of the mind, the other the things of sense; and they have need, the mind of knowledge that it may become cognizant of incorporeal objects, the eye of light for the apprehending of bodily forms.

Light has proved itself the source of many other boons to mankind, but pre-eminently of philosophy, the greatest boon of all. For man's faculty of vision, led upward by light, discerned the nature of the heavenly bodies and their harmonious movement. He saw the well-ordered circuits of fixed stars and planets, how the former moved in unchanging orbits and all alike, while the latter sped round in two revolutions out of harmony with each other. He marked the rhythmic dances of all these, how they were marshaled by the laws of a perfect music, and the sight produced in his soul an ineffable delight and pleasure. Banqueting on sights displayed to it one after another, his soul was insatiate in beholding. And then, as usually happens, it went on to busy itself with questionings, asking, "What is the essence of these visible objects? Are they in nature unoriginate, or had they a beginning of existence? What is the method of their movement? And what are the principles by which each is governed?" It was out of the investigation of these problems that philosophy grew, than which no more perfect good has come into the life of mankind.

It was with a view to that original intellectual light, which I have mentioned as belonging to the order of the incorporeal world, that he created the heavenly bodies of which our senses are aware. These are images divine and exceeding fair, which he established in heaven as in the purest temple belonging to corporeal being. This he did that they might serve many purposes. One purpose was to give light; another to be signs; a third duly to fix seasons of the year; and lastly for the sake of days, months, years, which (as we all know) have served as measures of time and given birth to number. The kind of useful service rendered by each of the bodies mentioned is self-evident; yet that the truth may be more precisely apprehended it may not be out of place to follow it step by step in a reasoned account.

All the time having been divided into two portions, day and night, the Father assigned the sovereignty of the day to the sun, as to a great king, and that of the night to the moon and the host of the other stars. The greatness of the sway and government pertaining to the sun finds its clearest proof in what has been already mentioned: one and alone it has by itself separately had day apportioned to it, half of the whole of time; while all the rest with the moon have had allotted to them the other half, which has received the name of night. And when the sun has risen, all that multitude of stars which were visible but now is not merely dimmed but becomes actually invisible through the pouring forth of its light; and upon its setting they begin all of them to shine out in their own true characters. . . .

. . . .

After all the rest, as I have said, Moses tells us that man was created after the image of God and after his likeness.[5] Right well does he say this, for nothing earthborn is more like God than man. Let no one represent the likeness as one to a bodily form; for neither is God in human form, nor is the human body godlike. No, it is in respect of the Mind, the sovereign element of the soul, that the word 'image' is used; for after the pattern of a single Mind, even the Mind of the Universe as an archetype, the mind in each of those who successfully came into being was molded. It is in a fashion a god to him who carries and enshrines it as an object of reverence; for the human mind evidently occupies a position in men precisely answering to that which the great Ruler occupies in all the world. It is invisible while itself seeing all things, and while comprehending the substance of others it is as to its own substance unperceived; and while it opens by arts and sciences roads branching in many directions, all of them great highways, it comes through land and sea investigating what either element contains. Again, when on soaring wing it has contemplated the atmosphere and all its phases, it is borne yet higher to the ether and the circuit of heavens, and is whirled round with the dances of planets and fixed stars, in accordance with the laws of perfect music, following that love of wisdom which guides its steps. And so, carrying its gaze beyond the confines of all substance discernible by sense, it comes to a point at which it reaches out after the intelligible world, and on descrying in that world sights of surpassing loveliness, even the patterns and the originals of the things of sense which it saw here, it is seized by a sober intoxication, like those filled with Corybantic frenzy, and is inspired, possessed by a longing far other than theirs and a nobler desire. Wafted by this to the topmost arch of the things perceptible to mind, it seems to be on its way to the Great King himself; but amid its longing to see him, pure and untempered rays of concentrated light stream forth like a torrent, so that by its gleams the eye of the understanding is dazzled. And since images do not always correspond to their archetype and pattern, but are in many instances unlike it, the writer further brought out his meaning by adding "after the likeness" to the words "after the image," thus showing that an accurate cast, bearing a clear impression, was intended.

THE EXCELLENCES OF THE JEWISH LAW [6]

Besides these there is a host of other things which belong to unwritten customs and institutions or are contained in the laws themselves. What a man would hate to suffer he must not do himself to others. What he has not laid down he must not take up, either from a garden or a wine press or a threshing floor. He must not filch anything great or small from a stack. He must not grudge to give fire to one who needs it or close off running water. If the poor or the cripple beg food of him, he must give it as an offering of religion to God. He must not debar dead bodies from burial, but throw upon them as much earth as piety demands, nor disturb in any way the resting places and monuments of the departed. He must not by fettering or any other means worsen the plight of him who is in hard straits; he must not make abortive the generative power of men by gelding nor that of women by sterilizing drugs and other devices. There must be no maltreatment of animals contrary to what is appointed by God or even by a lawgiver, no destroying of their seed nor defrauding of their offspring. No unjust scales, no false measurements, no fraudulent coinage must be substituted. The secrets of a friend must not be divulged in enmity. What need in Heaven's name have we of your Buzyges and his precepts? There are other matters to be

noted: children must not be parted from their parents even if
you hold them as captive, nor a wife from her husband even if
you are her owner by lawful purchase.

These no doubt are more important and serious matters, but
there are others, little things of casual occurrence. Do not render
desolate the nesting home of birds or make the appeals of animals
of none effect when they seem to fly to you for help as they sometimes do. Nor commit any lesser offense of the kind. These things
are of nothing worth, you may say, yet great is the law which
ordains them and ever watchful is the care which it demands.
Great, too, and appalling are the warnings and imprecations
which accompany it. And such deeds are everywhere surveyed
and avenged by God himself. . . .

.   .   .   .

Is it not a marvel that for a whole day they should have kept
from transgressing on any occasion any of the ordinances—or
rather for many days, not one only—days, too, which did not
follow straight on each other but only after intervals, and intervals of seven during which habits belonging to the secular days
naturally hold the mastery? You may ask: Is not this merely a
case of practicing self-control so that they should be capable of
abstaining from toil if necessary, no less than of toilsome activity?
No, it was a great and marvelous achievement which the lawgiver had in view. He considered that they should not only be
capable of both action and inaction in other matters, but also
should have expert knowledge of their ancestral laws and customs. What then did he do? He required them to assemble in the
same place on these seventh days and, sitting together in a re-
spectful and orderly manner, hear the laws read so that none
should be ignorant of them. And indeed they do always assemble
and sit together, most of them in silence, except when it is the
practice to add something to signify approval of what is read. But
some priest who is present or one of the elders reads the holy laws
to them and expounds them point by point till about the late
afternoon, when they depart, having gained both expert knowledge of the holy laws and considerable advance in piety. Do you
think that this marks them as idlers or that any work is equally
vital to them? And so they do not resort to persons learned in the

Law with questions as to what they should do or should not do, nor yet by keeping independent transgress in ignorance of the Law, but any one of them whom you attack with inquiries about their ancestral institutions can answer you readily and easily. The husband seems competent to transmit knowledge of the laws to his wife, the father to his children, the master to his slaves.

Again with regard to the seventh year, one can without difficulty use much the same though perhaps not identical words. For here it is not they themselves who abstain from work as on those seventh days, but it is the land which they leave idle against the days to come hereafter to give it fertility; for they believe that it gains much by getting a respite, and is then tilled in the next year without being exhausted by unbroken cultivation. You may see that the same treatment of our bodies tends to strengthen them. Physicians prescribe some intermissions and relaxations not merely when health has to be restored. For monotony without a break, particularly in work, is always seen to be injurious. Here is a proof that their object is as I describe. If anyone offered to cultivate this same land during the seventh year much more strenuously than before and to surrender to them the whole of the fruits, they would absolutely refuse. For they do not think that it is only themselves who should abstain from work, though if they did so it would be nothing to wonder at, but that the land should gain at their hands a respite and easing off to make a fresh start in receiving renewed attention and husbandry. For what in heaven's name was to hinder them from letting out the land during the year and collecting the produce of that year at its end from the others who tilled it? But, as I have said, they entirely refuse anything of the kind, doubtless out of consideration for the land. We have a truly great proof of their humanity in the following also. Since they themselves abstain from labor during that year, they think that they should not gather or lay by the fruits produced which do not accrue to them from their own toil; but since God has provided them, sprung from the soil by its own action, they should grant them to be used freely by wayfarers and others who desire or need them.

You have now had enough on this subject, for you will not require me to show that these rules for the seventh days are established firmly among them by the Law. Probably you have often heard ere now from many physicians, scientists, and philosophers what influence it has over the life of all things and of mankind in particular. This is what I have to say about the seventh day.

THE LAWGIVER AND HIS WORK

The Theophany Interpreted [7]

Now as he [8] was leading the flock to a place where the water and the grass were abundant, and where there happened to be plentiful growth of herbage for the sheep, he found himself at a glen where he saw a most astonishing sight. There was a bramblebush, a thorny sort of plant and of the most weakly kind, which, without anyone's setting it alight, suddenly took fire, and, though enveloped from root to twigs in a mass of fire, which looked as though it were spouted up from a fountain, yet remained whole, and, instead of serving as fuel to the fire, actually fed on it. In the midst of the flame was a form of the fairest beauty, unlike any visible object, an image supremely divine in appearance, refulgent with a light brighter than the light of fire. It might be supposed that this was the image of him that is; but let us rather call it an angel or herald, since, with a silence that spoke more clearly than speech, it employed as it were the miracle of sight to herald future events.

For the burning bramble was a symbol of those who suffered wrong, as the flaming fire of those who did it. Yet that which burned was not burned up, and this was a sign that the sufferers would not be destroyed by their aggressors, who would find that the aggression was vain and profitless, while the victims of malice escaped unharmed. The angel was a symbol of God's providence, which all silently brings relief to the greatest dangers, exceeding every hope.

But the details of the comparison must be considered. The bramble, as I have said, is a very weakly plant; yet it is prickly and will wound if one do but touch it. Again, though fire is naturally destructive, the bramble was not devoured thereby, but on the contrary was guarded by it, and remained just as it was before it took fire, lost nothing at all but gained an additional brightness. All this is a description of the nation's condition as it then stood, and we may think of it as a voice proclaiming to the sufferers: "Do not lose heart; your weakness is your strength, which can prick, and thousands will suffer from its wounds. Those who desire to consume you will be your unwilling saviors instead of your destroyers. Your ills will work you no ill. Nay, just when the enemy is surest of ravaging you, your fame will shine forth most gloriously." Again fire, the element which works destruction, convicts the cruel-hearted. "Exult not in your own strength," it says. "Behold your invincible might brought low, and learn wisdom. The property of flame is to consume, yet it is consumed, like wood. The nature of wood is to be consumed, yet it is manifested as the consumer, as though it were the fire."

The Character of Moses [9]

The departing emigrants had among them over six hundred thousand men of military age, while the rest of the multitude, consisting of old men, womenfolk, and children, could not easily be counted. They were accompanied by a promiscuous, nondescript, and menial crowd, a bastard host, so to speak, associated with the trueborn. These were the children of Egyptian women by Hebrew fathers into whose families they had been adopted, also those who, reverencing the divine favor shown to the people, had come over to them, and such as were converted and brought to a wiser mind by the magnitude and the number of the successive punishments.

The appointed leader of all these was Moses, invested with this office and kingship, not like some of those who thrust themselves into position of power by means of arms and engines of war and strength of infantry, cavalry, and navy, but on account of his goodness and his nobility of conduct and the universal benevolence which he never failed to show. Further, his office was bestowed upon him by God, the lover of virtue and nobility, as the reward due to him. For when he gave up the lordship of Egypt, which he held as son to the daughter of the then reigning king, because the sight of the iniquities committed in the land and his own nobility of soul and magnanimity of spirit and in-born hatred of evil led him to renounce completely his expected inheritance from the kinsfolk of his adoption, he who presides over and takes charge of all things thought good to requite him with the kingship of a nation more populous and mightier, a nation destined to be consecrated above all others to offer prayers forever on behalf of the human race, that it may be delivered from evil and participate in what is good. Having received this office, he did not, like some, take pains to exalt his own house and promote his sons, of whom he had two, to great power and make them his consorts for the present and his successors for the hereafter. For in all things great and small he followed a pure and guileless policy and, like a good judge, allowed the incorruptibility of reason to subdue his natural affection for his children. For he had set before him one essential aim: to benefit his subjects, and, in all that he said or did, to further their interests and neglect no opportunity which would forward the common well-being. In solitary contrast to those who had hitherto held the same authority, he did not treasure up gold and silver, did not levy tributes, did not possess houses or chattels or livestock or a staff of slaves or revenues, or any other accompaniment of costly and opulent living, though he might have had all in abundance. He held that to prize material wealth shows poverty of soul, and despised such wealth as blind; but the wealth of nature which has eyes to see he highly honored and zealously pursued, more perhaps than any other man. In dress and food and the other sides of life, he made no arrogant parade to increase his pomp and grandeur. But while in these he practiced the economy and unassuming ways of a private citizen, he was liberal in the truly royal expenditure of those treasures which the ruler may well desire to have in abundance. These treasures were the repeated exhibition of self-restraint, continence, temperance, shrewdness, good sense, knowledge, endurance of toil and hardships, contempt of pleasures, justice, advocacy of excellence, censure and chastisement according to law for wrongdoers, praise and honor for welldoers, again as the law directs.

And so, as he abjured the accumulation of lucre and the wealth whose influence is mighty among men, God rewarded him by giving him instead the greatest and most perfect wealth. That is the wealth of the whole earth and sea and rivers, and of all the other elements and the combinations which they form. For since God judged him worthy to appear as a partner of his own possessions, he gave into his hands the whole world as a portion well fitted for his heir. Therefore each element obeyed him as its master, changed its natural properties and submitted to his command, and this perhaps is no wonder. For if, as the proverb says, what belongs to friends is common, and the prophet is called the friend of God, it would follow that he shares also God's possessions, so far as it is serviceable. For God possesses all things but needs nothing; while the good man, though he possesses nothing in the proper sense, not even himself, partakes of the precious things of God so far as he is capable. And that is but natural, for he is a world citizen, and therefore not on the roll of any city of men's habitation, rightly so because he has received no mere piece of land but the whole world as his portion. Again, was not the joy of his partnership with the Father and Maker of all magnified also by the honor of being deemed worthy to bear the same title? For he was named god and king of the whole nation, and entered, we are told, into the darkness where God was, that is into the unseen, invisible, incorporeal, and archetypal essence of existing things. Thus he beheld what is hidden from the sight of mortal nature; and, in himself and his life displayed for all to see, he has set before us, like some well-wrought picture, a piece of work beautiful and godlike, a model for those who are willing to copy it. Happy are they who imprint, or strive to imprint, that image in their souls. For it were best that the mind should carry the form of virtue in perfection; but, failing this, let it at least have the unflinching desire to possess that form.

The Power of God [10]

Though this supply of food never failed and continued to be enjoyed in abundance, a serious scarcity of water again occurred. Sore-pressed by this, their mood turned to desperation, whereupon Moses, taking that sacred staff with which he accomplished the signs in Egypt, under inspiration smote the steep rock with it.[11] It may be that the rock contained originally a spring and now had its artery clean severed, or perhaps that then for the first time a body of water collected in it through hidden channels was forced out by the impact. Whichever is the case, it opened under the violence of the stream and spouted out its contents, so that not only then did it provide a remedy for their thirst but also abundance of drink for a longer time for all these thousands. For they filled all their water vessels, as they had done on the former occasion, from the springs that were naturally bitter but were changed and sweetened by God's directing care.[12]

If anyone disbelieves these things, he neither knows God nor has ever sought to know him; for if he did, he would at once have perceived—aye, perceived with a firm apprehension—that these extraordinary and seemingly incredible events are but child's play to God. He has but to turn his eyes to things which are really great and worthy of his earnest contemplation: the creation of heaven and the rhythmic movements of the planets and fixed stars; the light that shines upon us from the sun by day and from the moon by night; the establishment of the earth in the very center of the universe; the vast expanses of continents and islands, and the numberless species of animals and plants; and again the widespreading seas, the rushing rivers, spring-fed and winter torrents, the fountains with their perennial streams, some sending forth cold, other warm water, the air with its changes of every sort, the yearly seasons with their well-marked diversities and other beauties innumerable. He who should wish to describe the several parts, or rather any one of the cardinal parts of the universe, would find life too short, even if his years were prolonged beyond those of all other men. But these things, though truly marvelous, are held in little account because they are familiar. Not so with the unfamiliar; though they be but small matters, we give way before what appears so strange and, drawn by their novelty, regard them with amazement.

The Septuagint [13]

That the sanctity of our legislation has been a source of wonder, not only to the Jews but also to all other nations, is clear both from the facts already mentioned and those which I proceed to state. In ancient times the laws were written in the Chaldean tongue, and remained in that form for many years, without any change of language, so long as they had not yet revealed their beauty to the rest of mankind. But in course of time the daily, unbroken regularity of practice exercised by those who observed them brought them to the knowledge of others, and their fame began to spread on every side. For things excellent, even if they are beclouded for a short time through envy, shine out again under the benign operation of nature when their time comes. Then it was that some people, thinking it a shame that the laws should be found in one half only of the human race, the barbarians, and denied altogether to the Greeks, took steps to have them translated. In view of the importance and public utility of the task, it was referred, not to private persons or magistrates, who were very numerous, but to kings, and amongst them to the king of highest repute. Ptolemy, surnamed Philadelphus, was the third in succession to Alexander, the conqueror of Egypt. In all the qualities which make a good ruler, he excelled not only his contemporaries but all who have arisen in the past; and even till today, after so many generations, his praises are sung for the many evidences and monuments of his greatness of mind which he left behind him in different cities and countries, so that, even now, acts of more than ordinary munificence or buildings on a specially great scale are proverbially called Philadelphian after him. To put it shortly, as the house of the Ptolemies was highly distinguished, compared with other dynasties, so was Philadelphus among the Ptolemies. The creditable achievements of this one man almost outnumbered those of all the others put together, and, as the head takes the highest place in the living body, so he may be said to head the kings.

This great man, having conceived an ardent affection for our laws, determined to have the Chaldean translated into Greek, and at once dispatched envoys to the High Priest and King of Judaea, both offices being held by the same person,[14] explaining his wishes and urging him to choose by merit persons to make a full rendering of the Law into Greek. The High Priest was naturally pleased, and, thinking that God's guiding care must have led the King to busy himself in such an undertaking, sought out such Hebrews as he had of the highest reputation, who had received an education in Greek as well as in their native lore, and joyfully sent them to Ptolemy. When they arrived, they were offered hospitality and, having been sumptuously entertained, requited their entertainer with a feast of words full of wit and weight. For he tested the wisdom of each by propounding for discussion new instead of the ordinary questions, which problems they solved with happy and well-pointed answers in the form of apothegms, as the occasion did not allow of lengthy speaking.

After standing this test, they at once began to fulfill the duties of their high errand. Reflecting how great an undertaking it was to make a full version of the laws given by the voice of God, where they could not add or take away or transfer anything, but must keep the original form and shape, they proceeded to look for the most open and unoccupied spot in the neighborhood outside the city. For within the walls it was full of every kind of living creatures, and consequently the prevalence of diseases and deaths, and the impure conduct of the healthy inhabitants, made them suspicious of it. In front of Alexandria lies the island of Pharos, stretching with its narrow strip of land toward the city and enclosed by a sea not deep but most consisting of shoals, so that the loud din and booming of the surging waves grows faint through the long distance before it reaches the land. Judging this to be the most suitable place in the district where they might find peace and tranquility, and the soul could commune with the laws with none to disturb its privacy, they fixed their abode there; and, taking the sacred books, stretched them out toward heaven with the hands that held them, asking of God that they might not fail in their purpose. And he assented to their prayers, to the end that the greater part, or even the whole, of the human race might be profited and led to a better life by continuing to observe such wise and truly admirable ordinances.

Sitting here in seclusion, with none present save the elements of nature—earth, water, air, heaven—the genesis of which was to be the first theme of their sacred revelation, for the laws begin with the story of the world's creation, they became as it were possessed, and under inspiration wrote, not each several scribe something different, but the same word for word, as though dictated to each by an invisible prompter. Yet who does not know that every language, and Greek especially, abounds in terms, and that the same thought can be put in many shapes by changing single words and whole phrases, and suiting the expression to the occasion? This was not the case, we are told, with this Law of ours; but the Greek words used corresponded literally with the Chaldean, exactly suited to the things they indicated. For just as in geometry and logic, so it seems to me, the sense indicated does not admit of variety in the expression which remains unchanged in its original form, so these writers, as it clearly appears, arrived at a wording which corresponded with the matter and alone, or better than any other, would bring out clearly what was meant. The clearest proof of this is that, if Chaldeans have learned Greek or Greeks Chaldean, and read both versions, the Chaldean and the translation, they regard them with awe and reverence as sisters, or rather one and the same, both in matter and words, and speak of the authors not as translators but as prophets and priests of the mysteries, whose sincerity and singleness of thought has enabled them to go hand in hand with the purest of spirits, the spirit of Moses.[15]

THE PUNISHMENT TO FIT THE CRIME [16]

The legislators deserve censure who prescribe for malefactors punishments which do not resemble the crime, such as monetary fines for assaults, disfranchisement for wounding or maiming another, expulsion from the country and perpetual banishment for willful murder, or imprisonment for theft. For inequality and unevenness is repugnant to the commonwealth which pursues truth. Our law exhorts us to equality when it ordains that the penalties inflicted on offenders should correspond to their actions; that their property should suffer if the wrongdoing affected their neighbor's property, and their bodies if the offense was a bodily injury, the penalty being determined according to the limb, part, or sense affected, while if his malice extended to taking another's life his own life should be the forfeit. For to tolerate a system in which the crime and the punishment do not correspond, have no common ground, and belong to different categories, is to subvert rather than uphold legality. In saying this, I assume that the other conditions are the same; for to strike a stranger is not the same as to strike a father, nor the abuse of a ruler the same as abuse of an ordinary citizen. Unlawful actions differ according as they are committed in a profane or sacred place, or at festivals and solemn assemblies and public sacrifices, as contrasted with days which have no holiday associations or are even quite inauspicious. And all other similar facts must be carefully considered with a view to making the punishment greater or less.

Again he [17] says that if anyone knocks out the eye of a manservant or maidservant, he must set him at liberty. Why is this? Just as nature conferred the sovereignty of the body on the head when she granted it also possession of the citadel as the most suitable position for its kingly rank, conducted it thither to take command and established it on high with the whole framework from neck to foot set below it, like the pedestal under the statue, so too she has given the lordship of the senses to the eyes. Thus to them too as rulers she has assigned a dwelling right above the others, in her wish to give them, amongst other privileges, the most conspicuous and distinguished situation.

Now as for the services and benefits which the eyes render to the human race, it would take a long time to enumerate them, but one, the best, must be mentioned. Philosophy was showered down by heaven and received by the human mind, but the guide which brought the two together was sight, for sight was the first to discern the high roads which lead to the upper air. Now philosophy is the fountain of good things, all that are truly good, and he who draws from that spring deserves praise if he does so for the acquisition and practice of virtue, but blame if it is for knavish ends and to outwit another with sophistry. For in the first case he resembles the convivial man who makes himself and his fellow guests merry, in the second the drinker who swills himself with strong wine, only to play the sot and insult himself and his neighbors. Now let us describe the way in which sight acted as guide to philosophy; sight looked up to the ethereal region and beheld the sun and moon, and the fixed and wandering stars, the host of heaven in all its sacred majesty, a world within a world; then their risings and settings, their ordered rhythmic marchings, their conjunctions as the appointed times recur, their eclipses, their reappearances; then the waxing and waning of the moon, the courses of the sun from side to side as it passes from the south to the north and returns from the north to the south, thus producing the yearly seasons by which all things are brought to their consummation. Numberless other marvels did it behold, and after it had gazed around over earth and sea and the lower air, it made speed to show all these things to the mind. The mind, having discerned through the faculty of sight what of itself it was not able to apprehend, did not simply stop short at what it saw, but, drawn by its love of knowledge and beauty, and charmed by the marvelous spectacle, came to the reasonable conclusion that all these were not brought together automatically by unreasoning forces, but by the mind of God, who is rightly called their Father and Maker; also that they are not unlimited but are bounded by the ambit of a single universe, walled in like a city by the outermost sphere of the fixed stars; also that the Father who begat them according to the law of nature takes thought for his offspring, his providence watching over both the whole and the parts. Then it went on to inquire what is the substance of the world which we see and whether its constituents are all the same in substance or do some differ from others; what are the elements of which each particular part is composed, what are the causes which brought them into being, and what are the forces or properties which hold them together, and are these forces corporeal or incorporeal. We may well ask what title we can give to research into these matters but philosophy, and what more fitting name than philosopher to their investigator. For to make a study of God and the universe embracing all that is therein, both animals and plants, and of the conceptual archetypes and also the works which they produce for sense to perceive, and of the good and evil qualities in every created thing, shows a disposition which loves to learn, loves to contemplate, and is truly wisdom-loving or philosophical.

This is the greatest boon which sight bestowed on human life, and I think that this pre-eminence has been awarded to it because it is more closely akin to the soul than the other senses. They are all of the same family as the mind, but, just as it is with families, the place which is closest in birth and first and highest is held by sight. We may find many proofs of this, for who does not know that when we rejoice, the eyes are bright and smiling; when we are sad they are full of anxiety and dejection, and, if the burden is magnified and presses and crushes, they break out into tears; when anger prevails, they swell and their look is bloodshot and fiery; when the temper dies down, [they are][18] gentle and kindly; when we are reflecting or inquiring, the pupils are set and seem to share our thoughts; while in persons of little sense their silliness makes their vision roaming and restless. In general, the emotions of the soul are shared by the eyes, and as it passes through its numberless phases they change with it, a natural consequence of their affinity. Indeed it seems to me that nowhere else in God's creations is the inward and invisible so well represented by the outward and visible as reason is by sight.

AN ANTI-JEWISH EPISODE [19]

For it was perfectly clear that the rumor of the overthrowing of the synagogues beginning at Alexandria would spread at once to the rest of Egypt and speed from Egypt to the East and the nations of the East and from the Hypotaenia and Marea, which are the outskirts of Libya, to the West and the nations of the West. For so populous are the Jews that no one country can hold them, and therefore they settle in very many of the most prosperous countries in Europe and Asia both in the islands and on the mainland, and while they hold the Holy City where stands the sacred Temple of the most high God to be their mother city, yet those which are theirs by inheritance from their fathers, grandfathers, and ancestors even farther back, are in each case accounted by them to be their fatherland in which they were born and reared, while to some of them they have come at the time of their foundation as immigrants to the satisfaction of the founders. And it was to be feared that people everywhere might take their cue from Alexandria, and outrage their Jewish fellow citizens by rioting against their synagogues and ancestral customs. Now the Jews, though naturally well-disposed for peace, could not be expected to remain quiet whatever happened, not only because with all men the determination to fight for their institutions outweighs even the danger to life, but also because they are the only people under the sun who, by losing their meeting houses, were losing also what they would have valued as worth dying many thousand deaths, namely, their means of showing reverence to their benefactors, since they no longer had the sacred buildings where they could set forth their thankfulness. And they might have said to their enemies, "You have failed to see that you are not adding to, but taking from, the honor given to our masters; and you do not understand that everywhere in the habitable world the religious veneration of the Jews for the Augustan house has its basis as all may see in the meeting houses; and if we have these destroyed, no place, no method is left to us for paying this homage. If we neglect to pay it when our institutions permit we should deserve the utmost penalty for not tendering our requital with all due fullness. But if we fall short because it is forbidden by our own laws, which Augustus also was well pleased to confirm, I do not see what offense, either small or great, can be laid to our charge. The only thing for which we might be blamed would be that we transgressed, though involuntarily, by not defending ourselves against the defections from our customs, which even if originally due to others often ultimately affect those who are responsible for them." It was by saying what he should leave unsaid and leaving unsaid what he should say that Flaccus treated us in this iniquitous way. But what were the motives of those whose favor he was seeking? Was it that they really wished to honor the Emperor? Was there then any lack of temples in the city, so many parts of which are consecrated and give all that is needed for the installation of anything they wished? No, what we have described is an act of aggression by bitterly hostile and crafty plotters in which the authors of the outrages would not appear to be acting unjustly and the sufferers could not oppose them with safety. For surely, my good sirs, there is no honor given by overthrowing the laws, disturbing ancestral customs, outraging fellow citizens, and teaching the inhabitants of other cities to disregard the claims of fellow feeling.

II

JOSEPHUS THE HISTORIAN

Joseph, son of Mattathias, a priest of distinguished lineage and Pharisaic views, played a rather ambiguous role in the Roman-Jewish war of 66–70 A.D. After his surrender to Vespasian, he was taken to Rome by his imperial master. In accordance with Roman custom, when he was liberated he assumed the family name of his former owner and became known as Josephus Flavius. Because of his conduct during the war, he was accused of high treason by many fellow Jews; he composed, chiefly for the benefit of his coreligionists in Babylonia, a detailed story of *The Jewish War*, in Aramaic. Later he was encouraged to translate this work into Greek; only the Greek version is extant today. In addition, he was urged to expand this story into a regular history of the Jewish people from the beginning to his own time. Under this spur, he wrote *The Antiquities of the Jews*, in twenty books. He supplemented these major historical works by an autobiographical account of his life. All these works are permeated with an apologetic spirit. They were to serve principally the purpose of defending the Jewish people and religion at the bar of a frequently hostile Graeco-Roman public opinion. His most forthright apologetic work was his treatise *Against Apion*, a reply to a leading Alexandrian exponent of classical antisemitism.

THE JEWISH THEOCRACY [20]

THERE IS ENDLESS VARIETY in the details of the customs and laws which prevail in the world at large. To give but a summary enumeration: some peoples have entrusted the supreme political power to monarchies, others to oligarchies, yet others to the masses. Our lawgiver,[21] however, was attracted by none of these forms of polity, but gave to his constitution the form of what—if a forced expression be permitted—may be termed a 'theocracy,' placing all sovereignty and authority in the hands of God. To him he persuaded all to look, as the author of all blessings, both those which are common to all mankind and those which they had won for themselves by prayer in the crises of their history. He convinced them that no single action, no secret thought, could be hid from him. He represented him as One, uncreated and immutable to all eternity, in beauty surpassing all mortal thought, made known to us by his power, although the nature of his real being passes knowledge.

That the wisest of the Greeks learned to adopt these conceptions of God from principles with which Moses supplied them, I am not now concerned to urge; but they have borne abundant witness to the excellence of these doctrines, and to their consonance with the nature and majesty of God. In fact, Pythagoras, Anaxagoras, Plato, the Stoics who succeeded him, and indeed nearly all the philosophers appear to have held similar views concerning the nature of God. These, however, addressed their philosophy to the few, and did not venture to divulge their true beliefs to the masses, who had their own preconceived opinions; whereas our lawgiver, by making practice square with precept, not only convinced his own contemporaries but so firmly implanted this belief concerning God in their descendants to all future generations that it cannot be moved. The cause of his success was that the very nature of his legislation made it [always] far more useful than any other; for he did not make religion a department of virtue, but the various virtues—I mean justice, temperance, fortitude, and mutual harmony in all things between the members of the community—departments of religion. Religion governs all our actions and occupations and speech; none of these things did our lawgiver leave unexamined or indeterminate.

All schemes of education and moral training fall into two categories: instruction is imparted in the one case by precept, in the other by practical exercising of the character. All other legislators, differing in their opinions, selected the particular method which each preferred and neglected the other. . . . Our legislator, on the other hand, took great care to combine both systems. He did not leave practical training in morals inarticulate; nor did he permit the letter of the law to remain inoperative. Starting from the very beginning with the food of which we partake from infancy and the private life of the home, he left nothing, however insignificant, to the discretion and caprice of the individual. What meats a man should abstain from and what he may enjoy, with what persons he should associate, what period should be devoted respectively to strenuous labor and to rest—for all this our leader made the Law the standard and rule, that we might live under it as under a father and master, and be guilty of no sin through willfulness or ignorance.

For ignorance he left no pretext. He appointed the Law to be the most excellent and necessary form of instruction, ordaining, not that it should be heard once for all, or twice, or on several occasions, but that every week men should desert their other occupations and assemble to listen to the Law, and to obtain a thorough and accurate knowledge of it—a practice which all other legislators seem to have neglected.

Indeed, most men, so far from living in accordance with their own laws, hardly know what they are. Only when they have done wrong do they learn from others that they have transgressed the law. Even those of them who hold the highest and most important offices admit their ignorance, for they employ professional legal experts as assessors and leave them in charge of the administration of affairs. But should anyone of our nation be questioned about the laws, he would repeat them all more readily than his own name. The result, then, of our thorough grounding in the laws from the first dawn of intelligence is that we have them, as it were, engraven on our souls. A transgressor is a rarity, evasion of punishment by excuses an impossibility.

To this cause above all we owe our admirable harmony. Unity and identity of religious belief, perfect uniformity in habits and customs, produce a very beautiful concord in human character. Among us alone will be heard no contradictory statements about God, such as are common among other nations, not only on the lips of ordinary individuals under the impulse of some passing mood, but even boldly propounded by philosophers; some putting forward crushing arguments against the very existence of God, others depriving him of his providential care for mankind. Among us alone will be seen no difference in the conduct of our lives. With us all act alike, all profess the same doctrine about God, one which is in harmony with our Law and affirms that all things are under his eye. Even our womenfolk and dependents would tell you that piety must be the motive of all our occupations in life.

. . . .

For all that, the Lysimachuses and Molons and other writers of that class, reprobate sophists and deceivers of youth, rail at us as the very vilest of mankind. Gladly would I have avoided an investigation of the institutions of other nations, for it is our traditional custom to observe our own laws and to refrain from criticism of those of aliens. Our legislator has expressly forbidden us to deride or blaspheme the gods recognized by others, out of respect for the very word "God." But since our accusers expect to confute us by a comparison of the rival religions, it is impossible to remain silent. I speak with the more assurance because the statement which I am about to make is no invention of my own for the occasion, but has been made by many writers of the highest reputation.

Who, in fact, is there among the admired sages of Greece who has not censured their most famous poets and their most trusted legislators for sowing in the minds of the masses the first seeds of such notions about the gods? They represent them to be as numerous as they choose, born of one another, and engendered in all manner of ways. They assign them different localities and habits, like animal species, some living underground, others in the sea, the oldest of all being chained in Tartarus. Those to whom they have allotted heaven have set over them one who is nominally Father but in reality a tyrant and despot, with the result that his wife and brother and the daughter whom he begot from his own head conspire against him to arrest and imprison him, just as he himself had treated his own father.

Justly do these tales merit the severe censure which they receive from their intellectual leaders. Moreover, they ridicule the belief that some gods are beardless striplings, others old and bearded; that some are appointed to trades, this one being a smith, that goddess a weaver, a third a warrior who fights along with men, others lute players or devoted to archery; and again that they are divided into factions and quarrel about men, insomuch that they not only come to blows with each other but actually lament over and suffer from wounds inflicted by mortals. But—and here outrageousness reaches its climax—is it not monstrous to attribute those licentious unions and amours to well nigh all the deities of both sexes? Furthermore, the noblest and chief of them all, the Father himself, after seducing women and rendering them pregnant, leaves them to be imprisoned or drowned in the sea, and is so completely at the mercy of destiny that he cannot either rescue his own offspring or restrain his tears at their death. Fine doings are these, and others that follow, such as adultery in heaven, with the gods as such shameless onlookers that some of them confessed that they envied the united pair. And well they might, when even the eldest of them, the King, could not restrain his passion for his consort long enough to permit of withdrawal to his chamber. Then there are the gods in bondage to men, hired now as builders, now as shepherds; and others chained, like criminals, in a prison of brass. What man in his senses would not be stirred to reprimand the inventors of such fables and to condemn the consummate folly of those who believed them? They have even deified Terror and Fear, nay, Frenzy and Deceit (which of the worst passions have they not transfigured into the nature and form of a god?), and have induced cities to offer sacrifices to the more respectable members of this pantheon. Thus they have been absolutely compelled to regard some of the gods as givers of blessings and to call others '(gods) to be averted.' They then rid themselves of the latter, as they would of the worst scoundrels of humanity, by means of favors and presents, expecting to be visited by some serious mischief if they fail to pay them their price.

Now what is the cause of such irregular and erroneous conceptions of the deity? For my part, I trace it to the ignorance of the true nature of God with which their legislators entered on their task, and to their failure to formulate even such correct knowledge of it as they were able to attain and to make the rest of their constitution conform to it. Instead, as if this were the most trifling of details, they allowed the poets to introduce what gods they chose, subject to all the passions, and the orators to pass decrees for entering the name of any suitable foreign god on the burgess roll. Painters also, and sculptors, were given great license in this matter by the Greeks, each designing a figure of his own imagination, one molding it of clay, another using paints. The artists who are the most admired of all use ivory and gold as the material for the novelties which they are constantly producing. And now the gods who once flourished with honors are grown old—that is the kinder way of putting it—and others, newly introduced, are the objects of worship. Some temples are left to desolation, others are but now being erected, according to individual caprice; whereas they ought, on the contrary, to have preserved immutably their belief in God and the honor which they rendered to him.

Apollonius Molon [22] was but one of the crazy fools. The genuine exponents of Greek philosophy were well aware of all that I have said; nor were they ignorant of the worthless shifts to which the allegorists have resort. That was why they rightly despised them and agreed with us in forming a true and befitting conception of God. From this standpoint Plato declares that no poet ought to be admitted to the republic, and dismisses even Homer in laudatory terms, after crowning and anointing him with unguents, in order to prevent him from obscuring by his fables the correct doctrine about God. In two points, in particular, Plato followed the example of our legislator. He prescribed as the primary duty of the citizens a study of their laws, which they must all learn word for word by heart. Again, he took precautions to prevent foreigners from mixing with them at random and to keep the state pure and confined to law-abiding citizens. Of these facts Apollonius Molon took no account when he condemned us for refusing admission to persons with other preconceived ideas about God and for declining to associate with those who have chosen to adopt a different mode of life. Yet even this habit is not peculiar to us; it is common to all, and shared not only by Greeks but by Greeks of the highest reputation. The Lacedaemonians made a practice of expelling foreigners and would not allow their own citizens to travel abroad, in both cases apprehensive of their laws being corrupted. *They* might perhaps be justly reproached for discourtesy, because they accorded to no one the rights either of citizenship or of residence among them. We, on the contrary, while we have no desire to emulate the customs of others, yet gladly welcome any who wish to share our own. That, I think, may be taken as a proof both of humanity and magnanimity.

Of the Lacedaemonians I will say no more. But the Athenians, who considered their city open to all comers, what was their attitude in this matter? Apollonius was ignorant of this and of the inexorable penalty which they inflicted on any who uttered a single word about the gods contrary to their laws. On what other ground was Socrates put to death? He never sought to betray his city to the enemy; he robbed no temple. No: because he used to swear strange oaths and give out (in jest, surely, as some say) that he received communications from a spirit; he was therefore condemned to die by drinking hemlock. His accuser brought a further charge against him of corrupting young men, because he stimulated them to hold the constitution and laws of their country in contempt. Such was the punishment of Socrates, a citizen of Athens. Anaxagoras was a native of Clazomenae, but because he maintained that the sun, which the Athenians held to be a god, was an incandescent mass, he escaped by a few votes only from being condemned by them to death. They offered a talent for the head of Diagoras of Melos because he was reported to have jeered at their mysteries. Protagoras, had he not promptly fled, would have been arrested and put to death because of a statement about the gods in his writings which appeared to conflict with Athenian tenets. Can one wonder at their attitude toward men of such authority when they did not spare even women? They put Ninus, the priestess, to death because someone accused her of initiating people into the mysteries of foreign gods; this was forbidden by their law, and the penalty decreed for any who introduced a foreign god was death. Those who had such a law evidently did not believe that the gods of other nations were gods, else they would not have denied themselves the advantage of increasing the number of their own.

So much may be said to the credit of the Athenians. But even Scythians, who delight in murdering people and are little better than wild beasts, nevertheless think it their duty to uphold their national customs; and Anacharsis, whose wisdom won the admiration of the Greeks, was on his return put to death by his compatriots because he appeared to have come back infected with Greek habits. In Persia, also, numerous instances will be found of persons being executed for the same reason. Apollonius, however, had an affection for the laws of the Persians and a high opinion of the people, evidently because Greece had a taste of their courage and the benefit of their agreement with herself in religious beliefs! The latter she experienced when she saw her temples burned to the ground, their courage in her bare escape from subjection to their yoke. Apollonius actually imitated all the Persian practices, outraging his neighbors' wives and castrating their children.

With us such maltreatment even of a brute beast is made a capital crime. And from these laws of ours nothing has had power to deflect us, neither fear of our masters, nor envy of the institutions esteemed by other nations. We have trained our courage, not with a view to waging war for self-aggrandizement, but in order to preserve our laws. To defeat in any other form we patiently submit; but when pressure is put upon us to alter our statutes, then we deliberately fight, even against tremendous odds, and hold out under reverses to the last extremity. And why should we envy other nations their laws when we see that even their authors do not observe them? The Lacedaemonians were, of course, bound in the end to condemn their unsociable constitution and their contempt for marriage, and the people of Elis and Thebes the unnatural vice so rampant among them. At any rate, if they have not in fact altogether abandoned them, they no longer openly avow practices which once they considered very excellent and expedient. But they go further than this and repudiate their laws on the subject of these unions—laws which at one time carried such weight with the Greeks that they actually attributed to the gods the practice of sodomy and, on the same principle, the marriage of brother and sister, thus inventing an excuse for the monstrous and unnatural pleasures in which they themselves indulged.

In the present work I pass over the various penalties and all the modes of compounding for them which the majority of legislators provided in their codes at the outset for offenders—accepting fines in case of adultery, marriage in that of immorality—and, in matters of impiety, all the subterfuges which they left open for denying the facts, if anyone took the trouble to open an inquiry. Nowadays, indeed, violation of the laws has with most nations become a fine art. Not so with us. Robbed though we be of wealth, of cities, of all good things, our Law at least remains immortal; and there is not a Jew so distant from his country, so much in awe of a cruel despot, but has more fear of the Law than of him. If, then, our attachment to our laws is due to their excellence, let it be granted that they are excellent. If, on the contrary, it be thought that the laws to which we are so loyal are bad, what punishment could be too great for persons who transgress those which are better?

Now, since time is reckoned in all cases the surest test of worth, I would call time to witness to the excellence of our lawgiver and of the revelation concerning God which he has transmitted to us. An infinity of time has passed since Moses, if one compares the age in which he lived with those of other legislators; yet it will be found that throughout the whole of that period not merely have our laws stood the test of our own use, but they have to an ever-increasing extent excited the emulation of the world at large.

Our earliest imitators were the Greek philosophers, who, though ostensibly observing the laws of their own countries, yet in their conduct and philosophy were Moses' disciples, holding similar views about God and advocating the simple life and friendly communion between man and man. But that is not all. The masses have long since shown a keen desire to adopt our religious observances; and there is not one city, Greek or barbarian, nor a single nation, to which our custom of abstaining from work on the seventh day has not spread, and where the fasts and the lighting of lamps and many of our prohibitions in the matter of food are not observed. Moreover, they attempt to imitate our unanimity, our liberal charities, our devoted labor in the crafts, our endurance under persecution on behalf of our laws. The greatest miracle of all is that our Law holds out no seductive bait of sensual pleasure, but has exercised this influence through its own inherent merits; and, as God permeates the universe, so the Law has found its way among all mankind. Let each man reflect for himself on his own country and his own household, and he will not disbelieve what I say. It follows, then, that our accusers must either condemn the whole world for deliberate malice in being so eager to adopt the bad laws of a foreign country in preference to the good laws of their own or else give up their grudge against us. In honoring our own legislator and putting our trust in his prophetical utterances concerning God, we do not make any arrogant claim justifying such odium. Indeed, were we not ourselves aware of the excellence of our laws, assuredly we should have been impelled to pride ourselves upon them by the multitude of their admirers.

PART THREE

SECTARIAN MOVEMENTS

I

THE SAMARITANS[1]

Although Judaism often seems to the non-Jew to be a religious tradition of unusual consistency and unity, a closer study of its history reveals that at critical epochs in its development alternative ways of preserving the faith have been proposed by different groups in the Jewish population. These alternative courses have furnished the basis of sectarian movements in Judaism. Some of these movements have survived, for a shorter or longer time; others have so completely passed out of existence and out of the records of history that nothing is known of them beyond their names.

Whenever a minority movement has proved viable, the majority party has had to work out a program for co-existing with the rival sect. The first selection below, based on a compilation of early Amoraic times, possibly soon after the compilation of the Mishnah, summarizes the rules of the Pharisaic majority for co-existing with the Samaritans, who were the earliest Jewish sect. Some two hundred of the Samaritans survive today and maintain their corporate identity. The final separation of the Samaritans from the parent religion seems not to have taken place earlier than the time of Alexander the Great, although the antecedent contention dates from the attempts in the period of the kings to build, in the kingdom of Israel, a sanctuary to rival the Temple at Jerusalem. When the split came, the Samaritans had their temple on Mount Gerizim. At this time only the Pentateuch had been canonized, and the Samaritans accepted as their Scriptures these five books with the addition of the Book of Joshua. Their early history is obscure; most early references to the sect are found in unfriendly sources. Exceptional for its friendly tone toward the Samaritans is the parable of the Good Samaritan, in the New Testament.

I

THE USAGES OF THE SAMARITANS are at times like those of the heathens, at times like those of the Israelites, but most of the time like the Israelites.

We do not accept from them the bird sacrifices of men or women cured from gonorrhea, nor the bird sacrifices of women after confinement, nor sin offerings, nor trespass offerings. But we receive from them vows and free-will offerings.

We do not suffer them to acquire immovable property; nor do we sell them sheep for shearing, nor crops to cut, nor timber still standing. But we sell them timber, on condition that they shall cut it. R. Meir says, "We sell them only the timber which is cut." We sell to a Samaritan butcher an animal, on condition that he will slaughter it. R. Meir says, "We sell him only that which is slaughtered."

We do not sell them large cattle though wounded, nor foals, nor calves. But we may sell them cattle that are maimed beyond the possibility of cure.

We do not sell them weapons, nor anything with which they can cause damage to the public.

We do not give them Jewish women in marriage; nor do we marry their women. We lend them and borrow from them money on interest.

We let them have the gleanings, the forgotten sheaf, and the corner of the field. They observe the laws with regard to the gleanings, the forgotten sheaf, and the corner of the field. They may be relied upon regarding the gleanings, the forgotten sheaf, and the corner of the field, in their proper time, and concerning the tithe for the poor, in its proper time. Their fruit is considered as untithed, as that of heathens. They invalidate the *Erub*, as heathens.

A Jewess may not deliver a Samaritan woman, nor nurse her child. But a Samaritan woman may deliver a Jewess and nurse her child in the Jewish woman's quarters.

An Israelite may circumcise a Samaritan, and a Samaritan an

Israelite. R. Judah says, "A Samaritan should not circumcise an Israelite, for he circumcises in the name of Mount Gerizim."

We may lodge an animal in a Samaritan stable or hire a Samaritan to go behind the cattle of an Israelite, and an Israelite may hand over his cattle to a Samaritan herdsman. An Israelite may give his son in the charge of a Samaritan to teach him a trade. An Israelite may associate with Samaritans and may have his hair cut by them in any place, as is not the case with the heathen.

A Samaritan suffers the *Ḥaliẓah* from his sister-in-law and gives a letter of divorce to his wife. He may be trusted to bring a letter of divorce from outside of Palestine to an Israelite.

These are the things we may not sell them: carcasses not ritually slaughtered and animals with organic diseases; forbidden animals and reptiles; the hoof of a dead animal; oil that has been polluted or into which a mouse has fallen; meat of an animal that has been mortally ill and of an embryo, although Israelites eat them.

We do not sell them these things, for such sales are frauds. And as we do not sell such things to them, so do we not buy those things from them. For it is written, "For thou art a holy people unto the Lord thy God." [2] Inasmuch as thou art holy, thou shalt not make another people holier than thyself.

A Samaritan may be trusted to say whether or not he buried an abortion in a field or whether an animal has had its firstborn or not.

A Samaritan may be relied upon concerning the fruit of trees of the fourth year and of the first three years, and concerning gravestones. But he is not trusted concerning overhanging boughs or projecting stones, under which there may be places of uncleanliness; nor concerning the cleanliness of the lands outside of Palestine; nor concerning a field declared unclean on account of crushed bones carried over it from a plowed grave, because they are open to suspicion in all these things. This is the principle: they are not to be trusted in any matter in which they are open to suspicion.

II

We do not buy meat from a Samaritan butcher, except that of which he himself eats; nor baskets with slaughtered birds, unless he first puts them in his mouth, and does not select the ones to be given to the Israelite. For they have been suspected of giving Israelites flesh of carcasses.

The Samaritan is on the same footing as the Israelite with regard to all damages mentioned in the Torah. An Israelite who slays a Samaritan or a Samaritan who slays an Israelite, if unintentionally, is secluded in a city of refuge; if intentionally, he suffers death.

If the ox of an Israelite gores the ox of a Samaritan, the owner goes free. But if the ox of a Samaritan gores the ox of an Israelite, should it be the first offense, the Samaritan owner pays half the damage; should it be an offense of an animal whose owner stood forewarned, he pays the full damage. R. Meir says, "In the case of an ox of a Samaritan that gores the ox of an Israelite, whether for the first time or not, the owner pays the full damage, from his other possessions."

The cheese of Samaritans is allowed. R. Simeon, the son of Eleazar, says, "The cheese of a private individual is allowed, but that of the village dealers is forbidden."

The cooked or preserved foods of the Samaritans, which they prepare with wine or vinegar, are forbidden.

The priests of Israel may share the priestly dues with the Samaritan priests in the territory of the Samaritans, because they are thus, as it were, rescuing property from the Samaritans; but not in Israelite territory, lest people might consider the Samaritans as regular priests.

If a Samaritan priest, when he is unclean, eats and gives of his food to an Israelite, the latter may eat of that food. If the Samaritan priest is clean, the Israelite must not eat of his food.

. We buy no bread from a Samaritan baker at the end of the Passover until after three bakings, nor from private individuals until after three Sabbaths, nor from villagers until after three cycles of baking. This applies only when they have not made the unleavened bread together with the Israelites or have anticipated the Feast of Passover by a day. But if they have made the unleavened bread together with the Israelites, or have commenced to celebrate the Feast of Passover a day later, their leaven is permitted.

R. Simeon forbids the unleavened bread of the Samaritans, because they do not know how to observe the laws concerning the unleavened bread as the Israelites do.

Formerly the Sages said, "The wine of Gedur is forbidden, because of the wine of Kefar Paggashah." This they afterward modified, saying, "Wherever the Samaritans are suspected of mingling with the heathen, wine of open barrels is forbidden and that of sealed barrels is allowed." R. Meir says, "All their wine is allowed, except that which is open in the market." The Sages say, "That which is open in any place is forbidden, that which is sealed is permitted, and that which has been perforated and then sealed is as if it had always been sealed." Their jars, if new, are permitted; if old, are forbidden.

Why are the Samaritans forbidden to marry into Israel? Because they have intermingled with the priests of the high places.[3] R. Ishmael says, "At first they were genuine proselytes." Why are they then forbidden? Because there are cases of children of uncertain parentage, and because the Samaritans do not perform the levirate marriage in case one has died after the consummation of the marriage.

When shall we receive the Samaritans? When they shall renounce Mount Gerizim and acknowledge Jerusalem and the resurrection of the dead. Thereupon, he that robs a Samaritan shall be as one who robs an Israelite.

II

THE JEWISH SECTS [4]

During the period of the Second Commonwealth, a major division of the Jews took place. One group, generally regarded as the Temple or aristocratic party, held that the canonical Scriptures, without further interpretation by the oral law, constituted the full measure of Jewish piety; these were the Sadducees. A second group, destined to become the dominant party and the preserver and carrier of the Jewish religion, held that the oral law was a necessary and living supplement to the written law; these were the Pharisees. In the selection below Josephus, the historian, summarizes briefly the beliefs of these two major groups and two smaller ones, and estimates their worth as it appeared to an observer who had made a careful study of the rival doctrines before associating himself with the Pharisaic party.

THE JEWS HAD, for a great while, three sects of philosophy peculiar to themselves; the sect of Essenes, and the sect of the Sadducees, and the third sort of opinions was that of those called Pharisees, of which sects, although I have already spoken in the second book of the Jewish War, yet will I a little touch on them now.

Now for the Pharisees, they live meanly and despise delicacies in diet, and they follow the conduct of reason; and what that prescribes to them as good for them they do, and they think they ought earnestly to strive to observe reason's dictates for practice. They also pay a respect to such as are in years, nor are they so bold as to contradict them in anything which they have introduced; and when they determine that all things are done by fate they do not take away the freedom from men of acting as they think fit, since their notion is that it hath pleased God to make a temperament whereby what he wills is done, but so that the will of man can act virtuously or viciously. They also believe that souls have an immortal vigor in them, and that under the earth there will be rewards and punishments, according as they have lived virtuously or viciously in this life; and the latter are to be detained in an everlasting prison, but that the former shall have power to revive and live again; on account of which doctrines they are able greatly to persuade the body of the people; and whatsoever they do about divine worship, prayers, and sacrifices, they perform them according to their direction, insomuch that the cities gave great attestation to them on account of their entire virtuous conduct, both in the actions of their lives and their discourses also.

But the doctrine of the Sadducees is this: that souls die with the bodies; nor do they regard the observation of anything besides what the law enjoins them, for they think it an instance of virtue to dispute with those teachers of philosophy whom they frequent; but this doctrine is received but by a few, yet by those still of the greatest dignity. But they are able almost to do nothing of themselves; for when they become magistrates, as they are unwillingly and by force sometimes obliged to be, they addict themselves to the notions of the Pharisees, because the multitude would not otherwise bear them.

The doctrine of the Essenes is this: that all things are best ascribed to God. They teach the immortality of souls and esteem that the rewards of righteousness are to be earnestly striven for; and when they send what they have dedicated to God into the Temple, they do not offer sacrifices, because they have more pure lustrations of their own, on which account they are excluded from the common court of the Temple but offer their sacrifices themselves; yet is their course of life better than that of other men, and they entirely addict themselves to husbandry. It also deserves our admiration how much they exceed all other men that addict themselves to virtue, and this in righteousness; and indeed to such a degree that, as it hath never appeared among any other men, neither Greeks nor barbarians—no, not for a little time—so hath it endured a long while among them. This is demonstrated by that institution of theirs which will not suffer anything to hinder them from having all things in common, so that a rich man enjoys no more of his own wealth than he who hath nothing at all. There are about four thousand men that live in this way, and neither marry wives nor are desirous to keep servants, as thinking the latter tempts men to be unjust and the former gives the handle to domestic quarrels; but as they live by themselves, they minister to one another. They also appoint certain stewards to receive the incomes of their revenues and of the fruits of the ground, such as are good men and priests, who are to get their corn and their food ready for them. They none of them differ from others of the Essenes in their way of living, but do the most resemble those Dacae who are called *Polistae*.[5]

But of the fourth sect of Jewish philosophy, Judas the Galilean was the author. These men agree in all other things with the Pharisaic notions, but they have an inviolable attachment to liberty—and say that God is to be their only Ruler and Lord. They also do not value dying any kinds of death; nor indeed do they heed the deaths of their relations and friends, nor can any such fear make them call any man lord. And since this immovable resolution of theirs is well known to a great many, I shall speak no farther about that matter; nor am I afraid that anything I have said of them should be disbelieved, but rather fear that what I have said is beneath the resolution they show when they undergo pain. And it was in Gessius Florus'[6] time that the nation began to go mad with this distemper, who was our procurator and who occasioned the Jews to go wild with it by the abuse of his authority and to make them revolt from the Romans. And these are the sects of Jewish philosophy.

III

THE ESSENES[7]

In the selection immediately preceding this, Josephus mentioned a third Jewish sect, the Essenes; here the same historian, who went through the probationary period in an Essenic community before becoming a Pharisee, discusses in considerable detail the beliefs and practices of the semimystical, separatist, communalistic sect of Essenes. The value of this account is enormous, because although Josephus speaks of a sacred literature of the sect, we have no documents preserved that we know to be of Essenic origin. It has been conjectured that the influence of the Essenes is present in some of the Apocryphal writings, but this contention has never been fully substantiated. The Essenes, wherever possible, withdrew from contact with the pollutions of everyday life into the seclusion of their own monastic communities, where they emphasized meticulous ritual purity rather than religious or philosophic speculation.

FOR THERE ARE THREE PHILOSOPHICAL SECTS among the Jews. The followers of the first of which are the Pharisees, of the second the Sadducees, and the third sect, which pretends to a severer discipline, are called Essenes. These last are Jews by birth and seem to have a greater affection for one another than the other sects have. These Essenes reject pleasures as an evil, but esteem continence and the conquest over our passions as a virtue. They neglect wedlock, but choose out other persons' children while they are pliable and fit for learning, and esteem them to be of their kindred, and form them according to their own manners. They do not absolutely deny the fitness of marriage and the succession of mankind thereby continued, but they guard against the lascivious behavior of women and are persuaded that none of them preserve their fidelity to one man.

These men are despisers of riches and so very communicative as raises our admiration. Nor is there anyone to be found among them who hath more than another; for it is a law among them that those who come to them must let what they have be common to the whole order, insomuch that among them all there is no appearance of poverty or excess of riches, but everyone's possessions are intermingled with every other's possessions, and so there is, as it were, one patrimony among all the brethren. They think that oil is a defilement; and if any of them be anointed without his own approbation, it is wiped off his body, for they think to be sweaty is a good thing, as they do also to be clothed in white garments. They also have stewards appointed to take care of their common affairs, who every one of them have no separate business for any but what is for the use of them all.

They have no one certain city, but many of them dwell in every city; and if any of their sect come from other places, what they have lies open for them, just as if it were their own; and they go into such as they never knew before, as if they had been ever so long acquainted with them; for which reason they carry nothing at all with them when they travel into remote parts, though still they take their weapons with them, for fear of thieves. Accordingly, there is, in every city where they live, one appointed particularly to take care of strangers, and to provide garments and other necessities for them. But the habit and management of their bodies is such as children use who are in fear of their masters. Nor do they allow the change of garments or of shoes, till they be first entirely torn to pieces or worn out by time. Nor do they buy or sell anything to one another, but every one of them gives what he hath to him that wanteth it, and receives from him again in lieu of it what may be convenient for himself; and although there be no requital made, they are fully allowed to take what they want of whomsoever they please.

And as for their piety toward God, it is very extraordinary; for before sunrise they speak not a word about profane matters, but put up certain prayers, which they have received from their forefathers, as if they made supplication for its rising. After this every one of them is sent away by their curators to exercise some of those arts wherein they are skilled, in which they labor with great diligence till the fifth hour, after which they assemble themselves together again into one place; and when they have clothed themselves in white veils, they then bathe their bodies in cold water. And after this purification is over, they every one meet together in an apartment of their own, into which it is not permitted to anyone of another sect to enter; while they go, after a pure manner, into the dining room, as into a certain holy temple, and quietly set themselves down; upon which the baker lays them loaves in order; the cook also brings a single plate of one sort of food and sets it before every one of them; but a priest says grace before meat, and it is unlawful for anyone to taste of the food before grace be said. The same priest, when he hath dined, says grace again after meat; and when they begin and when they end they praise God, as he that bestows their food upon them; after which they lay aside their [white] garments and betake themselves to their labors again till the evening; then they return home to supper after the same manner, and if there be any strangers there, they sit down with them. Nor is there ever any clamor or disturbance to pollute their house, but they give every one leave to speak in their turn; which silence thus kept in their house appears to foreigners like some tremendous mystery, the cause of which is that perpetual sobriety they exercise and the settled measure of meat and drink that is allotted them, and that such as is abundantly sufficient for them.

And truly, as for other things, they do nothing but according to the injunctions of their curators; only these two things are done among them at everyone's own free will, which are to assist those that want it and to show mercy; for they are permitted of their own accord to afford succor to such as deserve it, when they stand in need of it, and to bestow food on those that are in distress, but they cannot give anything to their kindred without the curators. They dispense their anger after a just manner and restrain their passion. They are eminent for fidelity and are the ministers of peace; whatsoever they say also is firmer than an oath; but swearing is avoided by them, and they esteem it worse than perjury, for they say that he who cannot be believed without [swearing by] God is already condemned. They also take great pains in studying the writings of the ancients and choose out of them what is most for the advantage of their soul and body, and they inquire after such roots and medicinal stones as may cure their distempers.

But now, if anyone hath a mind to come over to their sect, he is not immediately admitted, but he is prescribed the same method of living which they use for a year, while he continues excluded; and they give him also a small hatchet, and the forementioned girdle and the white garment. And when he hath given evidence, during that time, that he can observe their continence, he approaches nearer to their way of living and is made a partaker of the waters of purification; yet is he not even now admitted to live with them; for after this demonstration of his fortitude, his temper is tried two more years, and if he appear to be worthy they then admit him into their society. And before he is allowed to touch their common food, he is obliged to take tremendous oaths, that, in the first place, he will exercise piety toward God, and then that he will observe justice toward men and that he will do no harm to anyone, either of his own accord or by the command of others; that he will always hate the wicked and be assistant to the righteous; that he will ever show fidelity to all men, and especially to those in authority, because no one obtains the government without God's assistance; and that if he be in authority, he will at no time whatever abuse his authority, nor endeavor to outshine his subjects, either in his garments or any other finery, that he will be perpetually a lover of truth, and propose to himself to reprove those that tell lies; that he will keep his hands clear from theft and his soul from unlawful gains; and that he will neither conceal anything from those of his own sect nor discover any of their doctrines to others, no, not though anyone should compel him so to do at the hazard of his life. Moreover he swears to communicate their doctrines to no one any otherwise than as he received them himself; that he will abstain from robbery, and will equally preserve the books belonging to their sect and the names of the angels. These are the oaths by which they secure their proselytes to themselves.

But for those that are caught in any heinous sins, they cast them out of their society, and he who is thus separated from them does often die after a miserable manner; for as he is bound by the oath he hath taken and by the customs he hath been engaged in, he is not at liberty to partake of that food that he meets with elsewhere, but is forced to eat grass and to famish his body with hunger till he perish, for which reason they receive many of them again, when they are at their last gasp, out of compassion to them, as thinking the miseries they have endured till they came to the very brink of death to be a sufficient punishment for the sins they had been guilty of.

But in the judgments they exercise they are most accurate and just; nor do they pass sentence by the votes of a court that is fewer than a hundred. And as to what is once determined by that number, it is unalterable. What they most of all honor, after God himself, is the name of their legislator,[8] whom if anyone blaspheme, he is punished capitally. They also think it a good thing to obey their elders and the majority. Accordingly, if ten of them be sitting together, no one of them will speak while the other nine are against it. They also avoid spitting in the midst of them, or on the right side. Moreover, they are stricter than any other of the Jews in resting from their labors on the seventh day; for they not only get their food ready the day before, that they may not be obliged to kindle a fire on that day, but they will not remove any vessel out of its place nor go to stool thereon. Nay, on the other days they dig a small pit a foot deep with a paddle (which kind of hatchet is given them when they are first admitted among them), and covering themselves round with their garment, that they may not affront the divine rays of light, they ease themselves into that pit, after which they put the earth that was dug out again into the pit; and even this they do only in the more lonely places, which they choose out for this purpose; and although this easement of the body be natural, yet it is a rule with them to wash themselves after it, as if it were a defilement to them.

Now after the time of their preparatory trial is over, they are parted into four classes; and so far are the juniors inferior to the seniors that if the seniors should be touched by the juniors, they must wash themselves, as if they had intermixed themselves with the company of a foreigner. They are long-lived also, insomuch that many of them live above a hundred years, by means of the simplicity of their diet—nay, as I think, by means of the regular course of life they observe also. They contemn the miseries of life and are above pain, by the generosity of their mind. And as for death, if it will be for their glory, they esteem it better than living always; and indeed our war with the Romans gave abundant evidence what great souls they had in their trials, wherein although they were tortured and distorted, burned and torn to pieces, and went through all kinds of instruments of torment, that they might be forced either to blaspheme their legislator or to eat what was forbidden them, yet could not they be made to do either of them—no, nor once to flatter their tormentors or to shed a tear; but they smiled in their very pains, and laughed those to scorn who inflicted the torments upon them, and resigned up their souls with great alacrity, as expecting to receive them again.

For their doctrine is this, that bodies are corruptible and that the matter they are made of is not permanent; but that the souls are immortal and continue forever; and that they come out of the most subtle air and are united to their bodies as to prisons, into which they are drawn by a certain natural enticement, but that when they are set free from the bonds of the flesh they then, as released from a long bondage, rejoice and mount upward. And this is like the opinion of the Greeks, that good souls have their habitations beyond the ocean, in a region that is neither oppressed with storms of rain or snow, or with intense heat, but that this place is such as is refreshed by the gentle breathing of a west wind, that is perpetually blowing from the ocean; while they allot to bad souls a dark and tempestuous den, full of never-ceasing punishments. And, indeed, the Greeks seem to me to have followed the same notion when they allot the islands of the blessed to their brave men, whom they call heroes and demigods, and to the souls of the wicked the region of the ungodly in Hades, where their fables relate that certain persons, such as Sisyphus and Tantalus and Ixion and Tityus, are punished—which is built on this first supposition, that souls are immortal; and thence are those exhortations to virtue and dehortations from wickedness collected whereby good men are bettered in the conduct of their life by the hope they have of reward after their death, and whereby the vehement inclinations of bad men to vice are restrained by the fear and expectation they are in that, although they should lie concealed in this life, they should suffer immortal punishment after their death. These are the divine doctrines of the Essenes about the soul which lay an unavoidable bait for such as have once had a taste of their philosophy.

There are also those among them who undertake to foretell things to come by reading the holy books and using several sorts of purifications and being perpetually conversant in the discourses of the prophets, and it is but seldom that they miss in their predictions.

Moreover, there is another order of Essenes who agree with the rest as to their way of living and customs and laws but differ from them in the point of marriage, as thinking that by not marrying they cut off the principal part of human life, which is the prospect of succession; nay, rather, that if all men should be of the same opinion, the whole race of mankind would fail. However, they try their spouses for three years, and if they find that they have their natural purgations thrice, as trials that they are likely to be fruitful, they then actually marry them. But they do not use to accompany with their wives when they are with child, as a demonstration that they do not marry out of regard to pleasure, but for the sake of posterity. Now the women go into the baths with some of their garments on, as the men do with somewhat girded about them. And these are the customs of this order of the Essenes.

IV

THE THERAPEUTAE [9]

The Therapeutae, an Alexandrian-Jewish sect described in loving detail by Philo in the next selection, resemble closely the Essenes of Palestine. Because of the resemblance, some scholars have suggested that the Therapeutae were an Essenic offshoot who had transplanted their community into Egypt. A suggestion of this sort, while it does justice to the striking similarity of the religious beliefs of the two groups, neglects two major differences: first, the Therapeutae differ sharply from the Essenes in revealing a concern for wisdom, that is, for intellectual insight into religion; and, second, the Alexandrian group is described by Philo as an upper-class group, turning to their contemplative mysticism out of weariness with the world, whereas most Essenes apparently were of the lower classes.

THE VOCATION OF THESE PHILOSOPHERS is at once made clear from their title of Therapeutae and Therapeutrides, a name derived from *therapeuo,* either in the sense of 'cure,' because they profess an art of healing better than that current in the cities which cures only the bodies, while theirs treats also souls oppressed with grievous and well-nigh incurable diseases, inflicted by pleasures and desires and griefs and fears, by acts of covetousness, folly, and injustice, and the countless host of the other passions and vices; or else in the sense of 'worship,' because nature and the sacred laws have schooled them to worship the Self-existent, who is better than the Good, purer than the One, and more primordial than the Monad. Who among those who profess piety deserve to be compared with these? . . .

[They] settle in a certain very suitable place, which they regard as their fatherland. This place is situated above the Mareotic Lake on a somewhat low-lying hill, very happily placed both because of its security and the pleasantly tempered air. The safety is secured by the farm buildings and villages round about, and the pleasantness of the air by the continuous breezes which arise both from the lake which debouches into the sea and from the open sea hard by. For the sea breezes are light, the lake breezes close; and the two combining together produce a most healthy condition of climate.

The houses of the society thus collected are exceedingly simple, providing protection against two of the most pressing dangers, the fiery heat of the sun and the icy cold of the air. They are neither near together as in towns, since living at close quarters is troublesome and displeasing to people who are seeking to satisfy their desire for solitude, nor yet at a great distance, because of the sense of fellowship which they cherish and to render help to each other if robbers attack them. In each house there is a consecrated room which is called a sanctuary or closet, and closeted in this they are initiated into the mysteries of the sanctified life. They take nothing into it, either drink or food or any other of the things necessary for the needs of the body, but laws and oracles delivered through the mouth of prophets, and psalms and anything else which fosters and perfects knowledge and piety. They keep the memory of God alive and never forget it, so that even in their dreams the picture is nothing else but the loveliness of divine excellences and powers. Indeed, many when asleep and dreaming give utterance to the glorious verities of their holy philosophy. Twice every day they pray, at dawn and at eventide: at sunrise they pray for a fine bright day, fine and bright in the true sense of the heavenly daylight which they pray may fill their minds. At sunset they ask that the soul may be wholly relieved from the press of the senses and the objects of sense, and, sitting where she is consistory and council chamber to herself, pursue the quest of truth. The interval between early morning and evening is spent entirely in spiritual exercise. They read the Holy Scriptures and seek wisdom from their ancestral philosophy by taking it as an allegory, since they think that the words of the literal text are symbols of something whose hidden nature is revealed by studying the underlying meaning.

They have also writings of men of old, the founders of their way of thinking, who left many memorials of the form used in allegorical interpretation; and these they take as a kind of archetype and imitate the method in which this principle is carried out. And so they do not confine themselves to contemplation, but also compose hymns and psalms to God in all sorts of meters and melodies, which they write down with the rhythms necessarily made more solemn.

For six days they seek wisdom by themselves in solitude in the closets mentioned above, never passing the outside door of the house or even getting a distant view of it. But every seventh day they meet together as for a general assembly and sit in order, according to their age, in the proper attitude, with their hands inside the robe, the right hand between the breast and the chin and the left withdrawn along the flank. Then the senior among them who also has the fullest knowledge of the doctrines which they profess comes forward, and with visage and voice alike quiet and composed, gives a well-reasoned and wise discourse. He does not make an exhibition of clever rhetoric, like the orators or sophists of today, but follows careful examination by careful expression of the exact meaning of the thoughts; and this does not lodge just outside of the ears of the audience, but passes through the hearing into the soul and there stays securely. All the others sit still and listen, showing their approval merely by their looks or nods.

This common sanctuary in which they meet every seventh day is a double enclosure, one portion set apart for the use of the men, the other for the women. For women, too, regularly make part of the audience, with the same ardor and the same sense of their calling. The wall between the two chambers rises up from the ground to three or four cubits built in the form of a breastwork, while the space above up to the roof is left open. This arrangement serves two purposes; the modesty becoming to the female sex is preserved; while the women, sitting within earshot, can easily follow what is said, since there is nothing to obstruct the voice of the speaker.

They lay self-control to be, as it were, the foundation of their soul and on it build the other virtues. None of them would put food or drink to his lips before sunset, since they hold that philosophy finds its right place in the light, the needs of the body in the darkness; and therefore they assign the day to the one and some small part of the night to the other. Some in whom the desire for studying wisdom is more deeply implanted even only after three days remember to take food. Others so luxuriate and delight in the banquet of truths which wisdom richly and lavishly supplies that they hold out for twice that time, and only after six days do they bring themselves to taste such sustenance as is absolutely necessary. They have become habituated to abstinence like the grasshoppers who are said to live on air, because, I suppose, their singing makes their lack of food a light matter. But to the seventh day, as they consider it to be sacred and festal in the highest degree, they have awarded special privileges as its due; and on it, after providing for the soul, refresh the body also, which they do as a matter of course with the cattle, too, by releasing them from their continuous labor. . . .

I wish also to speak of their common assemblages and the cheerfulness of their convivial meals as contrasted with those of other people. . . . Some perhaps may approve the method of banqueting, now prevalent everywhere, through hankering for the Italian expensiveness and luxury, emulated both by Greeks and non-Greeks, who make their arrangements for ostentation rather than festivity. . . . But since the story of these well-known banquets is full of such follies, and they stand self-convicted in the eyes of any who do not regard conventional opinions and the widely circulated report which declares them to have been all that they should be, I will describe in contrast the festal meetings of those who have dedicated their own lives and themselves to knowledge and the contemplation of the verities of nature, following the truly sacred instructions of the prophet Moses. First of all, these people assemble after seven sets of seven days have passed, for they revere not only the simple seven but its square also, since they know its chastity and perpetual virginity. This is the eve of the chief fast which fifty takes for its own [10]—fifty the most sacred of numbers and the most deeply rooted in nature, being formed from the square of the right-angled triangle, which is the source from which the universe springs.

So then they assemble, white-robed and with faces in which

cheerfulness is combined with the utmost seriousness; but before they recline, at a signal from a member of the Rota, which is the name commonly given to those who perform these services, they take their stand in a regular line in an orderly way, their eyes and hands lifted up to Heaven—eyes because they have been trained to fix their gaze on things worthy of contemplation, hands in token that they are clean from gain-taking and not defiled through any cause of the profit-making kind. So standing, they pray to God that their feasting may be acceptable and proceed as he would have it.

After the prayers, the seniors recline according to the order of their admission, since by 'senior' they do not understand the aged and gray-headed, who are regarded as still mere children if they have only in late years come to love this rule of life, but those who from their earliest years have grown to manhood and spent their prime in pursuing the contemplative branch of philosophy, which indeed is the noblest and most godlike part. The feast is shared by women also, most of them aged virgins, who have kept their chastity not under compulsion, like some of the Greek priestesses, but of their own free will in their ardent yearning for wisdom. Eager to have her for their life mate, they have spurned the pleasures of the body; and desire no mortal offspring, but those immortal children which only the soul that is dear to God can bring to the birth unaided because the Father has sown in her spiritual rays enabling her to behold the verities of wisdom.

The order of reclining is so apportioned that the men sit by themselves on the right and the women by themselves on the left. Perhaps it may be thought that couches, though not costly, still of a softer kind would have been provided for people of good birth and high character, and trained practice in philosophy. Actually, they are plank beds of the common kinds of wood, covered with quite cheap strewings of native papyrus, raised slightly at the arms to give something to lean on. For while they mitigate somewhat the harsh austerity of Sparta, they always and everywhere practice a frugal contentment worthy of the free, and oppose with might and main the love lures of pleasure. They do not have slaves to wait upon them, as they consider that the own-

ership of servants is entirely against nature. For nature has borne
all men to be free, but the wrongful and covetous acts of some
who pursued that source of evil, inequality, have imposed their
yoke and invested the stronger with power over the weaker. In
this sacred banquet there is, as I have said, no slave; but the
services are rendered by free men, who perform their tasks as attendants, not under compulsion nor yet waiting for orders, but
with deliberate good will, anticipating eagerly and zealously the
demands that may be made. For it is not just *any* free men who
are appointed for these offices, but young members of the asso-
ciation chosen with all care for their special merit, who, as becomes their good character and nobility, are pressing on to reach
the summit of virtue. They give their services gladly and proudly,
like sons to their real fathers and mothers, judging them to be
the parents of them all in common, in a closer affinity than that
of blood, since to the right-minded there is no closer tie than
noble living. And they come in to do their office ungirt and with
tunics hanging down, that in their appearance there may be no
shadow of anything to suggest the slave.

In this banquet—I know that some will laugh at this, but only
those whose actions call for tears and lamentation—no wine is
brought . . . but only water of the brightest and clearest—cold
for most of the guests, but warm for such of the older men as
live delicately. The table, too, is kept pure from the flesh of animals; the food laid on it is loaves of bread with salt as a season-
ing—sometimes also flavored with hyssop, as a relish for the
daintier appetites. Abstinence from wine is enjoined by right
reason, as for the priest when sacrificing, so to these for their
lifetime. For wine acts like a drug, producing folly; and costly
dishes stir up that most insatiable of animals, desire.

Such are the preliminaries. But when the guests have laid
themselves down arranged in rows, as I have described, and the
attendants have taken their stand, with eveything in order ready
for their ministry, the President of the company, when a general
silence is established—here it may be asked, when is there no
silence—well, at this point there is silence even more than before,
so that no one ventures to make a sound or breathe with more

force than usual—amid this silence, I say, he discusses some question arising in the Holy Scriptures or solves one that has been propounded by someone else. In doing this, he has no thought of making a display; for he has no ambition to get a reputation for clever oratory, but desires to gain a closer insight into some particular matters and, having gained it, not to withhold it selfishly from those who, if not so clear-sighted as he, have at least a similar desire to learn. His instruction proceeds in a leisurely manner; he lingers over it and spins it out with repetitions, thus permanently imprinting the thoughts in the souls of the hearers; since if the speaker goes on descanting with breathless rapidity, the mind of the hearers is unable to follow his language, loses ground, and fails to arrive at apprehension of what is said. His audience listens with ears pricked up and eyes fixed on him, always in exactly the same posture, signifying comprehension and understanding by nods and glances, praise of the speaker by the cheerful change of expression which steals over the face, difficulty by a gentler movement of the head and by pointing with a fingertip of the right hand. . . .

When then the President thinks he has discoursed enough . . . he rises and sings a hymn composed as an address to God. . . . After him all the others take their turn, as they are arranged and in the proper order; while all the rest listen in complete silence, except when they have to chant the closing lines or refrains, for then they all lift up their voices, men and women alike. When everyone has finished his hymn, the young men bring in the tables mentioned a little above, on which is set the truly purified meal of leavened bread seasoned with salt mixed with hyssop, out of reverence for the holy table enshrined in the sacred vestibule of the Temple, on which lie loaves and salt without condiments, the loaves unleavened and the salt unmixed. For it was meet that the simplest and purest food should be assigned to the highest caste—namely, the priests—as a reward for their ministry; and that the others, while aspiring to similar privileges, should abstain from seeking the same as they and allow their superiors to retain their precedence.

After the supper they hold the sacred vigil, which is conducted in the following way. They rise up all together and, standing in the middle of the refectory, form themselves first into two choirs, one of men and one of women, the leader and precentor chosen for each being the most honored amongst them and also the most musical. Then they sing hymns to God composed of many measures and set to many melodies, sometimes chanting together, sometimes taking up the harmony antiphonally, hands and feet keeping time in accompaniment; and, rapt with enthusiasm, reproduce sometimes the lyrics of the procession, sometimes of the halt and of the wheeling and counterwheeling of a choric dance.

Then, when each choir has separately done its own part in the feast, having drunk as in the Bacchic rites of the strong wine of God's love, they mix and both together become a single choir, a copy of the choir set up of old beside the Red Sea in honor of the wonders there wrought. For, at the command of God, the sea became a source of salvation to one party and of perdition to the other. As it broke in twain and withdrew under the violence of the forces which swept it back, there rose on either side, opposite to each other, the semblance of solid walls; while the space thus opened between them broadened into a highway smooth and dry throughout, on which the people marched under guidance right on until they reached the higher ground on the opposite mainland. But when the sea came rushing in with the returning tide and from either side passed over the ground where dry land had appeared, the pursuing enemy were submerged and perished. This wonderful sight and experience, an act transcending word and thought and hope, so filled with ecstasy both men and women that, forming a single choir, they sang hymns of thanksgiving to God their Savior, the men led by the prophet Moses and the women by the prophetess Miriam.[11]

It is on this model above all that the choir of the Therapeutae of either sex, note in response to note and voice to voice, the treble of the women blending with the bass of the men, create an harmonious concent, musical in the truest sense. Lovely are the thoughts, lovely the words, and worthy of reverence the choristers; and the end and aim of thoughts, words and choristers alike, is piety. Thus they continue till dawn, drunk with this drunkenness in which there is no shame; then, not with heavy heads or drowsy eyes, but more alert and wakeful than when they came to the banquet, they stand with their faces and whole body turned to the east, and when they see the sun rising they stretch their hands up to heaven and pray for bright days and knowledge of the truth and the power of keen-sighted thinking. And after the prayers they depart, each to his private sanctuary, once more to ply the trade and till the field of their wonted philosophy.

So much then for the Therapeutae, who have taken to their hearts the contemplation of nature and what it has to teach, and have lived in the soul alone, citizens of Heaven and the world, presented to the Father and Maker of all by their faithful sponsor, Virtue, who has procured for them God's friendship and added a gift going hand in hand with it, true excellence of life, a boon better than all good fortune and rising to the very summit of felicity.

V

THE NEW COVENANTERS [12]

Although the manuscript on which our knowledge of the Damascus sect, or New Covenanters, is based is probably fairly late (tenth century A.D.?), there is much justification for considering the sect to be one of the extremist manifestations of Jewish religious creativity in the period of the Second Commonwealth. This sect was composed of dissident members of the priesthood who sympathized, in part at least, with the Pharisaic position. They repudiated the Temple worship and animal sacrifices. They emphasized messianic expectations and seem to have spent their time in their place of exile near Damascus, awaiting the coming of the Messiah, hoping and believing that they would be among the "remnant" to be saved. Like the Essenes and Therapeutae, they had an oath of initiation for new members; there are some suggestions of initiation ritual in the fragmentary document from which the following selections are taken.

I

AND NOW, hearken unto me all ye who have entered into
    the covenant,
    And I will disclose to you the ways of the wicked.
God loveth wisdom:
And counsel he hath set before him:
Prudence and knowledge minister unto him.
Long-suffering is with him
And plenteousness of forgivenesses
To pardon those who repent of transgression
And power and might and great fury with flames of fire
For them who turned aside out of the way,
And abhorred the statute,
So that there should be no remnant,

Nor any to escape of them. . . .
Yet in all of them he raised him up men called by name,
In order to leave a remnant to the earth,
And to fill the face of the earth with their seed.
And through his Messiah he shall make them know his holy
            spirit,
And he is true, and in the true interpretation of his name
            are their names:
But them he hated he made to go astray.

II

Now therefore, children, hearken unto me,
And I will open your eyes to see,
And to understand the works of God.
And to choose what he approveth,
And to reject what he hateth
To walk uprightly in all his ways,
And not to go about in the thoughts of an evil imagination
And (with) eyes (full) of fornication. . . .

III

The priests are the penitents of Israel who went forth out of
the land of Judah, and [the Levites are] they who joined them.
And the sons of Zadok are the elect of Israel called by the name,
that are holding office in the end of the days. Behold the statement of their names according to their generations, and the
period of their office, and the number of their afflictions, and the
years of their sojournings, and the statement of their works. . . .

IV

In accordance with the covenant which God established with
            the forefathers
In order to pardon their sins,
So shall God make atonement for them.
And on the consummation of the period of these years

They shall no more join themselves to the house of Judah,
But shall everyone stand up against his net.
The wall shall have been built,
The boundary been far removed.

V

And during all these years Belial shall be let loose against
Israel, as God spake through Isaiah the prophet, the son of
Amos, saying, "Fear and the pit and the snare are upon thee, O
inhabitant of the land."[13]

This means the three nets of Belial, concerning which Levi
the son of Jacob spake, by which he caught Israel and directed
their faces to three kinds of unrighteousness. The first is fornication, the second is the wealth [of wickedness], the third is
the pollution of the Sanctuary. He that cometh up from this
shall be caught by that, and he that escapeth from this shall be
caught by that. . . .

VI

And during the period of the destruction of the land there
arose those who removed the landmark and led Israel astray.
And the land became desolate, because they spake rebellion
against the commandments of God through Moses and also
through his holy anointed one, and they prophesied a lie to turn
Israel away from God.

But God remembered the covenant with the forefathers:
And he raised up from Aaron men of understanding,
And from Israel wise men:
And he made them to hearken,
And they digged the well.
"A well the princes digged,
The nobles of the people delved it
By the order of the Lawgiver."

The well is the Law, and they who digged it are the penitents
of Israel who went forth out of the land of Judah and sojourned

in the land of Damascus, all of whom God called princes. For they sought him, and his glory was not turned back in the mouth of one (of them). And the Lawgiver is he who studies the Law, in regard to whom Isaiah said, "He bringeth forth an instrument for his work." [14] And the nobles of the people are those who came to dig the well by the precepts in which the Lawgiver ordained that they should walk throughout the full period of the wickedness. And save them they shall get nothing until there arises the Teacher of Righteousness in the end of the days. . . .

VII

When the two houses of Israel separated, all who proved faithless were delivered to the sword, and those who held fast escaped into the land of the North. As he said, "And I will cause to go into captivity Siccuth your King and Chiun your images, the star of your God which ye made for yourselves beyond Damascus." [15] The books of the Law are the tabernacle of the king, as he said, "And I will raise up the tabernacle of David that is fallen." [16] The king is the congregation, and Chiun the images are the books of the Prophets, whose words Israel has despised. And the star is he who studied the Law, who came to Damascus, as it is written. "There shall come forth a star out of Jacob, and a scepter shall rise out of Israel." [17] The scepter is the prince of all the congregation. . . ."

VI

A SECTARIAN MANUAL OF DISCIPLINE [18]

Some of the recently discovered Dead Sea Scrolls give evidence of having been the products of a sectarian fringe group, similar to the Essenes and the New Covenanters. The language used in these scrolls is striking in its parallel to that of the Zadokite New Covenant document from which the previous group of selections was taken. The following selections, translated from what may have been a "Manual of Discipline" of the sect, give a clear impression of the general character of the initiation ceremonies in all these sects.

I

To do that which is good and right before him, according to that which he has commanded through Moses and all his servants the Prophets. And to love all those whom he has chosen, and to hate all those whom he has rejected. To keep from all evil and to cling to all good works. And to practice truth, justice, and right upon the earth. And not to walk in the stubbornness of a guilty heart and lustful glances, so as to do evil. And to lead into the Covenant of Grace all those who incline to practice the precepts of God so that they may be united in the Party of God, and so that they may walk before him in perfection in all that has been revealed to their councils, and so that they may love all the sons of light, each according to his portion in the Party of God, and so that they may hate all the sons of darkness, each according to his guilt by virtue of the vengeance of God. And all those who incline toward the truth shall bring all their intelligence and their strength and their power to the Community of God so as to purify their intelligence in the truth of the precepts of God and to regulate their strength according to the perfection of his ways and all their power according to his just

Counsel. And not to take a single step outside any of the works of God, (but to accomplish them) in their time; not to anticipate their moments, not to be late for any of their feasts. And not to depart from their precepts of truth to go either to the right or to the left. . . .

. . . .

And all those who enter into the rule of the Community shall pass into the Covenant in the presence of God, (pledging themselves) to act according to all that he has commanded them and not to depart far from him through terror however great, or through fear or through ordeal, though they be tempted by the whole empire of Belial. And when they shall pass into the Covenant, the priests and the Levites shall bless God for their deliverance and for all his works of truth. And all those who pass into the Covenant shall say after them "Amen! Amen!"

And the priests shall narrate the exploits of God in his mighty works, and shall proclaim all his grace and love toward Israel. And the Levites shall narrate the iniquities of the sons of Israel and all their wicked rebellions and their sins (committed) under the empire of Belial.

[And all] those who enter into the Covenant shall make their confession after them, saying: "We have been perverse, we have rebelled, we have sinned, we have acted wickedly, we [and] our fathers before us, walking [contrary to the precepts of God. But] truth and justice [. . .] was his judgment against us and against our fathers. . . ."

II

And here is the rule for the members of the Community who have pledged themselves: to turn away from all evil and to cling to all that (God) has commanded, according to his will; to separate themselves from the congregation of the perverse so as to belong to the Community in matters of the Law and goods and administrative rules, in the manner of the sons of Zadok, the priests who keep the Covenant, and in the manner of the members of the Community, who have bound themselves to the Covenant in like manner. To execute the decree of destiny in all things relative to the Law and to possessions and to right. To practice the truth in common, along with humility, justice, and right; and to love piety; and to walk modestly in all their ways so that none walks in the stubbornness of his heart, erring after his heart and his eyes and the plottings of his instincts. But, on the contrary, to circumcise in the Community the foreskin of instinct and of insubordination, laying a foundation of truth for Israel, for the Community of the eternal Covenant. To expiate for all those who have pledged themselves to (practice) the same holiness as Aaron and (to belong) to the House of Truth in Israel, and (for) those who are united to them (in belonging) to the Community even in a matter of legal action and judgment. To condemn all those who transgress the Charter and the Covenant; to rule their ways according to all these precepts, when they have been received into the Community.

III

Whoever enters into the Party of the Community, let him enter into the Covenant of God in the presence of all those who have bound themselves to it; and let him vow on his soul, by a binding oath, to become converted to the Law of Moses in all that (God) has commanded, (to become converted) with all his heart and with all his soul in all that has been revealed (as issuing) from it to the sons of Zadok, the priests who keep the Covenant and seek his will, and to the body of the members of their Covenant, of those who have bound themselves in common (to practice) his truth and to walk in his will. . . .

PART FOUR

TANNAITIC COLLECTIONS

I

THE ORAL TRADITION

One of the chief arguments used by the Jewish apologists was that of the antiquity of Jewish law and religion. Even the conquerors of the Jewish people recognized, as a rule, the right of the Jews to live in accordance with "the law of their forefathers"—an oft-recurring phrase in the Greco-Roman enactments concerning the Jewish minority. The Jews themselves not only pushed the story of the patriarchs and Moses back to immemorial antiquity—Josephus spoke of five thousand years of Jewish history before his time—but also claimed that a large body of oral laws was revealed to the Jewish people simultaneously with the written law, the Bible. These oral traditions, carried down the ages by a succession of outstanding prophets and sages, were believed to have been implied in the biblical revelation from the outset, and it was held that they could still be reconstructed from the biblical text by an ingenious method of "hermeneutic" reinterpretation.

The two selections which follow offer both the basic outline of this historic chain of tradition and the hermeneutic methods of interpretation used by the rabbis. In the first of the two, the names of the chief bearers of the tradition are mentioned, starting with Simeon the Just, at the beginning of the Maccabean era. During that period pre-eminence fell to two outstanding leaders in each generation, the so-called 'pairs' (*zuggot*), until Hillel and Shammai, shortly before the Christian era. Hillel, a Babylonian immigrant, established a new dynasty which, before long, assumed the leaderhip of the Sanhedrin, the main legislative, judicial, and scholarly body in the country. Under the title of 'patriarchs,' after the Bar Kocheba revolt, Hillel's descendants were the official spokesmen of Palestinian Jewry until 429 A.D., and were recognized as acting in that capacity by the Roman authorities as well as by their own people.

Hillel was also the first to formulate the rabbinic modes of interpretation. Although they are basically different from the rules of inference of the Aristotelian logic, the seven modes, as stated by Hillel, adequately represented the accepted

Jewish—and, in some respects, the generally Near Eastern—
methods of rigorous reasoning from a body of truths given in
revelation. The seven modes of Hillel were later expanded
into thirteen by the school of R. Ishmael (second century
A.D.) and still further elaborated into thirty-two modes,
chiefly employed in nonlegal hermeneutics, by R. Eliezer, son
of R. Jose the Galilean (about 200 A.D.). Statements of the
seven modes of Hillel and the thirteen modes of R. Ishmael
are available in authentic texts of the tannaitic age; the
account of the thirty-two modes, in the so-called *Mishnah of
R. Eliezer,* is essentially a medieval compilation.

THE CHAIN OF TRADITION [1]

I

MOSES RECEIVED TORAH FROM SINAI and delivered it to
Joshua, and Joshua to the Elders, and the Elders to the
Prophets, and the Prophets delivered it to the Men of the
Great Synagogue. These said three things, "Be deliberate in judg-
ing, and raise up many disciples, and make a hedge for the
Torah."

Simeon the Just was of the survivors of the Great Synagogue.
He used to say, "Upon three things the world standeth; upon
Torah, upon worship, and upon the showing of kindness."

Antigonos of Socho received from Simeon the Just. He used to
say, "Be not like servants who serve the master on condition of
receiving a gift, but be like servants who serve the master not on
condition of receiving a gift. And let the fear of Heaven be upon
you."

Jose ben Joezer, of Zeredah, and Jose ben Johanan, of Jerusalem, received from them. Jose ben Joezer, of Zeredah, said, "Let
thy house be a place of meeting for the Wise, and dust thyself
with the dust of their feet, and drink their words with thirst."

Jose ben Johanan, of Jerusalem, said, "Let thy house be opened
wide, and let the poor be thy household, and talk not much with
a woman." He said it: in the case of his own wife, much more
in the case of his companion's wife. Hence the Wise have said,

Everyone that talketh much with a woman causes evil to himself, and desists from words of Torah, and his end is he inherits Gehinnom.

Joshua ben Perahyah and Nittai the Arbelite received from them. Joshua ben Perahyah said, "Make thee a Master, and get thee a companion, and judge every man by the scale of merit."

Nittai the Arbelite said, "Keep far from the evil neighbor, and consort not with the wicked, and be not doubtful of retribution."

Judah ben Tabbai and Simeon ben Shetah received from them. Judah ben Tabbai said, "Make not thyself as they that prepare the judges; and when the suitors are before thee, let them be as wrongdoers in thy sight; and when they have departed from before thee, let them be in thy sight as innocent men, seeing they have accepted the sentence upon themselves."

Simeon ben Shetah said, "Examine thoroughly the witnesses, and be careful in thy words; perchance through them they may learn to lie."

Shemaiah and Abtalion received from them. Shemaiah said, "Love work and hate mastery, and make not thyself known to the government."

Abtalion said, "Ye Wise, take heed to your words, lest ye incur the guilt [that deserves] exile, and ye be exiled to a place of evil waters, and the disciples that come after you drink and die, and the name of Heaven be found profaned."

Hillel and Shammai received from them. Hillel said, "Be of the disciples of Aaron, one that loves peace, that loves mankind and brings them nigh to Torah."

He used to say, "Whoso makes great his name loses his name, and whoso adds not makes to cease, and he who does not learn deserves killing, and one who serves himself with the crown passes away."

He used to say, "If I am not for myself who is for me? and when I am for myself what am I? and if not now, when?"

Shammai said, "Make thy Torah a fixed [duty]. Say little and do much, and receive every man with a cheerful expression of face."

Rabban Gamaliel [2] used to say, "Make thee a master and remove thyself from what is doubtful, and do not often tithe by conjecture."

Simeon his son said, "All my days I have grown up among the Wise, and I have not found anything better for one than silence; and not study is the chief thing, but action; and whoso multiplies words occasions sin."

Rabban Simeon ben Gamaliel said, "Upon three things the world stands: on truth, on judgment, and on peace. As it is said, 'Truth and judgment of peace judge ye in your gates.'" [3]

II

Rabbi [4] said, "Which is that right way which a man should choose for himself? Any that is an honor to him that does it and an honor to him in the sight of men. And be careful in the case of a light precept as in that of a weighty one, for thou knowest not how the rewards of the precepts are given. And count the loss by a precept against its reward, and the reward of a sin against its loss. Keep in view three things, and thou wilt not come into the power of sin; know what is above thee: a seeing eye, a hearing ear, and all thy deeds written in a book."

Rabban Gamaliel, son of Rabbi Judah the Prince said, "Study of Torah along with worldly occupation is seemly, for labor in the two of them makes sin forgotten. And all Torah without work ends in failure and occasions sin. And let all who labor with the congregation labor with them for the name of Heaven. For the merit of their fathers is their support, and their righteousness standeth forever. 'And ye—I confer upon you' [saith God] 'plenteous reward, as if ye had wrought.'"

Be cautious with the government, for they do not make advances to a man except for their own need. They seem like friends in the hour of their advantage, but they do not stand by a man in the hour of his adversity.

He used to say, "Make his will as thy will, so that he may make thy will as his will; make naught thy will before his will, so that he may make naught the will of others before thy will."

Hillel said, "Sever not thyself from the congregation, and be not sure of thyself till the day of thy death, and judge not thy associate until thou comest to his place; and say not of a word which is impossible to understand that it will be understood in the end; and say not, 'When I am at leisure I will study'—perchance thou wilt not be at leisure."

He used to say, "A rude man is not one that fears sin, nor is a man who knows not Torah a saint; nor does a shy person learn nor a passionate person teach, nor does one who engages much in business impart wisdom. And in a place where there are no men, strive to be a man."

Moreover, he saw a skull which floated on the face of the water, and he said, "Because thou drownedst, they drowned thee; and in the end they that drowned thee shall be drowned."

He used to say, "More flesh, more worms; more wealth, more care; more women, more witchcraft; more maidservants, more lewdness; more menservants, more thieving; more Torah, more life; more assiduity, more wisdom; more counsel, more understanding; more righteousness, more peace. He who has acquired a good name has acquired it for himself. He who has acquired words of Torah has acquired for himself the life of the world to come."

Rabban Johanan ben Zakkai received from Hillel and from Shammai. He used to say, "If thou hast learned much Torah, take not credit to thyself, for thereunto wast thou created."

Five disciples had Rabban Johanan ben Zakkai, and these are they: Rabbi Eliezer ben Horkenos, Rabbi Joshua ben Hananyah, Rabbi Jose the priest, Rabbi Simeon ben Nathanel, and Rabbi Eleazar ben Arach.

He used to sum up their praise: "Eliezer ben Horkenos is a plastered cistern that loseth not a drop. Joshua ben Hananyah, happy is she that bore him. Jose the priest is a saint. Simeon ben Nathanel is one that feareth sin. Eleazar ben Arach is as a full-flowing spring."

He used to say, "If all the Wise of Israel were in one scale of the balance and Eliezer ben Horkenos in the second scale, he would weigh them all down." Abba Shaul said, in his name, "If all the Wise of Israel were in one scale of the balance, yea and Eliezer ben Horkenos with them, and Eleazar ben Arach in the second scale, he would weigh them all down."

He said to them, "Go and see which is that good way to which a man should cleave?" R. Eliezer said, "A good eye." R. Joshua said, "A good associate." R. Jose said, "A good neighbor." R. Simeon said, "One who sees the event." R. Eleazar said, "A good heart." He said to them, "I approve the words of Eleazar ben Arach more than your words, for in his words are included yours."

He said to them: "Go and see which is that evil way which a man should shun." R. Eliezer said, "An evil eye." R. Joshua said, "An evil associate." R. Jose said, "An evil neighbor." R. Simeon said, "He who borrows and does not pay. He that borrows from man is as he that borrows from the Omnipresent; as it is said: 'The wicked borroweth and payeth not, but the righteous showeth favor and giveth.' " [5] R. Eleazar said, "An evil heart." He said to them, "I approve the words of Eleazar ben Arach more than your words, for in his words are included yours."

These said three things. R. Eliezer said, "Let the honor of thine associate be dear to thee as thine own; and be not quick to anger; and repent a day before thy death; and warm thyself at the fire of the Wise, and beware of their glowing coal lest thou be scorched. For their bite is the bite of a fox, and their sting the sting of a scorpion, and their hiss the hiss of a serpent, and all their words like coals of fire."

R. Joshua said, "The evil eye and the evil principle and hatred of mankind drive a man out of the world."

R. Jose said, "Let the property of thine associate be dear to thee as thine own. And dispose thyself to learn Torah, for it is not an inheritance. And let all thine actions be for the name of Heaven."

R. Simeon said, "Be careful in reading the Shema' and in prayer. And when thou prayest, make not thy prayer a fixed form, but beseeching and entreaty before God; as it is said: 'For he is gracious and merciful, long-suffering and plenteous in mercy, and repenteth him of the evil.' [6] And be not wicked in thine own sight."

R. Eleazar said, "Be alert to learn Torah and know what an-

give an *Epicuros*.[7] And know before whom thou laborest
o is the master of thy work to give thee the wages of thy

arphon said, "The day is short, and the work is great; and
borers are sluggish, and the wages are high, and the house-
:r is urgent."

e used to say, "The work is not upon thee to finish; nor art
u free to desist from it. If thou hast learned much Torah, they
ve thee much wages, and faithful is the master of thy work who
will pay thee the wages of thy toil. And know that the giving of
the reward to the righteous is in the time to come."

THE METHODS OF RABBINIC INTERPRETATION [8]

Rabbi Ishmael says: "There are thirteen exegetical principles
by which the Law is expounded: (1) The inference from minor
to major. (2) The inference from a similarity of phrases. (3) A
general law may be derived by induction from different cases
which, occurring in the same or in different verses, have yet some
feature in common. (4) A general proposition followed by the
enumeration of particulars already comprehended in the general
proposition, (in which case the scope of the proposition is limited
by the things specified). (5) An enumeration of particulars followed by a general proposition in which they are also comprehended, (in which case the scope of the proposition extends also
to the things not specified). (6) Two general propositions, separated from each other by an enumeration of particulars, include
only such things as are similar to those specified. (7) An inference drawn from a general proposition complemented by a particular term, and an inference drawn from a particular term complemented by a general proposition. (8) If anything is included
in a general proposition and is then made the subject of a special
statement, that which is predicated of it is not to be understood
as limited to itself alone, but is to be applied to the whole of the
general proposition. (9) If anything is included in a general
proposition and is then singled out in order to be made the sub-

ject of a special statement, similar to the general proposition, this particularization is intended, so far as its subject is concerned, to lessen and not to add to its restrictions. (10) If anything is included in a general proposition and is then singled out in order to be made the subject of a special statement, not similar to the general proposition, this particularization is intended in some respects to lessen and in others to add to its restrictions. (11) If anything is included in a general proposition and is then made the subject of a fresh statement (not in harmony with the former), the terms of the general proposition will not apply to it, unless the Scripture distinctly indicates that they shall apply. (12) The meaning of a passage may be deduced from its context, or from some subsequent passage. (13) Similarly, when two passages are in contradiction to each other, the explanation can be determined only when a third text is found, capable of harmonizing the two."

II

THE MISHNAH

Few of the ancients, and still fewer of the ancient Jews, drew any distinction whatever between the domains of religion, law, and morality, between *jus* and *fas*. Everything relating to human conduct was placed under the surveillance of the divinely ordained law. The most trivial aspect of business dealings or of ritualistic ceremonies was subjected to the same thorough scrutiny and detailed elaboration, as were the more lofty commandments. A rationalization of this may be read in the selection from Josephus' *Against Apion*, reproduced above, pp. 54 ff. Although no generally accepted classification of commandments is recorded in any ancient source, there was an early acceptance of the figure of six hundred and thirteen (*taryag*) as the number of basic biblical laws. These were divided into three hundred and sixty-five prohibitions, or negative commandments, and two hundred and forty-eight positive commandments. Opinions may have differed in antiquity, as they still differed in the Middle Ages, about the inclusion or exclusion of individual laws in this classification, or about the derivation of specific laws from particular biblical injunctions. There was, however, virtual unanimity about the equally obligatory character of them all. The following excerpts from the Mishnah (in addition to the section of the "Sayings of the Fathers," given above) furnish a few examples, which could readily be multiplied, of the all-pervasive unity and comprehensiveness of rabbinic law.

SABBATH REGULATIONS [9]

I

A GREAT GENERAL RULE have they laid down concerning the Sabbath: whosoever, forgetful of the principle of the Sabbath, committed many acts of work on many Sabbaths, is liable only to one sin offering; but if, mindful of the principle of the Sabbath, he yet committed many acts of work on many Sabbaths, he is liable for every Sabbath which he profaned. If he knew that it was the Sabbath and he yet committed many acts of work on many Sabbaths, he is liable for every main class of work which he performed; if he committed many acts of work of one main class, he is liable only to one sin offering.

The main classes of work are forty save one: sowing, ploughing, reaping, binding sheaves, threshing, winnowing, cleansing crops, grinding, sifting, kneading, baking, shearing wool, washing or beating or dyeing it, spinning, weaving, making two loops, weaving two threads, separating two threads, tying a knot, loosening a knot, sewing two stitches, tearing in order to sew two stitches, hunting a gazelle, slaughtering or flaying or salting it or curing its skin, scraping it or cutting it up, writing two letters, erasing in order to write two letters, building, pulling down, putting out a fire, lighting a fire, striking with a hammer and taking out aught from one domain into another. These are the main classes of work: forty save one. . . .

II

There are two (which are indeed four) kinds of 'going out' on the Sabbath for him that is inside, and two (which are indeed four) for him that is outside. Thus, if a poor man stood outside and the householder inside, and the poor man stretched his hand inside and put aught into the householder's hand or took aught from it and brought it out, the poor man is culpable and the householder is not culpable; if the householder stretched his hand outside and put aught into the poor man's hand or took aught from it and brought it in, the householder is culpable and the poor man is not culpable. But if the poor man stretched his hand inside and the householder took aught from it, or put aught into it, and [the poor man] brought it out, neither is culpable; and if the householder stretched his hand outside and the poor man took aught from it or put aught into it and [the householder] brought it in, neither is culpable.

A man should not sit down before the barber near to the time of the afternoon *Tefillah* unless he has already prayed it; a man should not enter a bathhouse or a tannery; nor should he [begin to] eat a meal or decide a suit, though if any have begun [a like deed] they need not interrupt it. They must interrupt [their doings] to recite the *Shema'*, but they need not interrupt them for the *Tefillah*.

A tailor should not go out with his needle [on Friday] near to nightfall, lest he forget and 'go out'; nor should a scrivener [go out then] with his pen; nor should a man search his clothes [for fleas] or read by lamplight. Rightly have they said, "A schoolmaster may look where the children are reading, but he himself may not read." In like manner a man that has a flux may not eat with a woman that has a flux, since it lends occasion to transgression.

These are among the rulings which the Sages enjoined while in the upper room of Ḥananiah b. Hezekiah b. Gorion. When they went up to visit him they voted, and they of the School of Shammai outnumbered them of the School of Hillel; and eighteen things did they decree on that day.

The School of Shammai say, "Ink, dyestuffs, or vetches may not be soaked [on a Friday] unless there is time for them to be [wholly] soaked the same day." And the School of Hillel permit it.

The School of Shammai say, "Bundles of flax may not be put in an oven unless there is time for them to steam off the same day; nor may wool be put into a [dyer's] caldron unless there is time for it to absorb the color the same day." And the School of Hillel permit it. The School of Shammai say, "Nets may not be spread for wild animals, birds, or fishes unless there is time for them to be caught the same day." And the School of Hillel permit it.

The School of Shammai say, "They may not sell aught to a Gentile or help him to load his beast or raise [a burden] on his shoulders unless there is time for him to reach a place near by [the same day]." And the School of Hillel permit it.

The School of Shammai say, "Hides may not be given to a [Gentile] tanner nor clothes to a Gentile washerman unless there is time for the work to be done the same day." And all these the School of Hillel permit such time as the sun is up.

Rabban Simeon b. Gamaliel said, "In my father's house they used to give white clothes to a Gentile washerman three days before Sabbath." Both [the School of Shammai and the School of Hillel] agree that men may lay down the olivepress beams or the winepress rollers.

Flesh and onions and eggs may not be roasted unless there is time for them to be roasted the same day; nor may bread be put into the oven when darkness is falling, nor may cakes be put upon the coals unless there is time for their top surface to form into crust. R. Eliezer says, "Time for their bottom surface [only] to form into crust."

The Passover offering may be let down into the oven when darkness is falling; and fire may be kindled in the fireplace on the chamber of the hearth, but elsewhere only if there is time [before the Sabbath] for the fire to take hold on the greater part [of the wood]. R. Judah says, "With charcoal [it is permitted if there is time for the fire to take hold on] any quantity soever."

III

With what may they light [the Sabbath lamp] and with what may they not light it? They may not use cedar fiber or uncarded flax or raw silk or a wick of bast or a wick of the desert or duck weed; or pitch or wax or castor oil or [heave offering] oil that [is become unclean and] must be burned, or [grease from] the fatty tail or tallow. Nahum the Mede says, "They may use melted tallow." But the sages say, "It is all one whether it is melted or not melted; they may not light therewith."

[Heave offering] oil that [is become unclean and] must be burned may not be used for lighting on a festival day. R. Ishmael says, "Tar may not be used out of respect for the Sabbath."

But the Sages permit all kinds of oils: sesame oil, nut oil, fish oil, colocynth oil, tar, and naphtha. R. Tarphon says, "They may use only olive oil."

Naught that comes from a tree may be used for lighting [the Sabbath lamp] excepting flax, and naught that comes from a tree can contract uncleanness by overshadowing excepting flax. If a wick made from [a piece of] cloth was twisted but not singed, R. Eliezer declares it susceptible to uncleanness and not to be used for lighting [the Sabbath lamp]; but R. Akiba says, "It is not susceptible to uncleanness and it may be used for lighting [the Sabbath lamp]."

A man may not pierce an eggshell and fill it with oil and put it on the opening of the lamp so that the oil will drip from it, [it is forbidden] even if it was made of earthenware (but R. Judah permits it); but if the potter had joined it [with the lamp] from the first it is permitted, in that it is a single vessel. A man may not fill a dish with oil and put it beside a lamp, and put the end of the wick in it so that it will absorb [the oil]. But R. Judah permits it.

If a man put out the lamp [on the night of Sabbath] from fear of the Gentiles or of thieves or of an evil spirit, or to suffer one that was sick to sleep, he is not culpable; [but if he did it with a mind] to spare the lamp or to spare the oil or to spare the wick, he is culpable. But R. Jose declares him exempt in every case excepting that of the wick, since he thereby forms charcoal.

For three transgressions do women die in childbirth: for heedlessness of the laws of the menstruant, the dough offering, and the lighting of the [Sabbath] lamp.

Three things must a man say within his house when darkness is falling on the eve of the Sabbath, "Have ye tithed? Have ye prepared the Erub? and, Light the lamp." If it is in doubt whether darkness has already fallen or not, they may not set apart tithes from what is known to be untithed or immerse utensils or light the lamps, but they may set apart tithes from Demai produce and prepare the Erub and cover up what is to be kept hot.

SOME COMMERCIAL REGULATIONS [10]

What is usury (*neshek*) and what is increase (*tarbith*)? It is usury (*neshek*) when a man lends a *sela* for five *denars* or two *seahs* of wheat for three, because he is a usurer (*noshek*). And what is increase? When a man increases [his gains] in [trafficking with] produce. How? If one man bought wheat [from another] at a golden *denar* the *kor* when such was the market price, and then wheat rose to thirty [silver] *denars* the *kor* and he said, "Deliver me my wheat, since I would sell it to buy wine with the price," and the other said, "Let thy wheat be reckoned to me at thirty *denars*, and thus thou hast now a claim on me for wine [to that value]," although he has no wine.

The creditor may not dwell without charge in the debtor's courtyard or hire it from him at a reduced rate, since that counts as usury. A man may increase rent charge but not purchase value. Thus if the owner hired his courtyard to a tenant and said, "If thou payest me now it is thine for ten *selas* a year, but if [thou payest] month by month it will be one *sela* a month," this is permitted; but if he sold him his field and said, "If thou payest me now it is thine for 1,000 *zuz*, but if at the time of threshing it will be 1,200 *zuz*," this is forbidden.

If a man sold his field and was given a part of the price and said to the buyer, "Pay me [the rest of] the price when thou wilt, and then take what is thine," this is forbidden. If a man lent another money on the security of his field and said to him, "If thou dost not pay me within three years it shall be mine," then it becomes his. Thus used Boethus b. Zunin to do with the consent of the Sages.

None may set up a shopkeeper on the condition of receiving half the profit, or give him money to buy produce therewith on the condition of receiving half the profit, unless he is paid his wage as a laborer. None may set [another's] hens [to hatch out his eggs] on the condition of sharing the profit, or give another calves or foals to rear on the condition of sharing half the estimated loss or gain, unless he is paid his wage for his labor and the cost of the food. But a man may undertake the care of calves and foals in return for half the profits, and rear them until they reach the third of their growth; and asses, until they can bear a burden.

A cow or an ass, and whatsoever works and eats, may be put out to rear with the condition of sharing in the profits. Where the custom is to share offspring immediately at birth, they do so; and where the custom is [first] to rear them, they do so. Rabban Simeon b. Gamaliel says, "A calf may be put out to rear with its dam and a foal with its dam." A tenant may offer increased rent in exchange for a loan to improve his field, without fearing that this is of the nature of usury.

A flock may not be accepted from an Israelite on "iron" terms, since that counts as usury; but it may be accepted from a Gentile. Money may be borrowed from Gentiles on usury and lent to them on usury, and the same applies with a resident alien. An Israelite may lend the money of a Gentile with the knowledge of the Gentile; but [if it was money which the Gentile had borrowed from an Israelite,] he may not lend it with the knowledge of the Israelite.

No bargain may be made over produce before its market price is known. After its market price is known, a bargain may be made; for even if one dealer has not the produce, another will have it. If he was the first to reap his crop, he may make a bargain with his fellow over grain stacked on the threshing floor, or over grapes in their harvesting baskets, or over olives in the vat, or over the clay balls of the potter, or over lime so soon as the limestone is sunk in the kiln. Moreover, a bargain may be made over manure at any time in the year. R. Jose says, "No bargain may be made over manure unless the seller has it on the dungheap." But the Sages permit it. A bargain may be made [to pay for wares] at the cheapest rate [that prevails at the time of delivery]. R. Judah says, "Even if the bargain was not made [to pay for wares] at the cheapest rate, he may say, 'Give me the wares at such a price, or give me back my money.'"

The owner may lend his tenants wheat to be repaid in kind if it is for sowing, but not if it is for food, for Rabban Gamaliel used to lend his tenants wheat to be repaid in kind when it was for sowing; and if he lent it when the price was high and it afterward fell, or when it was low and it afterward rose, he used to take wheat back from them at the lower rate—not because such was the rule, but because he was minded to apply to himself the more stringent ruling.

A man may not say to his fellow, "Lend me a *kor* of wheat and I will repay thee at threshing time," but he may say, "Lend it to me until my son comes," or "until I find the key." But Hillel used to forbid this. Moreover Hillel used to say, "A woman may not lend a loaf of bread to her neighbor unless she determines its value in money, lest wheat should rise in price and they be found partakers in usury."

A man may say to his fellow, "Help me to weed, and I will help thee to weed," or "Help me to hoe, and I will help thee to hoe." But he may not say, "Help me to weed, and I will help thee to hoe," or "Help me to hoe, and I will help thee to weed." All days of the dry season are accounted alike, and all days of the rainy season are accounted alike. A man may not say to another, "Help me to plow in the dry season, and I will help thee to plow in the rainy season." Rabban Gamaliel says, "There is usury that is paid in advance and usury that is paid afterward. Thus, if a man purposed to borrow from another and made him a present, and said, 'That thou mayest lend me money,' that is usury paid in advance. If a man borrowed from another and repaid it to him, and then sent him a present and said, 'This is for thy money of which thou hadst not the use while it was with me,' this is usury that is paid afterward." R. Simeon says, "There may be usury paid in words: a man may not say to his creditor, 'Know thou that such a man has come from such a place.'"

These transgress a negative command: the lender, the borrower, the guarantor, and the witnesses. And the Sages say, "The scribe also." They transgress the command: *Thou shalt not give him thy money upon usury,*[11] and *Take thou no usury* of him,[12] and *Thou shalt not be to him as a creditor,* and *Neither shall ye lay upon him usury,*[13] and *Thou shalt not put a stumbling block before the blind, but thou shalt fear thy God. I am the Lord.*[14]

DEGREES OF HOLINESS [15]

There are ten degrees of holiness. The land of Israel is holier than any other land. Wherein lies its holiness? In that from it they may bring the *Omer,* the First Fruits, and the Two Loaves,[16] which they may not bring from any other land.

The walled cities [of the land of Israel] are still more holy, in that they must send forth the lepers from their midst; moreover they may carry around a corpse therein wheresoever they will, but once it is gone forth [from the city] they may not bring it back.

Within the wall [of Jerusalem] is still more holy, for there [only] they may eat the Lesser Holy Things and the Second Tithe. The Temple Mount is still more holy, for no man or woman that has a flux, no menstruant, and no woman after childbirth may enter therein. The Rampart is still more holy, for no Gentiles and none that have contracted uncleanness from a corpse may enter therein. The Court of the Women is still more holy, for none that had immersed himself the self-same day [because of uncleanness] may enter therein; yet none would thereby become liable to a sin offering. The Court of the Israelites is still more holy, for none whose atonement is yet incomplete may enter therein, and they would thereby become liable to a sin offering. The Court of the Priests is still more holy, for Israelites may not enter therein save only when they must perform the laying on of hands, slaughtering, and waving.

Between the Porch and the Altar is still more holy, for none that has a blemish or whose hair is unloosed may enter there. The Sanctuary is still more holy, for none may enter therein with hands and feet unwashed. The Holy of Holies is still more holy, for none may enter therein save only the High Priest on the Day of Atonement at the time of the [Temple] service. R. Jose said, "In five things is the space between the Porch and the Altar equal to the Sanctuary, for they may not enter there that have a blemish or that have drunk wine or that have hands and feet unwashed, and men must keep far from between the Porch and the Altar at the time of burning the incense."

BLESSING THE GOOD AND THE EVIL [17]

If a man saw a place where miracles had been wrought for Israel he should say, "Blessed is he that wrought miracles for our fathers in this place." [If he saw] a place from which idolatry had been rooted out he should say, "Blessed is he that rooted out idolatry from our land."

[If he saw] shooting stars, earthquakes, lightnings, thunders, and storms he should say, "Blessed is he whose power and might fill the world." [If he saw] mountains, hills, seas, rivers, and deserts he should say, "Blessed is the author of creation." R. Judah says, "If a man saw the Great Sea [18] he should say: 'Blessed is he that made the Great Sea'—but only if he sees it at intervals of time." For rain and good tidings he should say: "Blessed is he, the true Judge."

If a man built a house or bought new vessels he should say, "Blessed is he that hath given us life." A man should say the benediction for misfortune regardless of [any consequent] good, and for good fortune regardless of [any consequent] evil. If a man cries out [to God] over what is past, his prayer is vain. Thus if his wife was with child and he said, "May it be thy will that my wife shall bear a male," this prayer is vain. If he was returning from a journey and heard a sound of lamentation in the city and said, "May it be thy will that they [which make lamentation] be not of my house," this prayer is vain.

He that enters into town should pray twice: once on his coming in and once on his going forth. Ben Azzai says, "Four times: twice on his coming in and twice on his going forth, offering thanks for what is past and making supplication for what is still to come."

Man is bound to bless [God] for the evil even as he blesses [God] for the good, for it is written: *And thou shalt love the Lord thy God with all thy heart and with all thy soul and with all thy might* [19]—*with all thy heart* (lebab), with both thine impulses, thy good impulse and thine evil impulse; *and with all thy soul,* even if he take away thy soul; *and with all thy might,* with all thy wealth. . . .

A man should not behave himself unseemly while opposite the Eastern Gate [of the Temple], since it faces toward the Holy of Holies. He may not enter into the Temple Mount with his staff or his sandal or his wallet, or with the dust upon his feet, nor may he make of it a short bypath; still less may he spit there.

At the close of every benediction in the Temple they used to say, "for everlasting"; but after the heretics had taught corruptly and said that there is but one world, it was ordained that they should say, "from everlasting to everlasting." And it was ordained that a man should salute his fellow with [the use of] the name [of God]; for it is written: *And, behold, Boaz came from Bethlehem, and said unto the reapers, The Lord be with you. And they answered him, The Lord bless thee.* [20] And it is written: *The Lord is with thee, thou mighty man of valor.* [21] And it is written: *And despise not thy mother when she is old.* [22] And it is written: *It is time to work for the Lord: they have made void the Law.* [23] R. Nathan says, "They have made void thy Law because it was a time to work for the Lord."

III

THE HALAKHIC MIDRASH

From the time when the institution of the synagogue was first created, rabbis have delivered sermons in the synagogues, especially in connection with divine services on Sabbaths and holidays. Philo described a service of this sort, at which some priest or leader "reads the holy laws to them, and expounds them point by point till about the late afternoon."[24] Most of the rabbinic homilies were based on scriptural passages, preferably drawn from the portion of the Pentateuch assigned for reading on the particular Sabbath or holiday on which the homily was delivered, and supplemented or embellished by quotations drawn from other parts of the Scriptures. The most salient points made by the orators were recorded orally and circulated in academic schools. Many of these summaries, of varying lengths, were arranged in the sequence of the scriptural lessons by some of the outstanding rabbis of the second century A.D. Known under the generic name of *"halakhic midrashim,"* they have more specific titles for particular collections: *Mekhilta,* on Exodus, *Sifra,* on Leviticus, and *Sifre,* on both Numbers and Deuteronomy. The following three excerpts give an inkling of the rich religious and ethical content of some of these rabbinic discourses.

I AM THE LORD THY GOD [25]

I AM THE LORD THY GOD. Why were the Ten Commandments not said at the beginning of the Torah? They give a parable. To what may this be compared? To the following: A king who entercd a province said to the people, "May I be your king?" But the people said to him, "Have you done anything good for us that you should rule over us?" What did he do then? He built the city wall for them, he brought in the water supply for them, and he fought their battles. Then when he said to them, "May I be your king?" They said to him: "Yes,

yes." Likewise, God. He brought the Israelites out of Egypt, divided the sea for them, sent down the manna for them, brought up the well for them, brought the quails for them. He fought for them the battle with Amalek. Then he said to them, "I am to be your king." And they said to him, "Yes, yes." Rabbi says: "This proclaims the excellence of Israel. For when they all stood before Mount Sinai to receive the Torah, they all made up their mind alike to accept the reign of God joyfully. Furthermore, they pledged themselves for one another. And it was not only concerning overt acts that God, revealing himself to them, wished to make his covenant with them but also concerning secret acts, as it is said, 'The secret things belong unto the Lord our God, but the things that are revealed,' etc.[26] But they said to him, 'Concerning overt acts we are ready to make a covenant with thee, but we will not make a covenant with thee in regard to secret acts lest one of us commit a sin secretly and the entire community be held responsible for it.'"

I am the Lord thy God. Why is this said? For this reason: At the sea he appeared to them as a mighty hero doing battle, as it is said, "The Lord is a man of war."[27] At Sinai he appeared to them as an old man full of mercy. It is said, "And they saw the God of Israel," etc.[28] And of the time after they had been redeemed what does it say? "And the like of the very heaven for clearness."[29] Again it says, "I beheld till thrones were placed."[30] And it also says, "A fiery stream issued and came forth from before him," etc.[31] Scripture, therefore, would not let the nations of the world have an excuse for saying that there are two Powers, but declares, "I am the Lord thy God." I am he who was in Egypt, and I am he who was at the sea. I am he who was at Sinai. I am he who was in the past, and I am he who will be in the future. I am he who is in this world, and I am he who will be in the world to come, as it is said, "See now that I, even I, am he," etc.[32] And it says, "Even to old age I am the same."[33] And it says, "Thus saith the Lord, the King of Israel, and his Redeemer the Lord of Hosts: I am the first, and I am the last."[34] And it says, "Who hath wrought and done it? He that called the generations from the beginning. I,

the Lord, who am the first," etc.[35] Rabbi Nathan says, "From
this one can cite a refutation of the heretics who say, 'There
are two Powers.' For when the Holy One, blessed be he, stood
up and exclaimed, 'I am the Lord thy God,' was there anyone
who stood up to protest against him? If you should say that it
was done in secret, but has it not been said, 'I have not spoken
in secret,' etc.?[36] 'I said not unto the seed of Jacob'[37]—that is,
to those only will I give it. 'They sought me in the desert.'[38] Did
I not give it in broad daylight? And thus it says, 'I the Lord
speak righteousness, I declare things that are right.'"[39]

Another interpretation: *I am the Lord thy God*. When the
Holy One, blessed be he, stood up and said, "I am the Lord
thy God," the mountains trembled and the hills wavered. Tabor
was coming from Beth Elim and Carmel from Aspamea, as it
is said, "As I live, saith the king whose name is the Lord of
Hosts, surely as Tabor among the mountains and Carmel by the
sea would come."[40] This one was saying, "I have been called."
And that one was saying, "I have been called." But when they
heard from his mouth, "Who brought thee out of the land of
Egypt," each one of them remained standing in its place, and
they said, "He is dealing only with those whom he brought out
from Egypt."

Another interpretation: *I am the Lord thy God*. When the
Holy One, blessed be he, stood up and said, "I am the Lord thy
God," the earth trembled; as it is said, "Lord, when thou didst
go forth out of Seir, when thou didst march out of the field of
Edom, the earth trembled."[41] And it goes on to say, "The mountains quaked at the presence of the Lord."[42] And it also says,
"The voice of the Lord is powerful; the voice of the Lord is
full of majesty," etc., up to "And in his palace everyone says,
'Glory!'"[43] And their houses even were filled with the splendor
of the *Shekinah*. At that time all the kings of the nations of the
world assembled and came to Balaam, the son of Beor. They
said to him; "Perhaps God is about to destroy his world by a
flood." He said to them: "Fools that ye are! Long ago God swore
to Noah that he would not bring a flood upon the world, as

it is said, "For this is as the water of Noah unto me; for as I have sworn that the waters of Noah should no more go over the earth.'"[44] They then said to him, "Perhaps he will not bring a flood of water, but he may bring a flood of fire." But he said to them, "He is not going to bring a flood of water or a flood of fire. It is simply that the Holy One, blessed be he, is going to give the Torah to his people. For it is said, 'The Lord will give strength unto his people', etc."[45] As soon as they heard this from him, they all turned back and went each to his place.

And it was for the following reason that the nations of the world were asked to accept the Torah, in order that they should have no excuse for saying, "Had we been asked, we would have accepted it." For, behold, they were asked and they refused to accept it, for it is said, "And he said: 'The Lord came from Sinai,'" etc.[46] He appeared to the children of Esau, the wicked, and said to them, "Will you accept the Torah?" They said to him, "What is written in it?" He said to them, "'Thou shalt not murder.'"[47] They then said to him, "The very heritage which our father left us was: 'And by thy sword shalt thou live.'"[48] He then appeared to the children of Amon and Moab. He said to them, "Will you accept the Torah?" They said to him, "What is written in it?" He said to them, "'Thou shalt not commit adultery.'"[49] They, however, said to him that they were all of them children of adulterers, as it is said, "Thus were both the daughters of Lot with child by their father."[50] Then he appeared to the children of Ishmael. He said to them, "Will you accept the Torah?" They said to him, "What is written in it?" He said to them, "'Thou shalt not steal.'"[51] They then said to him, "The very blessing that had been pronounced upon our father was: 'And he shall be as a wild ass of a man; his hand shall be upon everything.'[52] And it is written, 'For indeed I was stolen away out of the land of the Hebrews.'"[53] And when he came to the Israelites and "at his right hand was a fiery law unto them,"[54] they all opened their mouths and said, "All that the Lord hath spoken will we do and obey."[55] And thus it says, "He stood and measured the earth; he beheld and drove asunder the nations." [56] R. Simon b. Eleazar says, "If the sons of Noah could not endure the seven commandments enjoined upon them, how much less could they have endured all the commandments of the Torah! To give a parable. A king had appointed two administrators. One was appointed over the store of straw and the other was appointed over the treasure of silver and gold. The one appointed over the store of straw was held in suspicion. But he used to complain about the fact that they had not appointed him over the treasure of silver and gold. The people then said to him, 'Reka.[57] If you were under suspicion in connection with the store of straw, how could they trust you with the treasure of silver and gold?' " Behold, it is a matter of reasoning by the method of *kal vahomer:* [58] If the sons of Noah could not endure the seven commandments enjoined upon them, how much less could they have endured all the commandments of the Torah?

Why was the Torah not given in the land of Israel? In order that the nations of the world should not have the excuse for saying, "Because it was given in Israel's land, therefore we have not accepted it." Another reason: To avoid causing dissension among the tribes. Else one might have said, "In my territory the Torah was given." And the other might have said, "In my territory the Torah was given." Therefore, the Torah was given in the desert, publicly and openly, in a place belonging to no one. To three things the Torah is likened: to the desert, to fire, and to water. This is to tell you that, just as these three things are free to all who come into the world, so also are the words of the Torah free to all who come into the world.

Who brought thee out of the land of Egypt, out of the house of bondage. They were slaves to kings. You interpret it to mean that they were servants of kings. Perhaps it is not so, but means that they were slaves of servants. When it says, "And redeemed you out of the house of bondage, from the hand of Pharaoh King of Egypt." [59] it indicates that they were servants of kings and not servants of slaves. Another interpretation: *out of the house of servants.* Out of the house of worshipers, for they worshiped idols.

BELOVED ARE THE STRANGERS [60]

And a stranger shalt thou not vex, neither shalt thou oppress him; for ye were strangers in the land of Egypt. You shall not vex him—with words. Neither shall you oppress him—in money matters. You should not say unto him, "But yesterday you were worshiping Bel, Kores, Nebo, and until now swine's flesh was sticking out from between your teeth, and now you dare to stand up and to speak against me!" And how do we know that if you vex him he can also vex you? It is said, "And a stranger shalt thou not vex, neither shalt thou oppress him; for ye were strangers in the land of Egypt." In connection with this passage, R. Nathan used to say, "Do not reproach your fellow man with a fault which is also your own."

Beloved are the strangers.[61] For in ever so many passages Scripture warns about them: "And a stranger thou shalt not vex," etc.; "Love ye therefore the stranger," etc.;[62] "For ye know the heart of a stranger," etc.[63] R. Eliezer says, "It is because there is a bad streak in the stranger that Scripture warns about him in so many passages." R. Simeon b. Yohai says, "Behold, it says, 'But they that love him be as the sun when he goeth forth in his might.'[64] Now who is the greater, he who loves the king or he whom the king loves? You must say, 'It is he whom the king loves.' And it is written, 'And loveth the stranger,' etc."[65]

Beloved are the strangers. For in ever so many passages Scripture applies to them the same designations as it does to the Israelites. The Israelites are called 'servants,' as it is said, "For unto me the children of Israel are servants."[66] And so also the strangers are called 'servants,' as it is said, "And to love the name of the Lord, to be his servants."[67] The Israelites are referred to as 'ministers,' as it is said, "But ye shall be named the priests of the Lord; men shall call you the ministers of our God."[68] And so also the strangers are referred to as 'ministers,' as it is said, "Also the aliens that join themselves to the Lord, to minister unto him."[69] The Israelites are referred to as 'friends,' as it is

said, "But thou, Israel, my servant, Jacob whom I have chosen,
the seed of Abraham, my friend." [70] And the strangers are also
referred to as 'friends,' as it is said, "And loveth the stranger." [71]
A 'covenant' is mentioned in connection with the Israelites, as it
is said, "And my covenant shall be in your flesh." [72] And a
'covenant' is also mentioned in connection with the strangers, as
it is said, "And holdeth fast by my covenant." [73] 'Acceptance'
is mentioned in regard to the Israelites, as it is said, "That they
may be accepted before the Lord." [74] And 'acceptance' is also
mentioned in regard to the strangers, as it is said, "Their burnt
offerings and their sacrifices shall be acceptable upon mine
altar." [75] 'Guarding' is mentioned in regard to the Israelites, as
it is said, "Behold, he that guardeth Israel doth neither slumber
nor sleep." [76] And 'guarding' is also mentioned in regard to the
strangers, as it is said, "The Lord guardeth the strangers." [77]
Abraham called himself a 'stranger,' as it is said, "I am a stranger
and a sojourner with you." [78] David called himself a 'stranger,'
as it is said, "I am a stranger in the earth." [79] And he also says,
"For we are strangers before thee, and sojourners, as all our
fathers were; our days on the earth are as a shadow, and there
is no abiding." [80] And it also says, "For I am a stranger with
thee, a sojourner, as all my fathers were." [81]

Beloved are the strangers. It was for their sake that our father
Abraham was not circumcised until he was ninety-nine years
old. Had he been circumcised at twenty or at thirty years of
age, only those under the age of thirty could have become proselytes to Judaism. Therefore, God bore with Abraham until he
reached ninety-nine years of age, so as not to close the door to
future proselytes. Also to determine the reward according to the
days and years, thus increasing the reward of him who does his
will. This is to confirm what has been said, "The Lord was
pleased, for his righteousness' sake, to make the teaching great
and glorious." [82] And you find them [the proselytes] also among
the four groups who respond and speak before him by whose
word the world came into being: "One shall say, 'I am the
Lord's,'" that is, "All of me is the Lord's, and there is no admix-
ture of sin in me." "And another shall call himself by the name
of Jacob"; these are the righteous proselytes. "And another shall

subscribe with his hand unto the Lord"; these are the repentant sinners. "And surname himself by the name of Israel"; [83] these are the God-fearing ones.

Ye shall not afflict any widow or fatherless child. From this I know only about the widow and the fatherless child. How about any other person? It says, "Ye shall not afflict them"; these are the words of R. Ishmael. R. Akiba says, "'Any widow or fatherless child'; Scripture mentions them because they are likely to be afflicted."

If thou afflict in any wise, whether by a severe affliction or a light affliction. Another interpretation: *If thou afflict in any wise.* This tells us that one becomes guilty of oppression only after he has repeated the act. At the time when R. Simeon and R. Ishmael were led out to be killed, R. Simeon said to R. Ishmael, "Master, my heart fails me, for I do not know why I am to be killed." R. Ishmael said to him, "Did it never happen in your life that a man came to you for a judgment or with a question, and you let him wait until you had sipped your cup, or had tied your sandals, or had put on your cloak? And the Torah has said, 'If thou afflict in any wise,' whether it be a severe affliction or a light affliction." Whereupon R. Simeon said to him, "You have comforted me, master."

When R. Simeon and R. Ishmael were killed, R. Akiba said to his disciples, "Be prepared for trouble. For if something good had beeen destined to come upon our generation, R. Simeon and R. Ishmael—and none else—would have been the first ones to receive it. Now then, it must therefore be that these two men have been taken from our midst only because it is revealed before him by whose word the world came into being that great suffering is destined to come upon our generation." This confirms what has been said, "The righteous perisheth, and no man layeth it to heart, and godly men are taken away, none considering that the righteous is taken away from the evil to come."[84] And it also says, "He entereth into peace, they rest in their beds, each one that walketh in his uprightness."[85] And then, "But draw near hither, ye sons of the sorceress, the seed of the adulterer and the harlot."[86]

For if they cry at all unto me, I will surely hear their cry.

Does it mean only if he cries I will hear, and if he does not cry I will not hear? But Scripture says, "I will surely hear their cry!" Behold, then, what does Scripture mean by saying, "If they cry at all unto me, I will surely hear?" Simply this: I will punish more quickly when there is one crying than when there is no one crying. Now it may be reasoned, by using the method of *kal vaḥomer*: If God hears when an individual cries, how much more will he hear when many cry. And it is further to be reasoned, by using the method of *kal vaḥomer*: If with regard to meting out evil, which is of less importance, the rule is that when the individual cries against the group God hears his cry, how much more should this be the rule with regard to meting out good, which is of greater importance, and especially in the case when the group prays for the individual.

My anger shall wax hot. R. Ishmael says, "Here God's anger is spoken of, and there God's anger is spoken of. Just as there it means drought and exile, as it is said, 'And the anger of the Lord be kindled against you, and he shut up the heaven, so that there shall be no rain,' etc.,[87] so here also it means drought and exile. And just as here it means punishment by means of the sword, so also there it means punishment by the sword."

And your wives shall be widows and your children fatherless. But do I not know from the very literal meaning of the passage "And I will kill you" that your wives will be widows and your children fatherless? What need then is there of saying, "And your wives shall be widows and your children fatherless?" It is but to indicate that they will be widowed and yet not widows, in the same sense as when it is said, "So they were shut up unto the day of their death, in widowhood, with their husband alive."[88] And your children will be fatherless and yet not orphans, in that the court will not permit them to sell any of the property of their fathers on the presumption that the latter are still alive. Now it is to be reasoned, by using the method of *kal vaḥomer*: If for mere refraining from violating justice your reward will be that your wives will not become widows and your children will not be fatherless, how much more so when you actually execute justice. And thus it says, "Execute true judgment."[89] And it also says, "Execute the judgment of truth and peace in your gates."[90] And

it also says, "Thus saith the Lord: 'Keep ye justice, and do righteousness; for my salvation is near to come.'"[91] All the more is
it to be expected that your wives will not become widows and
your children will not become fatherless. And thus it says, "That
thou mightest fear the Lord thy God, to keep all his statutes and
his commandments, which I command thee, thou, and thy son,
and thy son's son, all the days of thy life; and that thy days may
be prolonged."[92] And it says, "And ye shall teach them your
children . . . that your days may be multiplied," etc.[93] And it also
says, "For as the days of a tree shall be the days of my people,"
etc.[94] And it also says, "They shall not labor in vain, nor bring
forth for terror; for they are the seed blessed of the Lord, and
their offspring with them."[95] And it also says, "Thy seed also
would be as the sand," etc.[96] And it also says, "Oh that they had
such a heart as this alway . . . that it might be well with them
and with their children forever."[97] And it also says, "For as the
new heavens . . . so shall your seed and your name remain."[98]
And it also says, "And a redeemer will come to Zion . . ."; and
it continues to say, "'And as for me, this is my covenant with
them,' saith the Lord; 'my spirit that is upon thee, and my words
which I have put in thy mouth shall not depart out of thy mouth,
nor out of the mouth of thy seed, nor out of the mouth of thy
seed's seed,' saith the Lord, 'from henceforth and forever.'"[99] All
the more is it to be expected that in this world your days will be
prolonged, and you will live to see children and grandchildren,
and that you will also merit the life in the world to come.

ON PEACE [100]

And give thee peace. 'Peace' at thy coming in and *'peace'* at
thy going out. Peace with all men. R. Ḥananya, the segan of the
priests, says, "*And give thee peace,* i.e., in thine own house."
R. Nathan says, "This refers to the peace of the kingdom of the
house of David (the Messianic kingdom), as it is said, *Of the
increase of his government and peace there shall be no end.*"[101]
Another interpretation: *And give thee peace;* the peace [which
comes from the study] of the Torah, as it is said, *The Lord will*

give strength unto his people, the Lord will bless his people with peace.[102]

Great is peace! For the sake of peace, [the angel who reported to Abraham] the words of Sarah altered the saying from, *My lord is old,* to, *I am old.*[103] Great is peace! The Holy One made a change for peace's sake.[104] Great is peace, for the angel made a change for peace's sake.[105] Great is peace, for the Name of God which was written in holiness is blotted out in the water (of the ordeal of jealousy), for peace's sake, to bring peace between husband and wife.

R. Eleazar says, "Great is peace, for the prophets have implanted it above all things in the mouth of humanity."

R. Simeon ben Ḥalafta says, "Great is peace, for it is the greatest channel of blessing, as it is said, *The Lord will give strength unto his people, the Lord will bless his people with peace.*" [106]

R. Eleazar Ha-Kapar says, "Great is peace, for it is the seal of all blessings, as it says, *The Lord bless thee and keep thee, etc., and give thee peace.*" R. Eleazar, his son, says, "Great is peace, so that even when Israel is idolatrous but there is peace among them, God, as it were, says that Satan should not [have power to] touch them; as it is said, *Ephraim is bound up with images, let him alone.*[107] But what do we read concerning them when they were divided among themselves? *Their heart is divided, now they will be punished.* Lo, great is peace and hateful is division!"

Great is peace, so that even during war the heart longs for peace, as it is said, *When thou comest near to a city to war against it and callest it to peace.*[108]

Great is peace, for even the dead need it, as it is said, *And thou shalt go to thy fathers in peace.*[109] Again it says, *In peace thou shalt die.*[110] Great is peace, for it is given [as a gift] to those who repent, as it is said, *Peace, peace, to them that are afar off and to them that are nigh.*[111] Great is peace, for it is the reward of the righteous, as it is said, *He (the righteous) cometh unto peace, they (the righteous) rest in their beds.*[112]

Great is peace, for the wicked are deprived of it, as it is said, *There is no peace for the wicked, saith my God.*[113]

Great is peace, for it is given [as a gift] to those who *love* the

Torah, as it is said, *Great peace is there to those who love thy Torah.*[114] Great is peace, for it is given as a gift to those who study the Torah, as it is said, *And all thy children shall be taught of the Lord and great shall be the peace of thy children.*[115] Great is peace, for it is given as a gift to the meek ones, as it is said, *And the meek shall possess the land and shall delight themselves in the abundance of peace.*[116] Great is peace, for it is given as a gift to those who do righteousness, as it is said, *And the work of righteousness shall be peace.*[117]

Great is peace, for the name of the Holy One is Peace, as it is said, *And he called him Yahweh Shalom* (the Lord is Peace).[118] R. Ḥananya, the segan of the priests, said, "Great is peace, for it is equal in importance to the whole work of Creation; as it is said, *Who formeth light and createth darkness, and maketh peace.*"[119] Great is peace, for even the dwellers in the highest heavens (the angels) need it, as it is said, *He makes peace in his heights.*[120] Now, if in the realm where there is no [natural] enmity or strife, no hatred or dissension, peace is considered to be the highest good, the more so [in this world] where all these forces operate.

One passage says, *He makes peace in his heights,* and another, *Is there any number of his hosts?*[121] and yet another, *Ten thousands will serve him and myriads are before him.*[122] How are these passages to be explained? Before Israel was driven out of their land, *there was no number to God's hosts;* after they had been driven out, [only] *Thousands and myriads serve him.* As it were, the *family* above had been diminished.

PART FIVE

AMORAIC COLLECTIONS

I

COMMANDMENTS, CUSTOMS, AND COURTS

Although rabbinic Judaism insisted on the absolute equality of all divinely ordained laws, for practical as well as pedagogic purposes its exponents needed some classification of the existing commandments and prohibitions. A major distinction was that drawn between the six hundred and thirteen 'biblical' commandments and so-called 'rabbinic' elaborations. True, the latter, too, were absolutely binding, but at least in cases of doubt one was allowed to give the rabbinic laws a more lenient interpretation, whereas biblical laws were to be rigorously applied at all times. In view of the necessities of the far-flung diaspora, and especially of the wide divergences between practices observed in Palestine and in Babylonia, the sages also recognized the binding force of local customs. At times, indeed, local customs were allowed to supersede the formal law. Much leeway had, therefore, to be given to legal experts and judges in the practical application of such conflicting regulations as had developed. Furthermore, as a more humane attitude came to prevail, methods were sought whereby the harsh biblical laws might be mitigated in situations calling for a penalty of capital punishment, and yet the law itself might not be abrogated. The following selections from the Babylonian Talmud illustrate these various points in the discussion of legal fundamentals. The Talmud consists of commentaries (called 'Gemara') by later teachers (third to fifth centuries) on the Mishnah, which was completed in the second century. Both the compilers of the Mishnah (*Tannaim*) and the compilers of the Talmud (*Amoraim*) acknowledged the authority of Scriptures and quoted from them constantly. In addition, the Amoraim quoted from the Mishnah. In order to differentiate the sources of the quoted matter in this section, quotations from Scripture are set in italic type and quotations from the Mishnah are set in small capitals.

HOW MANY COMMANDMENTS?[1]

[THEREFORE GAVE HE THEM TORAH (TEACHINGS) AND MANY COMMANDMENTS. . . .]

R. Simlai, when preaching, said, "Six hundred and thirteen precepts were communicated to Moses, three hundred and sixty-five negative precepts, corresponding to the number of solar days [in the year], and two hundred and forty-eight positive precepts, corresponding to the number of the members of man's body." Said R. Hamnuna, "What is the [authentic] text for this?" It is, *Moses commanded us torah, an inheritance of the* congregation of Jacob,[2] *'torah'* being in letter value equal to six hundred and eleven.[3] *I am* and *Thou shalt have no [other Gods]* [not being reckoned, because] we heard from the mouth of the Might [Divine]. David came and reduced them to eleven [principles], as it is written, *A Psalm of David. Lord, who shall sojourn in Thy tabernacle? Who shall dwell in Thy holy mountain?*—[i] *He that walketh uprightly, and* [ii] *worketh righteousness, and* [iii] *speaketh truth in his heart; that* [iv] *hath no slander upon his tongue* [v] *nor doeth evil to his fellow,* [vi] *nor taketh up a reproach against his neighbor,* [vii] *in whose eyes a vile person is despised, but* [viii] *he honoreth them that fear the Lord,* [ix] *He sweareth to his own hurt and changeth not,* [x] *He putteth not out his money on interest,* [xi] *nor taketh a bribe against the innocent. He that doeth these things shall never be moved.*[4] *He that walketh uprightly;* that was Abraham, as it is written, *Walk before me and be thou whole-hearted.*[5] *And worketh righteousness,* such as Abba Hilkiahu. *Speaketh truth in his heart,* such as R. Safra. *Hath no slander upon his tongue;* that was our Father Jacob, as it is written, *My father peradventure will feel me and I shall seem to him as a deceiver.*[6] *Nor doeth evil to his fellow;* that is he who does not set up in opposition to his fellow craftsman. *Nor taketh up a reproach against his neighbor;* that is he who befriends his near ones [relatives]. *In whose eyes a vile person is despised;* that was Hezekiah, the King of [Judah], who dragged his father's bones on a rope truckle bed. *He honoreth them that fear the Lord*; that was Jehoshapet, King of Judah, who, every time he beheld a scholar-disciple, rose from his throne, and embraced and kissed him, calling him, "Father, Father; *Rabbi, Rabbi; Mari, Mari!*" *He sweareth to his own hurt and changeth not*, like R. Johanan; for R. Johanan [once] said, "I shall remain fasting until I reach home." *He putteth not out money on interest*, not even interest from a heathen. *Nor taketh a bribe against the innocent*, such as R. Ishmael, son of R. Jose. It is written [in conclusion], *He that doeth these things shall never be moved*. Whenever R. Gamaliel came to this passage, he used to weep, saying, "[Only] one who practiced all these shall not be moved; but anyone falling short in any of these [virtues] would be moved!" Said his colleagues to him, "Is it written, *He that doeth all these things [shall not fall]?* It reads, *He that doeth these things*, meaning even if only he practices one of these things [he shall not be moved]. For if you say otherwise, what of that other [similar] passage, *Defile not ye yourselves in all these things?* [7] Are we to say that one who seeks contact with all these vices, he is become contaminated, but if only with one of those vices he is not contaminated? [Surely] it can only mean there that if he seeks contact with any one of these vices he is become contaminated; and likewise here, if he practices even one of these virtues [he will not be moved]."

Isaiah came and reduced them to six [principles], as it is written, [i] *He that walketh righteously, and* [ii] *speaketh uprightly*, [iii] *He that despiseth the gain of oppressions*, [iv] *that shaketh his hand from holding of bribes*, [v] *that stoppeth his ear from hearing of blood*, [vi] *and shutteth his eyes from looking upon evil; he shall dwell on high*. [8] *He that walketh righteously*; that was our Father Abraham, as it is written. *For I have known him, to the end that he may command his children and his household after him, etc.*, [9] *and speaketh uprightly*; that is one who does not put an affront on his fellow in public. *He that despiseth the gain of oppressions*, as, for instance, R. Ishmael b. Elisha; *that shaketh his hand from holding of bribes*, as, for instance, R. Ishmael son of Jose; *that stoppeth his ear from hearing of blood,* one who hears not aspersions made against a rabbinic student and remains silent, as once did R. Eleazar, son of R. Simeon; *and shutteth his eyes from looking upon evil,* as R. Ḥiyya b. Abba [taught]; for R. Ḥiyya b. Abba said, "This refers to one who does not peer at women as they stand washing clothes [in the courtyard] and [concerning such a man] it is written, *He shall dwell on high.*"

Micah came and reduced them to three [principles], as it is written, *It hath been told thee, O man, what is good, and what the Lord doth require of thee* [i] *only to do justly, and* [ii] *to love mercy, and* [iii] *to walk humbly with thy God.*[10] 'To do justly,' that is, maintaining justice; 'and to love mercy,' that is, rendering every kind office; 'and walking humbly before thy God,' that is, walking in funeral and bridal processions. And do not these facts warrant an *a fortiori* conclusion that if in matters that are not generally performed in private the Torah enjoins 'walking humbly,' is it not ever so much more requisite in matters that usually call for modesty?

Again came Isaiah and reduced them to two [principles], as it is said, *Thus saith the Lord,* [i] *Keep ye justice and* [ii] *do righteousness* [etc.].[11] Amos came and reduced them to one [principle], as it is said, *For thus saith the Lord unto the house of Israel, Seek ye me and live.*[12] To this R. Naḥman b. Isaac demurred, saying, "[Might it not be taken as,] 'Seek me by observing the whole Torah and live?' But it is Habakkuk who came and based them all on one [principle], as it is said, *But the righteous shall live by his faith.*"[13]

ON LOCAL CUSTOMS[14]

The citizens of Beyshan were accustomed not to go from Tyre to Sidon on the eve of the Sabbath. Their children went to R. Joḥanan and said to them, "For our fathers this was possible; for us it is impossible." Said he to them, "Your fathers have already taken it upon themselves, as it is said, *Hear my son, the instruction of thy father, and forsake not the teaching of thy mother.*"[15]

The inhabitants of Ḥozai were accustomed to separate *ḥallah* [16] on rice. [When] they went and told it to R. Joseph, he said to them, "Let a lay Israelite eat it in their presence." Abaye raised an objection against him, "Things which are permitted, yet others treat them as forbidden, you may not permit it in their presence?" Said he to him, "Yet was it not stated thereon," R. Ḥisda said, "This refers to Cutheans. What is the reason in the case of Cutheans? Because they confound one thing [with another]! Then these people too [being ignorant] confound one thing [with another]?" "Rather," said R. Ashi, "we consider: if most of them eat rice [bread], a lay Israelite must not eat it [the *ḥallah*] in their presence, lest the law of *ḥallah* be [altogether] forgotten by them; but if most of them eat corn [bread], let a lay Israelite eat it in their presence, lest they come to separate *[ḥallah]* from what is liable upon what is exempt and from what is exempt upon what is liable."

[It was stated in] the text, "Things which are permitted, yet others treat them as forbidden, you may not permit it in their presence." Said R. Ḥisda, "This refers to Cutheans." Yet not [to] all people? Surely it was taught: Two brothers may bathe together, yet two brothers do not bathe [together] in Cabul. And it once happened that Judah and Hillel, the sons of R. Gamaliel, bathed together in Cabul, and the whole region criticized them, saying, "We have never seen such [a thing] in [all] our days"; whereupon Hillel slipped away and went to the outer chamber, but he was unwilling to tell them, "You are permitted [to do this]." [Again,] one may go out in slippers on the Sabbath, yet people do not go out in slippers in Beri. And it once happened that Judah and Hillel, the sons of R. Gamaliel, went out in slippers on the Sabbath in Beri, whereupon the whole district criticized them, saying, "We have never seen such [a thing] in [all] our days"; so they removed them and gave them to their [non-Jewish] servants, but they were unwilling to tell them, "You are permitted [to wear these]." Again, one may sit on the stools of Gentiles on the Sabbath, yet people do not sit on the stools of Gentiles on the Sabbath in Acco. And it once happened that R. Simeon b. Gamaliel sat down on the stools of Gentiles on the Sabbath in Acco, and the whole district criticized him, saying, "We have never seen such [a thing] in [all] our days." [Accordingly] he slipped down on to the ground, but he was unwilling to tell them, "You are permitted [to do this]." The people of the coastal region, since Rabbis are not common among them, are like Cutheans.

As for [not sitting on] Gentiles' stools, that is well, [the reason being] because it looks like [engaging] in buying and selling. [That they do not go out] in slippers too [is understandable], lest they fall off and they come to carry them four cubits in the street. But what is the reason that [brothers] do not bathe [together]? As it was taught: A man may bathe with all except with his father, his father-in-law, his mother's husband and his sister's husband. But R. Judah permits [a man to bathe] with his father, on account of his father's honor, and the same applies to his mother's husband. Then they [the people of Cabul] came and forbade [it] in the case of two brothers on account of [bathing with] his sister's husband.

It was taught: A disciple must not bathe with his teacher; but if his teacher needs him, it is permitted.

When Rabbah b. Bar Ḥanah came, he ate of the stomach fat. Now R. 'Awira the Elder and Rabbah son of R. Huna visited him; as soon as he saw them, he hid it [the fat] from them. When they narrated it to Abaye, he said to them, "He has treated you like Cutheans." But does not Rabbah b. Bar Ḥanah agree with what we learned, WE LAY UPON HIM THE RESTRICTIONS OF THE PLACE WHENCE HE DEPARTED AND THE RESTRICTIONS OF THE PLACE WHITHER HE HAS GONE? Said Abaye, "That is only [when he goes] from [one town in] Babylonia to [another in] Babylonia, or from [a town in] Palestine to [another in] Palestine, or from [a town in] Babylonia to [another in] Palestine; but not [when he goes] from [a place in] Palestine to [another in] Babylonia, [for] since we submit to them, we do as they." R. Ashi said, "You may even say [that this holds good when a man goes] from Palestine to Babylonia; this is, however, where it is not his intention to return; but Rabbah b. Bar Ḥanah had the intention of returning."

Rabbah b. Bar Ḥanah said to his son, "My son, do not eat

[this fat], whether in my presence or not in my presence. As for me who saw R. Johanan eat [it], R. Johanan is sufficient [an authority] to rely upon in his presence and not in his presence. [But] you have not seen him [eat it]; [therefore] do not eat, whether in my presence or not in my presence." Now, [one statement] of his disagrees with [another statement] of his. For Rabbah b. Bar Hanah said, "R. Johanan b. Eleazar related to me: 'I once followed R. Simeon, son of R. Jose b. Lakunia, into a kitchen garden, and he took the aftergrowth of the cabbage and ate it, and he gave [some] to me and said to me, "My son, in my presence you may eat; when not in my presence, you may not eat [it]. I who saw R. Simeon b. Yohai eat [it]"— R. Simeon b. Yohai is [great] enough to rely upon in his presence and not in his presence; [but] you may eat in my presence, but do not eat [when] not in my presence.'" What is [this reference to] R. Simeon? For it was taught, R. Simeon said, "All aftergrowths are forbidden, except the aftergrowth of the cabbage, because there is none like them among the vegetables of the field; but the Sages maintain: all aftergrowths are forbidden. Now, both [state their views] on the basis of R. Akiba. For it was taught, *Behold, we may not sow, nor gather in our increase.*[17] R. Akiba said, "Now, since they do not sow, whence can they gather? Hence it follows that the aftergrowth is forbidden."

A SANHEDRIN AND CAPITAL PUNISHMENT[18]

A SANHEDRIN HAS JURISDICTION WITHIN THE LAND . . . AND OUTSIDE IT.

What [Scriptural] authority is there for this?—Our Rabbis taught, "[From the text:] *And these things shall be for a statute of judgment unto you throughout your generations* in all your dwellings,[19] we learn that a Sanhedrin has jurisdiction both in and outside Palestine." If that be so, what is the import of [the limitation in] the text, *Judges and officers shalt thou make thee* in all thy gates *which the Lord thy God giveth thee tribe by tribe?* [20] [It means that] in your [own] gates you set up tribunals in every district as well as in every city, whereas outside the land [of Palestine] you set up tribunals only in every district but not in every city.

A SANHEDRIN THAT EFFECTS AN EXECUTION ONCE IN SEVEN YEARS IS BRANDED A DESTRUCTIVE TRIBUNAL; R. ELIEZER B. AZARIAH SAYS, "ONCE IN SEVENTY YEARS." The question was raised whether the comment [of R. Eliezer b. Azariah was a censure, namely,] that even one death sentence in seventy years branded the Sanhedrin as a destructive tribunal, or [a mere observation] that it ordinarily happened but once in seventy years? It stands [undecided].

R. TARPHON AND R. AKIBA SAY, "WERE WE MEMBERS OF A SANHEDRIN, NO PERSON WOULD EVER BE PUT TO DEATH." How could they [being judges,] give effect to that [policy]? Both R. Johanan and R. Eleazar suggested that the witnesses might be plied with [intimate] questions, such as, "Did you take note whether the victim was [perchance] suffering from some fatal affection, or was he perfectly healthy?" R. Ashi [enlarging on this,] said, "And should the reply be, 'Perfectly healthy,' they might further be embarrassed by asking, 'Maybe the sword only severed an internal lesion?' " [21]

And what would be asked, say, in a charge of incest? Both Abaye and Raba suggested asking the witnesses whether they had seen the offenders as intimate as "kohl flask and probe?"

Now [with regard to] the Rabbis, what kind of evidence [in such a charge] would they deem sufficient to convict? According to Samuel's maxim, for Samuel said that being caught in the attitude of the unchaste is sufficient evidence.

II

ATONEMENT

The idea of repentance (in Hebrew, *teshubah,* meaning the sinner's total return from his sinful ways), and with it the idea of atonement for sins, was already prominent in biblical religion, particularly of the postexilic era. Before long, the Day of Atonement on the tenth of Tishre had been elevated into the position of a supreme Jewish holiday, the "Sabbath of Sabbaths." The services at the Second Temple on that day were marked, not only by their exceptional solemnity and by the high priest's prayers for a divine judgment that would favor the nation in the coming year, but also by the unique feature of the public utterance of the divine name (YHWH) by the high priest before the assembled congregation. Poetic descriptions of the Day of Atonement services in the Second Temple are still recited annually in all orthodox Jewish congregations.

THE DAY OF ATONEMENT [22]

MISHNAH. THE SIN OFFERING AND THE GUILT OFFERING [FOR THE] UNDOUBTED COMMISSION OF CERTAIN OFFENSES PROCURE ATONEMENT; DEATH AND THE DAY OF ATONEMENT PROCURE ATONEMENT TOGETHER WITH PENITENCE. PENITENCE PROCURES ATONEMENT FOR LIGHTER TRANSGRESSIONS: [THE TRANSGRESSION OF] POSITIVE COMMANDMENTS AND PROHIBITIONS. IN THE CASE OF SEVERE TRANSGRESSION, IT [PENITENCE] SUSPENDS [THE DIVINE PUNISHMENT] UNTIL THE DAY OF ATONEMENT COMES TO PROCURE ATONEMENT. IF ONE SAYS, "I SHALL SIN AND REPENT, SIN AND REPENT," NO OPPORTUNITY WILL BE GIVEN TO HIM TO REPENT. [IF ONE SAYS,] I SHALL SIN, AND THE DAY OF ATONEMENT WILL PROCURE ATONEMENT FOR ME, THE DAY OF ATONEMENT PROCURES FOR HIM NO ATONEMENT. FOR TRANSGRESSIONS AS BETWEEN MAN AND THE OMNIPRESENT THE DAY OF ATONE-

MENT PROCURES ATONEMENT, BUT FOR TRANSGRESSIONS AS BE-
TWEEN MAN AND HIS FELLOW THE DAY OF ATONEMENT DOES NOT
PROCURE ANY ATONEMENT UNTIL HE HAS PACIFIED HIS FELLOW.
THIS WAS EXPOUNDED BY R. ELEAZAR B. AZARIAH, "FROM ALL
YOUR SINS BEFORE THE LORD SHALL YE BE CLEAN," [23] I.E., FOR
TRANSGRESSIONS AS BETWEEN MAN AND THE OMNIPRESENT THE
DAY OF ATONEMENT PROCURES ATONEMENT, BUT FOR TRANS-
GRESSIONS AS BETWEEN MAN AND HIS FELLOW THE DAY OF
ATONEMENT DOES NOT PROCURE ATONEMENT UNTIL HE HAS
PACIFIED HIS FELLOW. R. AKIBA SAID, "HAPPY ARE YOU, ISRAEL!
WHO IS IT BEFORE WHOM YOU BECOME CLEAN? AND WHO IS IT
THAT MAKES YOU CLEAN, YOUR FATHER WHICH IS IN HEAVEN;
AS IT IS SAID, 'AND I WILL SPRINKLE CLEAN WATER UPON YOU
AND YE SHALL BE CLEAN.' [24] AND IT FURTHER SAYS, 'THOU HOPE
OF ISRAEL, THE LORD!' [25] JUST AS THE FOUNTAIN RENDERS CLEAN
THE UNCLEAN, SO DOES THE HOLY ONE, BLESSED BE HE, RENDER
CLEAN ISRAEL."

GEMARA. Only the undoubted guilt offering [atones], but
not the suspensive one? But is not the word 'forgiveness' written
with regard to it too? These [others] procure complete atonement; the suspensive guilt offering does not procure complete
atonement. Or else, as for these [others] another can effect their
atonement, whereas in the case of the suspensive guilt offering
nothing else can effect their atonement. For it was taught: If
those who were liable to sin offerings, or guilt offerings [for the]
undoubted [commission of offenses] permitted the Day of Atonement to pass, they are still obliged to offer them up; but in the
case of those who were liable to suspensive guilt offerings, they
are exempt.

DEATH AND THE DAY OF ATONEMENT PROCURE ATONEMENT,
TOGETHER WITH PENITENCE. Only 'TOGETHER WITH PENITENCE,'
but not in themselves! Shall we say that this teaching is not in
accord with Rabbi? For it is taught: Rabbi said, "For all transgressions [of commands of] the Torah, whether one had repented
or not, does the Day of Atonement procure atonement, except
in the case of one who throws off the yoke [of the Torah], in-

terprets the Torah unlawfully, or breaks the covenant of Abraham our father." In these cases, if he repented, the Day of Atonement procures atonement; if not, not! You might even say that this is in accord with Rabbi, "Repentance needs the Day of Atonement, but the Day of Atonement does not need repentance."

PENITENCE PROCURES ATONEMENT FOR LIGHTER TRANSGRESSIONS: [THE TRANSGRESSION OF] POSITIVE COMMANDMENTS AND PROHIBITIONS. If it procures atonement for the transgression of negative commandments, is it necessary [to state that it procures it for the transgression of] positive ones? Rab Judah said, "This is what he means: [It procures atonement] for [the transgression of] a positive commandment, or a negative commandment that is to be remedied into a positive one." But not [for the transgression] of an actual negative commandment? Against this the following contradiction is to be raised: These are light transgressions [for which penitence procures atonement, transgression of] positive commandments and negative commandments, with the exceptions of *Thou shalt not take [in vain]* [26]—*Thou shall not take* and others of the same kind.

Come and hear: R. Judah said, "For everything from *Thou shalt not take* and down, repentance procures atonement; for everything from *Thou shalt not take* and up, penitence procures suspension [of punishment] and the Day of Atonement procures atonement—*Thou shalt not take* and others of the same kind."

Come and hear: Since, in connection with Horeb, penitence and forgiveness are stated, one might assume that includes the [transgression of] *Thou shalt not take,* and therefore it says, *He will not clear the guilty.* [27] Then I might have assumed that, with all others guilty of having transgressed negative commandments, the same is the case; therefore the text reads, *[Will not clear the guilt of him who taketh] his name [in vain],* i.e., he does not clear the guilt in [the taking in vain of] his name, but he clears the guilt in the transgression of other negative commandments? This is indeed a point of dispute between Tannaim, for it was taught: For what transgression does peni-

tence procure atonement? For that of a positive commandment.
And in what case does repentance suspend punishment and the
Day of Atonement procure atonement? In such as involve extirpation, death penalty through the Beth Din, and in actual
negative commandments.

The Master said, "In connection with Horeb [penitence and]
forgiveness is stated." Whence do we know that? Because it was
taught: R. Eleazar said, "It is impossible to say *He will clear
the guilt*,[28] since it says *He will not clear the guilt*;[29] nor is it
possible to say: *He will not clear the guilt*, since it is said *He
will clear the guilt*—how is that to be explained? He 'clears the
guilt' of those who repent, and does not 'clear the guilt' of
those who do not repent."

R. Matthia b. Heresh asked R. Eleazar b. Azariah in Rome,
"Have you heard about the four kinds of sins, concerning which
R. Ishmael has lectured?" He answered: "They are three, and
with each is repentance connected. If one transgressed a positive commandment, and repented, then he is forgiven before he
has moved from his place; as it is said, *Return, O backsliding
children*.[30] If he has transgressed a prohibition and repented,
then repentance suspends [the punishment] and the Day of
Atonement procures atonement; as it is said, *For on this day
shall atonement be made for you . . . from all your sins*.[31] If
he has committed [a sin to be punished with] extirpation or
death through the Beth Din and repented, then repentance and
the Day of Atonement suspend [the punishment thereon], and
suffering finishes the atonement; as it is said, *Then will I visit
their transgression with the rod, and their iniquity with strokes*.[32]
But if he has been guilty of the profanation of the Name, then
penitence has no power to suspend punishment, nor the Day
of Atonement to procure atonement, nor suffering to finish it,
but all of them together suspend the punishment and only
death finishes it; as it is said, *And the Lord of hosts revealed
himself in my ears; surely this iniquity shall not be expiated by
you till ye die*."[33] What constitutes profanation of the Name?
Rab said, "If, e.g., I take meat from the butcher and do not pay
him at once." Abaye said, "That we have learned [to regard

as profanation] only in a place wherein one does not go out to collect payment; but in a place where one does go out to collect, there is no harm in it [not paying at once]." Rabina said, "And Matha Meḥasia is a place where one goes out collecting payments due." Whenever Abaye bought meat from two partners, he paid money to each of them, afterward bringing them together and squaring accounts with both. R. Joḥanan said, "In my case [it is a profanation if] I walk four cubits without [uttering words of] Torah or [wearing] *tefillin*."

Isaac, of the School of R. Jannai, said, "If one's colleagues are ashamed of his reputation, that constitutes a profanation of the Name." R. Naḥman b. Isaac commented, "E.g., if people say, 'May the Lord forgive So-and-so.'" Abaye explained, "As it was taught, *And thou shalt love the Lord thy God,*[34] i.e., that the Name of Heaven be beloved because of you. If someone studies Scripture and Mishnah, and attends on the disciples of the wise, is honest in business, and speaks pleasantly to persons, what do people then say concerning him? 'Happy the father who taught him Torah, happy the teacher who taught him Torah, woe unto people who have not studied the Torah; for this man has studied the Torah—look how fine his ways are, how righteous his deeds!' Of him does Scripture say, *And He said unto me: Thou art My servant, Israel, in whom I will be glorified.*[35] But if someone studies Scripture and Mishnah, attends on the disciples of the wise, but is dishonest in business and discourteous in his relations with people, what do people say about him? 'Woe unto him who studied the Torah, woe unto his father who taught him Torah, woe unto his teacher who taught him Torah!' This man studied the Torah: Look, how corrupt are his deeds, how ugly his ways; of him Scripture says, *In that men said of them: These are the people of the Lord, and are gone forth out of His Land.*"[36]

R. Ḥama b. Ḥanina said, "Great is penitence, for it brings healing to the world; as it is said, *I will heal their backsliding, I will love them freely.*"[37] R. Ḥama b. Ḥanina pointed out a contradiction, "It is written, *Return, ye backsliding children,* i.e., you who were formerly backsliding; and it is written, *I will heal your backsliding?"* [38] This is no difficulty: in the one case, the reference is where they return out of love; in the other, out of fear.

Rab Judah pointed out this contradiction, "It is written, *Return ye backsliding children, I will heal your backsliding;* but it is also written *For I am a lord unto you, and I will take you one of a city and two of a family?"* [39] This is no contradiction: the one verse speaks [of a return] out of love or fear, the other when it comes as a result of suffering.

R. Levi said, "Great is repentance, for it reaches up to the Throne of Glory, as it is said *Return, O Israel, unto the Lord thy God."* [40] R. Johanan said, "Great is repentance, for it overrides a prohibition of the Torah; as it is said, . . . *saying: If a man put away his wife, and she go from him, and become another man's, may he return unto her again? Will not that land be greatly polluted? But thou hast played the harlot with many lovers, and wouldst thou yet return to me? saith the Lord."* [41] R. Jonathan said, "Great is repentance, because it brings about redemption; as it is said, *And a redeemer will come to Zion, and unto them that turn from transgression in Jacob,* [42] i.e., why will a redeemer come to Zion? Because of those that turn from transgression in Jacob." Resh Lakish said, "Great is repentance, for because of it premeditated sins are accounted as errors; as it is said, *Return, O Israel, unto the Lord, thy God; for thou hast stumbled in thy iniquity."* [43] 'Iniquity' is premeditated, and yet he calls it 'stumbling.' But that is not so! For Resh Lakish said that repentance is so great that premeditated sins are accounted as though they were merits: as it is said, *And when the wicked turneth from his wickedness, and doeth that which is lawful and right, he shall live thereby!* [44] That is no contradiction: one refers to a case [of repentance] derived from love, the other to one due to fear. R. Samuel b. Nahmani said, in the name of R. Jonathan, "Great is repentance, because it prolongs the [days and] years of man; as it is said, *And when the wicked turneth from his wickedness . . . he shall live thereby."* R. Isaac said, "In the West [Palestine] they said, in the name of Rabbah b. Mari, 'Come and see how different from the character of one of flesh and blood is the action of the Holy One, blessed be he. As to the character of one of flesh and blood, if one angers his fellow it is doubtful whether he [the latter] will be pacified or not by him. And even if you would say he can be pacified, it is doubtful whether he will be pacified by mere words. But with the Holy One, blessed be he, if a man commits a sin in secret he is pacified by mere words; as it is said, *Take with you words, and return unto the Lord.*[45] Still more, he even accounts it to him as a good deed; as it is said, *And accept that which is good.*[46] Still more, Scripture accounts it to him as if he had offered up bullocks; as it is said, *So will we render for bullocks the offerings of our lips.*[47] Perhaps you will say [the reference is to] obligatory bullocks. Therefore it is said, *I will heal their backsliding, I will love them freely.'"* [48]

It was taught: R. Meir used to say, "Great is repentance, for on account of an individual who repents the sins of all the world are forgiven; as it is said, *I will heal their backsliding. I will love them freely, for mine anger is turned away from him."* 'From *them*' it is not said, but 'from *him*.' How is one proved a repentant sinner? Rab Judah said, "If the object which caused his original transgression comes before him on two occasions and he keeps away from it." Rab Judah indicated, "With the same woman, at the same time, in the same place." Rab Judah said, "Rab pointed out the following contradictions: It is written, *Happy is he whose transgression is covered, whose sin is pardoned;* [49] and it is also written, *He that covereth his transgression shall not prosper."* [50] This is no difficulty; one speaks of sins that have become known [to the public], the other of such as did not become known. R. Zutra b. Tobiah, in the name of R. Naḥman, said, "Here we speak of sins committed by a man against his fellow, there of sins committed by man against the Omnipresent." It was taught: R. Jose b. Judah said, "If a man commits a transgression, the first, second, and third time he is forgiven, the fourth time he is not forgiven; as it is said, *Thus saith the Lord: For three transgressions of Israel, yea for four, I will not reverse it;* [51] and furthermore it says, *Lo, all these things does God work, twice, yea, thrice, with a man."* [52] What does 'furthermore' serve for? One might have assumed that applies only to a community, but not to an individual; therefore come and hear [the additional verse], *Lo, all these things does God work, twice, yea, thrice with a man.*

Our Rabbis taught: As for the sins which one has confessed on one Day of Atonement, he should not confess them on another Day of Atonement; but if he repeated them, then he should confess them on another Day of Atonement. And if he had not committed them again, yet confessed them again, then it is with regard to him that Scripture says, *As a dog that returneth to his vomit, so is a fool that repeateth his folly.*[53] R. Eliezer b. Jacob said, "He is the more praiseworthy, as it is said, *For I know my transgression, and my sin is ever before me.*[54] How then do I [explain], *As a dog that returneth to his vomit,*" etc.? In accord with R. Huna; for R. Huna said, 'Once a man has committed a sin once and twice, it is permitted to him.'" 'Permitted?' How could that occur to you? Rather, it appears to him as if it were permitted.

It is obligatory to confess the sin in detail [explicitly], as it is said, *This people have sinned a great sin, and have made them a god of gold.*[55] These are the words of R. Judah b. Baba. R. Akiba said, "[This is not necessary], as it is said, *Happy is he whose transgression is covered, whose sin is pardoned.*"[56] Then why did Moses say, *and have made them a god of gold?* That is [to be explained] in accord with R. Jannai, for R. Jannai said, "Moses said before the Holy One, blessed be he: 'The silver and gold which thou has increased unto Israel until they said "Enough!" has caused them to make golden gods.'"

Two good administrators arose unto Israel, Moses and David. Moses begged, "Let my sin be written down," as it is said, *Because ye believed not in me to sanctify me.*[57] David begged that his sin be not written down, as it is said, *Happy is he whose transgression is forgiven, whose sin is pardoned.* This case of Moses and Aaron may be compared to the case of two women who received in court the punishment of stripes; one had committed an indecent act, the other had eaten the unripe figs of the seventh year. Whereupon the woman who had eaten unripe figs of the seventh year said, "I beg of you, make known for what offense I have been punished with stripes, lest people say, 'The one woman was punished for the same sin that the other was punished for.'" They brought unripe fruits of the seventh year and hanged them on her neck, and they were calling out before her, "This woman was punished with stripes because she ate the unripe figs of the seventh year."

One should expose hypocrites to prevent the profanation of the Name, as it is said, *Again, when a righteous man doth turn from righteousness, and commit iniquity, I will lay a stumblng block before him.*[58] The repentance of the confirmed sinner delays punishment, even though the decree of punishment for him had been signed already. The careless ease of the wicked ends in calamity. Power buries those who wield it. Naked did man come into the world, naked he leaves it. Would that his coming forth be like his coming in. Whenever Rab went to the court, he used to say thus, "Out of his own will he goes toward death, the wishes of his household he is unable to fulfill, for he returns empty to his home. Would that the coming forth be like the going in." (Whenever Raba went to the court he used to say thus, "Out of his own will he goes toward death, the wishes of his household he is unable to fulfill, for he returned empty to his house. Would that the coming forth be like the going in.") And when he [Rab] saw a crowd escorting him, he would say, *"Though his excellency mount up to heaven and his head reach unto the clouds, yet shall he perish forever like his own dung; they that have seen him shall say, 'Where is he?'"* [59] When R. Zutra was carried shoulder-high on the Sabbath before the Pilgrimage festivals, he would say, *"For riches are not forever, and doth the crown endure unto all generations?"* [60]

It is not good to respect the person of the wicked.[61] It is not good for the wicked that they are being favored [by the Holy One, blessed be he] in this world. It was not good for Ahab that he was favored in this world, as it is said, *Because he humbled himself before Me, I will not bring the evil in his days.*[62] *So as to turn aside the righteous in judgment;*[63] it is good for the righteous that they are not favored in this world. It was good for Moses that he was not favored in this world, as it is said, *Because ye believed not in me, to sanctify me* [etc.]. But had you believed in me, your time to depart this world would not yet have come.

Happy are the righteous! Not only do they acquire merit, but they bestow merit upon their children and children's children, to the end of all generations; for Aaron had several sons who deserved to be burned like Nadab and Abihu—as it is said, *That were left,* [64]—but the merit of their father helped them. Woe unto the wicked! Not alone that they render themselves guilty, but they bestow guilt upon their children and children's children, unto the end of all generations. Many sons did Canaan have who were worthy to be ordained like Tabi, the slave of R. Gamaliel, but the guilt of their ancestor caused them [to lose their chance].

Whosoever causes a community to do good, no sin will come through him; and whosoever causes the community to sin, no opportunity will be granted him to become repentant. "Whosoever causes a community to do good, no sin will come through him." Why? Lest he be in Gehinnom and his disciples in *Gan Eden* [Paradise], as it is said, *For thou wilt not abandon my soul to the nether world, neither wilt thou suffer thy godly one to see the pit.* [65] "And whosoever causes the community to sin, no opportunity will be granted him for repentance," lest he be in *Gan Eden* and his disciples in Gehinnom, as it is said, *A man that is laden with the blood of any person shall hasten his steps unto the pit; none will help him.* [66]

IF ONE SAYS, "I SHALL SIN AND REPENT, SIN AND REPENT." Why is it necessary to state "I SHALL SIN AND I SHALL REPENT" twice? That is in accord with what R. Huna said in the name of Rab; for R. Huna said in the name of Rab, "Once a man has committed a transgression once or twice, it becomes permitted to him." 'Permitted?' How could that come into your mind—Rather, it appears to him like something permitted.

I SHALL SIN, AND THE DAY OF ATONEMENT SHALL PROCURE ATONEMENT; THEN THE DAY OF ATONEMENT DOES NOT PROCURE ATONEMENT. Shall we say that our Mishnah is not in accord with Rabbi, for Rabbi said, "It was taught: For all transgression of Biblical commandments, whether he repented or not, whether positive or negative, does the Day of Atonement procure atonement"? You may even say it will be in agreement with Rabbi. It is different when he relies on it.

FOR TRANSGRESSIONS COMMITTED BY MAN AGAINST THE OMNI-

PRESENT. R. Joseph b. Helbo pointed out to R. Abbahu the following contradiction, "[We learned:] FOR TRANSGRESSIONS COMMITTED BY MAN AGAINST HIS FELLOW MAN THE DAY OF ATONEMENT PROCURES NO ATONEMENT; but it is written, *If one man sin against his fellow man, God* [Elohim] *will pacify him?* [67] *'Elohim'* here means 'the Judge.' But how then is the second half of the clause to be understood, *But if a n an sin against the Lord, who shall entreat for him?*" This is what he means to say: *If a man sins against his fellow man, the judge will judge him, he [his fellow] will forgive him, but if a man sins against the Lord God, who shall entreat for him?* Only repentance and good deeds.

R. Isaac said, "Whosoever offends his neighbor, and he does it only through words, must pacify him, as it is written, *My son, if thou art become surety for thy neighbor, if thou hast struck thy hands for a stranger—thou art snared by the words of thy mouth . . . do this, now, my son, and deliver thyself, seeing thou art come into the hands of thy neighbor; go, humble thyself, and urge thy neighbor.* [68] If he has a claim of money upon you, open the palm of your hand to him; and if not, send many friends to him." R. Hisda said, "He should endeavor to pacify him through three groups of three people each, as it is said, *He cometh before men and saith: I have sinned and perverted that which was right, and it profited me not.*" [69] R. Jose b. Hanina said, "One who asks pardon of his neighbor need do so no more than three times, as it is said, *Forgive, I pray thee now . . . and now we pray thee.* [70] And if he [against whom he had sinned] had died, he should bring ten persons and make them stand by his grave and say, 'I have sinned against the Lord, the God of Israel, and against this one, whom I have hurt.'" R. Abba had a complaint against R. Jeremiah: He [R. Jeremiah] went and sat down at the door of R. Abba, and as the maid poured out water some drops fell upon his head. Then he said, "They have made a dungheap of me," and he cited this passage about himself, *He raiseth up the poor out of the dust.* [71] R. Abba heard that and came out toward him, saying, "Now, I must come forth to appease you, as it is written, *"Go humble thyself and urge thy neighbor."* When R. Zera had any complaint against any man, he would repeatedly pass by him, show-

ing himself to him, so that he may come forth to [pacify] him.
Rab once had a complaint against a certain butcher, and when
on the eve of the Day of Atonement he [the butcher] did not
come to him, he said, "I shall go to him to pacify him." R. Huna
met him and asked, "Whither are you going, Sir?" He said,
"To pacify So-and-so." He thought, "Abba [72] is about to cause
one's death." He went there and remained standing before him
[the butcher], who was sitting and chopping an [animal's] head.
He raised his eyes and saw him [Rab], then said, "You are
Abba, go away; I will have nothing to do with you." Whilst he
was chopping the head, a bone flew off, struck his throat, and
killed him.

Once Rab was expounding portions of the Bible before Rabbis,
and there entered R. Ḥiyya, whereupon Rab started again from
the beginning; as Bar Ḳappara entered, he started again from
the beginning, as R. Simeon, the son of Rabbi entered, he started
again from the beginning. But when R. Ḥanina b. Ḥama entered, he said, "So often shall I go back?" And he did not go
over it again. R. Hanina took that amiss. Rab went to him on
thirteen eves of the Day of Atonement, but he would not be
pacified. But how could he do so, did not R. Jose b. Ḥanina
say, "One who asks pardon of his neighbor need not do so more
than three times?" It is different with Rab. But how could R.
Ḥanina act so [unforgivingly]? Had not Raba said that if one
passes over his rights, all his transgressions are passed over [for-
given]? Rather, R. Hanina had seen in a dream that Rab was
being hanged on a palm tree; and since the tradition is that one
who in a dream is hanged on a palm tree will become head
[of an Academy], he concluded that authority will be given to
him, and so he would not be pacified, to the end that he departed to teach Torah in Babylon.

Our Rabbis taught: The obligation of confession of sins comes
on the eve of the Day of Atonement, as it grows dark. But the
Sages said: "Let one confess before one has eaten and drunk,
lest one becomes upset in the course of the meal. And although
one has confessed before eating and drinking, he should confess again after having eaten and drunk, because perchance
some wrong has happened in the course of the meal. And al-

though he has confessed during the evening prayer, he should confess again during the morning prayer: [and although he has confessed] during the morning prayer, he should do so again during the *Musaf* [additional prayer]. And although he had confessed during the *Musaf*, he should do so again during the afternoon prayer; and although he had done so in the afternoon prayer, he should confess again in the *Ne'ilah* [concluding prayer]." And when shall he say [the confession]? The individual after his *'Amidah* Prayer;[73] the public reader in the middle thereof. What is it [the confession]? Rab said, "Thou knowest the secrets of eternity."[74] Samuel said, "From the depths of the heart." Levi said, "And in thy Torah it is said . . ." R. Johanan said, "Lord of the Universe," [etc.]. Rab Judah, "Our iniquities are too many to count, and our sins too numerous to be counted." R. Jamnuna said, "My God, before I was formed, I was of no worth, and now that I have been formed, it is as if I had not been formed. I am dust in my life, how much more in my death. Behold I am before thee like a vessel full of shame and reproach. May it be thy will that I sin no more, and what I have sinned wipe away in thy mercy, but not through suffering." That was the confession [of sins] used by Rab all the year round, and by R. Hamnuna the younger on the Day of Atonement. Mar Zutra said, "All that [is necessary only] when he did not say, 'Truly, we have sinned,' but if he had said, 'Truly, we have sinned,' no more is necessary; for Bar Hamdudi said, 'Once I stood before Samuel, who was sitting, and when the public reader came up and said, "Truly, we have sinned," he rose.'" Hence he inferred that this was the main confession.

SACRIFICES AND ATONEMENT [75]

R. 'Inyani b. Sason also said, "Why are the sections on sacrifices and the priestly vestments close together?"[76] To teach you: as sacrifices make atonement, so do the priestly vestments make atonement. The coat atones for bloodshed, for it is said, *And they killed a he-goat, and dipped the coat in the blood.*[77]

The breeches atoned for lewdness, as it is said, *And thou shalt make them linen breeches to cover the flesh of their nakedness.* [78] The miter made atonement for arrogance. How do we know it? Said R. Ḥanina, "Let an article placed high up come and atone for an offense of hauteur." The girdle atoned for [impure] meditations of the heart, i.e., where it was placed. The breastplate atoned for [neglect] of civil laws, as it is said, *And thou shalt make a breastplate of judgment.* [79] The ephod atoned for idolatry, as it is said, *Without ephod there are teraphim.* [80] The robe atoned for slander. How do we know it? Said R. Ḥanina, "Let an article of sound come and atone for an offense of sound." The headplate atoned for brazenness; of the headplate it is written, *And it shall be upon Aaron's forehead,* [81] whilst of brazenness it is written, *Yet thou hadst a harlot's forehead.* [82]

But that is not so, for surely R. Joshua b. Levi said, "For two things we find no atonement through sacrifices, but find atonement for them through something else, and they are bloodshed and slander." Bloodshed [is atoned for] by the beheaded heifer,[83] while slander [is atoned for] by incense. For R. Hanania recited, "How do we know that incense atones? Because it is said, *And he put on the incense, and made atonement for the people.*" [84] And the school of R. Ishmael taught [likewise]: For what does incense atone? for slander; let that which is done in secret come and atone for an offense committed in secret. Thus slander contradicts slander, and bloodshed contradicts bloodshed? There is no difficulty: in the one case the murderer is known, in the other the murderer is unknown. If the murderer is known, he is liable to death? It means [where he committed murder] deliberately, but was not warned. Slander, too, does not contradict slander: here it was done in secret, there it was done in public.

III

PROSELYTISM

Since the days of the Israelitic prophets, the Jewish people had been imbued with a deep sense of its religious mission; its spokesmen led the people to the idea that it was to serve as a "light to the nations." At the same time, living as a minority among many nations, the Jewish group often faced the realization that, by letting the bars down and indiscriminately admitting strangers to full participation in its faith, the people might be endangering its very survival. For this reason there is a general ambivalence in the attitude of the ancient Jewish leadership toward proselytism. Especially after the rise of Christianity and its great missionary successes among the half-converted "God-fearing" Gentiles, the rabbis formulated the rule that "the left hand should repel, and the right should attract."[85] The history of ancient Jewish proselytism is most complex because of this, and there are numerous and often sharply divergent views held by students. The following selections illustrate the way in which the general attitude of the rabbinic leaders toward proselytism was worked out in specific detail.

THE STATUS OF THE PROSELYTE [86]

ONE WHO IS ABOUT TO BECOME A PROSELYTE is not received at once. But he is asked, "What has induced you to join us? Do you not know that this nation is downtrodden and afflicted more than all the other nations; that they are subjected to many ills and sufferings; that they would have their children and grandchildren die, and would even themselves suffer death because of the observances of circumcision, immersion, and all other commands; and that they do not assume an air of ostentation before the eyes of the world as all the other nations do?" If the candidate replies, "I am unworthy to take

157

upon myself the obligations of him who created the world by mere uttering of words, blessed be he," he is received at once; if not, he takes leave and departs.

After he has taken upon himself to accept Judaism, he is taken to the immersion house. Having covered his nakedness with water, they instruct him in some of the details of the commands, with special reference to the laws concerning the Gleanings, the Forgotten Sheaf, the Corner of the Fields, and the Tithes.

Just as they instruct a man, so do they instruct a woman, with special reference to the laws concerning menstruation, the priest's share of the dough, and the Sabbath lights.

After the immersion, they speak to him words of welcome, words of comfort, "Whom have you joined, O happy one? You have joined him who created the world by mere uttering of words, blessed be he. For the world was created only for the sake of Israel. There are none called the children of God, except Israel. There are none beloved of God, except Israel. All that we have spoken to you before your conversion, was only to increase your reward. . . . "

He who embraces Judaism through the desire to marry a Jewish woman, through personal love for the Jews, or through fear of the Jews is not a genuine proselyte. And so used R. Judah and R. Nehemiah to say, "All those who embraced Judaism in the days of Mordecai and Esther were no genuine proselytes, for it is said, *And many from among the peoples of the land became Jews; for the fear of the Jews was fallen upon them.*" [87] And he who embraces Judaism, not for the sake of God, is no genuine proselyte . . .

In the case of an Israelite who has lent money to a heathen or of a heathen who has lent money to an Israelite, if the heathen afterward becomes a proselyte, only the principal, and not the interest, may be collected. R. Judah says, "If the creditor, before the conversion, formally included the interest with the principal, he may collect all."

Similarly, in case a first son has been born to the proselyte, or in case his cow has borne a calf, or in case his cow has been slaughtered, if any of these occurred before he became a proselyte, he is free of the priestly dues; if after he became a proselyte, he is not free of the priestly dues. If there is a doubt whether it occurred before or after he became a proselyte, he is free of the priestly dues. . . .

Who is a 'resident alien'? He who took upon himself not to worship idolatry, according to the view of R. Meir. R. Judah says, "He who took upon himself not to eat animals which were not slaughtered according to the ritual law. . . . "

Israelites dealing with the resident alien are commanded not to transgress the following laws, *Ye shall not do him wrong;* [88] *Thou shalt not oppress a hired servant,*[89] *The wages of a hired servant shall not abide with thee all night.*[90]

We do not give them Jewish women in marriage, nor do we marry their women. And we do not lend them, nor borrow from them, money on interest.

We do not settle the resident alien in a border district nor in a bad section, but in an attractive section, in the midst of Palestine, where his trade may develop. For it is said, *He shall dwell with thee, in the midst of thee, in the place which he shall choose within one of thy gates, where it liketh him best; thou shalt not wrong him.*[91] . . .

In the case of a proselyte who has died and has left a son or a daughter who had become proselytes with him, his possessions are free, like the deer, and his slaves go free. If the slaves are prudent, they can acquire the possessions by 'drawing' them toward themselves. For the Sages said, "Movable property is acquired by 'drawing,' and immovable property is acquired by taking possession."

R. Eliezer says, "Immovable property is acquired, not only by taking possession, but even in the following case: If one is walking in the field of a proselyte who has died, and if another man comes to whom the first one has said, 'The field is mine,' the field is the first one's." The Sages say: "He does not acquire the field, until he has taken possession of it. . . . . "

If a proselyte who has died has had slaves tending his sheep, and someone now comes and says, "The slaves and the cattle are mine," they are his. But if the slaves are prudent, they can say to him, "We are free men, and the cattle are ours." The slaves then are free, and the cattle are theirs.

And a stranger shalt thou not wrong, neither shalt thou oppress him.[92] You shall not wrong the proselyte through words, nor shall you oppress him economically. . . .

The proselytes are favored by God, for the Scriptures always compare them to Israel, of whom it is said, *Behold thou, Israel, my servant, Jacob whom I have chosen.*[93] Love is mentioned in connection with Israel, as it is said, *I have loved you, saith the Lord.*[94] And love is mentioned in connection with proselytes, as it is said, *And loveth the stranger, in giving him food and raiment.*[95] The Israelites are called servants, as it is said, *For unto Me the children of Israel are servants;*[96] and the proselytes are called servants, as it is said, *To be his servants.*[97] Acceptability is mentioned in connection with Israel, as it is said, *"And it shall be always upon his forehead, that they may be accepted before the Lord;*[98] and acceptability is mentioned in connection with proselytes, as it is said, *Their burnt offerings and their sacrifices shall be acceptable upon mine altar.*[99] Safeguarding is mentioned in connection with Israel, as it is said, *The Lord is thy keeper; the Lord is thy shade upon thy right hand,*[100] and safeguarding is mentioned in connection with proselytes, as it is said, *The Lord preserveth the strangers.*[101] Ministry is mentioned in connection with Israel, as it is said, *But ye shall be named the priests of the Lord; men shall call you the ministers of our God;*[102] and ministry is mentioned in connection with proselytes, as it is said, *Also the aliens, that join themselves to the Lord, to minister unto him.*[103]

Palestine is favored, for the mere presence of the proselyte in the Holy Land qualifies him for acceptance in Israel. If one should say in Palestine, "I am a proselyte," we receive him at once. But outside of Palestine, we receive him only when he has his witnesses with him. . . .

THE TREATMENT OF PROSELYTES [104]

Our Rabbis taught: As it might have been assumed that if a man came and said, "I am a proselyte," he is to be accepted; hence it was specifically stated in the Scripture *with thee* [105] only when he is well known to thee. Whence is it inferred that if he came and had his witnesses with him [that his word is accepted]? It was specifically stated in Scripture, *And if a proselyte sojourn . . . in your land.* [106] From this I only know [that the law is applicable] within the land of Israel; whence is it inferred [that it is also applicable] within the countries outside the land? It was specifically stated in Scripture *with thee,* i.e., "wherever he is with thee." If so, why was the land of Israel specified? "In the land of Israel proof must be produced; outside the land of Israel no such proof need be produced"; these are the words of R. Judah. But the Sages said, "Proof must be produced both within the land of Israel and outside the land."

If he came and had witnesses with him, what need is there for a Scriptural text? R. Shesheth replied, "Where they state, 'We heard that he became a proselyte at a certain particular court.' As it might have been taught that we are not to believe them, we were taught [that we do believe them]."

In your land: from this I only know [that the law is applicable] within the land of Israel, whence is it inferred [that it is also applicable] within the countries outside the land? It was specifically stated in Scripture *with thee,* i.e., "wherever he is with thee." But this, surely, had been expounded already. One is derived from *with thee* and the other from *with you.* [107]

But the Sages said, "Proof must be produced both within the land of Israel and outside the land." But, it is written, surely, *in your land!* That expression is required [for the deduction] that proselytes may be accepted even in the land of Israel. As it might have been assumed that there they become proselytes only on account of the prosperity of the land of Israel, and at the present time also, when there is no prosperity, they might still be attracted by the Gleanings, the Forgotten Sheaf, the Corner and the Poor Man's Tithe; hence we were taught [that they may nevertheless be accepted].

R. Ḥiyya b. Abba stated in the name of R. Joḥanan, "The *halakhah* is that proof must be produced both in the land of Israel and outside the land." Is this not obvious? [In a dispute between] an individual and a majority, the *halakhah* is of course in agreement with the majority. It might have been suggested that R. Judah's view is more acceptable, since he is supported by Scriptural texts; hence we were taught [that the *halakhah* is in agreement with the Sages].

Our Rabbis taught, *And judge righteously between a man and his brother, and the proselyte that is with him.*[108] From this text did R. Judah deduce that a man who becomes a proselyte in the presence of a Beth Din is deemed to be a proper proselyte, but he who does so privately is no proselyte.

It once happened that a man came before R. Judah and told him, "I have become a proselyte privately." "Have you witnesses?" R. Judah asked. "No," the man replied. "Have you children?" "Yes," the man replied. "You are trusted," the Master said to him, "as far as your own disqualification is concerned, but you cannot be relied upon to disqualify your children."

Did R. Judah, however, state that a proselyte is not trusted in respect of his children? Surely it was taught: *He shall acknowledge*[109] implies "he shall be entitled to acknowledge him before others"? From this did R. Judah deduce that a man is believed when he declares, "This son of mine is firstborn." And as a man is believed when he declares, "This son of mine is firstborn," so is he believed when he declares, "This son of mine is the son of a divorced woman" or "the son of a *haluzah*." But the Sages say, "He is not believed." R. Naḥman b. Isaac replied, "It is this that he really told him, 'According to your own statement you are an idolater, and no idolater is eligible to tender evidence.'"

Rabina said, "It is this that he really told him, 'Have you children?' [And when the other replied] 'Yes' [he asked] 'Have you grandchildren?' [The reply being again] 'Yes,' he told him, 'You are trusted so far as to disqualify your own children, but you cannot be trusted so far as to disqualify your grandchildren.'"

Thus it was also taught elsewhere: R. Judah said, "A man is trusted in respect [of the status of] his young son, but not in respect of that of his grown-up son;" and R. Hiyya b. Abba explained in the name of R. Johanan that 'young' does not mean actually a minor and 'grown-up' does not mean one who is actually of age, but any young son who has children is regarded as of age while any grown-up son who has no children is deemed to be a minor. And the law is in agreement with R. Nahman b. Isaac. But surely [a Baraitha] was taught in agreement with Rabina. That statement was made with reference to the law of acknowledgment.

Our Rabbis taught: If at the present time a man desires to become a proselyte, he is to be addressed as follows, "What reason have you for desiring to become a proselyte? Do you not know that Israel at the present time are persecuted and oppressed, despised, harassed, and overcome by afflictions?" If he replies, "I know and yet am unworthy," he is accepted forthwith and is given instruction in some of the minor and some of the major commandments. He is informed of the sin [of the neglect of the commandments of] Gleanings, the Forgotten Sheaf, the Corner, and the Poor Man's Tithe. He is also told of the punishment for the transgression of the commandments. Furthermore, he is addressed thus, "Be it known to you that before you came to this condition, if you had eaten suet you would not have been punishable with *kareth;* if you had profaned the Sabbath you would not have been punishable with stoning; but now were you to eat suet you would be punished with *kareth,* were you to profane the Sabbath you would be punished with stoning." And as he is informed of the punishment for the transgression of the commandments, so is he informed of the reward granted for their fulfillment. He is told, "Be it known to you that the world to come was made only for the righteous, and that Israel at the present time are unable to bear either too much prosperity or too much suffering." He is not, however, to be persuaded or dissuaded too much. If he is accepted, he is circumcised forthwith. Should any shreds which render the circumcision invalid remain, he is to be circumcised a second time. As soon as he is healed, arrangements are made for his immediate ablution, when two learned men must stand by his side and acquaint him with some of the other minor commandments and with some of the major ones. When he comes up after his ablution, he is deemed to be an Israelite in all respects.

In the case of a woman proselyte, women make her sit in the water up to her neck, while two learned men stand outside and give her instruction in some of the minor commandments and some of the major ones.

The same law applies to a proselyte and to an emancipated slave; and only where a menstruant may perform her ablution may a proselyte and an emancipated slave perform this ablution; and whatever is deemed an interception in ritual bathing is also deemed to be an interception in the ablutions of a proselyte, an emancipated slave, and a menstruant.

The Master said, "If a man desires to become a proselyte . . . he is to be addressed as follows, 'What reason have you for desiring to become a proselyte . . . ?' and he is made acquainted with some of the minor and with some of the major commandments." What is the reason? In order that, if he desire to withdraw, let him do so; for R. Ḥelbo said, "Proselytes are as hard for Israel [to endure] as a sore, because it is written in Scripture, *And the proselyte shall join himself with them, and they shall cleave to the house of Jacob.*" [110]

"He is informed of the sin [of the neglect of the commandment of] Gleanings, the Forgotten Sheaf, the Corner, and the Poor Man's Tithe." What is the reason?—R. Ḥiyya b. Abba replied in the name of R. Joḥanan, "Because a Noahide would rather be killed than spend so much as a *perutah*, which is not returnable."

"He is not, however, to be persuaded or dissuaded too much." R. Eleazar said, "What is the Scriptural proof? It is written: *And when she saw that she was steadfastly minded to go with*

her, she left off speaking unto her.[111] 'We are forbidden,' she
told her, '[to move on the Sabbath beyond the] Sabbath boundaries'—'Whither thou goest,' [the other replied] 'I will go.'[112]
'We are forbidden private meeting between man and woman.'
'Where thou lodgest, I will lodge.' 'We have been commanded
six hundred and thirteen commandments.'—'Thy people shall
be my people.' 'We are forbidden idolatry.' 'And thy God my
God.' 'Four modes of death were entrusted to Beth Din.'—
'Where thou diest, will I die.' 'Two graveyards were placed at
the disposal of the Beth Din.' 'And there will I be buried.'
Presently *she saw that she was steadfastly minded* etc."

IV

COMMUNAL RESPONSIBILITY

Jewish survival in the dispersion was made possible in part by the strong communal organization developed by the Jews, usually with the support of the states under whose rule they lived. The ethnic-religious autonomy of the Jewish people found expression in powerful self-governing institutions, particularly the synagogue, the court of justice, and the school, and in a ramified system of social welfare. In many of these areas Judaism performed pioneering services for all of Western civilization. Talmudic Jewry transformed the meaning of the ancient biblical term *zedakah* from 'righteousness' to 'charity.' It declared charity to be a matter of sheer justice, and prided itself on being, more than any other group in the world, "merciful, bashful and charitable."[113] Similarly, talmudic Judaism stressed learning as both a supreme duty and an achievement, and early introduced a system of popular education for boys which was unparalleled among other groups until the nineteenth century.

A LAW OF LOVING-KINDNESS [114]

THE SCHOOL OF R. ANAN TAUGHT: It is written, *The roundings of thy thighs*.[115] Why are the words of the Torah compared to the thigh? To teach you that, just as the thigh is hidden, so should the words of the Torah be hidden, and this is the import of what R. Eleazar said, "What is the implication of the text, *It hath been told thee, O man, what is good, and what the Lord doth require of thee: Only to do justly, and to love mercy, and to walk humbly with thy God?*[116] 'To do justly' means [to act in accordance with] justice; 'to love mercy' refers to acts of loving-kindness; 'and to walk humbly with thy God' refers to attending to funerals and dowering a bride for her wedding. Now can we not make a deduction *a fortiori*: if in matters which are normally performed publicly the Torah enjoins 'to walk humbly,' how much more so in matters that are normally done privately?"

R. Eleazar stated, "Greater is he who performs charity than [he who offers] all the sacrifices, for it is said, *To do charity and justice is more acceptable to the Lord than sacrifice*." [117]

R. Eleazar further stated, "*Gemiluth Ḥasadim* is greater than charity, for it is said, *Sow to yourselves according to your charity, but reap according to your ḥesed.*[118] If a man sows, it is doubtful whether he will eat the harvest or not; but when a man reaps, he will certainly eat." R. Eleazar further stated, "The reward of charity depends entirely upon the extent of the kindness in it, for it is said, *Sow to yourselves according to charity but reap according to the kindness.*"

Our Rabbis taught: In three respects is *Gemiluth Ḥasadim* superior to charity. Charity can be done only with one's money, but *Gemiluth Ḥasadim* can be done with one's person and one's money. Charity can be given only to the poor, *Gemiluth Ḥasadim* both to the rich and the poor. Charity can be given to the living only, *Gemiluth Ḥasadim* can be done both to the living and to the dead.

R. Eleazar further stated, He who executes charity and justice is regarded as though he had filled all the world with kindness, for it is said, *He loveth charity and justice, the earth is full of the loving-kindness of the Lord.*[119] But lest you say that whoever wishes to do good succeeds without difficulty, Scripture expressly says, *How precious is thy loving-kindness, O God,* etc.[120] As one might say that this applies also to a man who fears God, Scripture expressly says, *But the loving-kindness of the Lord is from everlasting to everlasting upon them that fear him.*" [121]

R. Ḥama b. Papa stated, "Every man who is endowed with grace is without doubt a God-fearing man, for it is said, *But the loving-kindness of the Lord is from everlasting to everlasting to them that fear him.*" R. Eleazar further stated, "What is the purport of what was written, *She openeth her mouth with wisdom, and the Torah of loving-kindness is on her tongue?* [122] Is there then a Torah of loving-kindness and a Torah which is not of loving-kindness? But the fact is that Torah [which is studied] for its own sake is a Torah of loving-kindness, whereas Torah [which is studied] for an ulterior motive is a Torah which is not of loving-kindness."

Some there are who say, "Torah [which is studied] in order [subsequently] to teach it is a Torah of loving-kindness, but Torah [which is] not [studied subsequently] to teach it is a Torah which is not of loving-kindness."

THE SOCIAL WELFARE SYSTEM [123]

Our Rabbis taught: The charity fund is collected by two persons [jointly] and distributed by three. It is collected by two, because any office conferring authority over the community must be filled by at least two persons. It must be distributed by three, on the analogy of money cases [which are tried by a Beth Din of three]. Food for the soup kitchen is collected by three and distributed by three, since it is distributed as soon as it is collected. Food is distributed every day, the charity fund every Friday. The soup kitchen is for all comers, the charity fund for the poor of the town only. The townspeople, however, are at liberty to use the soup kitchen like the charity fund, and vice versa, and to apply them to whatever purpose they choose. The townspeople are also at liberty to fix weights and measures, prices, and wages, and to inflict penalties for the infringement of their rules.

The Master said above, "Any office conferring authority over the community must be filled by at least two persons." Whence is this rule derived? R. Naḥman said, "Scripture says, *And they shall take the gold* etc.[124] This shows that they were not to exercise authority over the community, but that they were to be trusted." This supports R. Ḥanina, for R. Ḥanina reported [with approval] the fact that Rabbi once appointed two brothers to supervise the charity fund.

What authority is involved [in collecting for charity]? As was stated by R. Naḥman in the name of Rabbah b. Abbuha, because the collectors can take a pledge for a charity contribution even on the eve of Sabbath. Is that so? Is it not written, *I will punish all that oppress them.*[125] even, said R. Isaac b. Samuel b. Martha in the name of Rab, the collectors for charity? There is no contradiction. The one [Rab] speaks of a well-to-do man, the other of a man who is not well-to-do; as, for instance, Raba compelled R. Nathan b. Ammi to contribute four hundred *zuz* for charity.

[It is written], *And they that be wise shall shine as the brightness of the firmament;* [126] this applies to a judge who gives a true verdict on true evidence. *And they that turn many to righteousness (zedakah) as the stars forever and ever;* [127] these are the collectors for charity [*zedakah*]. In a Baraitha it was taught: *They that are wise shall shine as the brightness of the firmament;* this applies to a judge who gives a true verdict on true evidence and to the collectors for charity. *And they that turn many to righteousness like the stars forever and ever;* this applies to the teachers of young children. Such as who, for instance? Said Rab, "To such as R. Samuel b. Shilath." For Rab once found R. Samuel b. Shilath in a garden, whereupon he said to him, "Have you deserted your post?" He replied, "I have not seen this garden for thirteen years, and even now my thoughts are with the children." And what does Scripture say of the Rabbis? Rabina answered, *They that love him shall be as the sun when he goeth forth in his might.*[128]

Our Rabbis taught: The collectors of charity, [when collecting,] are not permitted to separate from one another, though one may collect at the gate while the other collects at a shop [in the same courtyard]. If one of them finds money in the street, he should not put it into his purse but into the charity box, and when he comes home he should take it out. In the same way, if one of them has lent a man a *mina* and he pays him in the street, he should not put the money into his own purse but into the charity box, and take it out again when he comes home.

Our Rabbis taught: If the collectors [still have money but] no poor to whom to distribute it, they should change the small coins into larger ones with other persons, but not from their own money. If the stewards of the soup kitchen [have food over and] no poor to whom to distribute it, they may sell it to others, but not to themselves. In counting out money collected for charity, they should not count the coins two at a time, but only one at a time.

Abaye said, "At first the Master would not sit on the mats in the synagogue; but when he heard that it had been taught that the townspeople can apply it to any purpose they choose he did sit on them." Abaye also said, "At first the Master used to keep two purses, one for the poor from outside and one for the poor of the town. When, however, he heard of what Samuel had said to R. Taḥalifa b. Abdimi, 'Keep one purse only and stipulate [with the townspeople] that it may be used for both,' he also kept only one purse and made this stipulation." R. Ashi said, "I do not even need to stipulate, since whoever comes [to give me money for charity] relies on my judgment and leaves it to me to give to whom I will."

There were two butchers who made an agreement with one another that if either killed on the other's day, the skin of his beast should be torn up. One of them actually did kill on the other's day, and the other went and tore up the skin. Those who did so were summoned before Raba, and he condemned them to make restitution. R. Yemar b. Shelemiah thereupon called Raba's attention to [the Baraitha which says] that the townspeople may inflict penalties for breach of their regulations. Raba did not deign to answer him. Said R. Papa, "Raba was quite right not to answer him; this regulation holds good only where there is no distinguished man in the town, but where there is a distinguished man they certainly have not the power to make such stipulations."

Our Rabbis taught: The collectors for charity are not required to give an account of the moneys entrusted to them for charity, nor the treasurers of the Sanctuary of the moneys given for holy purposes. There is no actual proof of this [in the Scriptures], but there is a hint of it in the words. *They reckoned not with the men into whose hand they delivered the money, to give to them that did the work, for they dealt faithfully.*[129]

R. Eleazar said, "Even if a man has in his house a steward on whom he can rely, he should tie up and count out [any money that he hands to him], as it says, *They put in bags and told the money.*"[130]

R. Huna said, "Applicants for food are examined, but not applicants for clothes." This rule is based, if you like, on Scripture; or, if you prefer, on common sense. It can be based, if you like, on common sense, because the one [who has no clothing] is exposed to contempt, but not the other. "Or, if you prefer, on Scripture," on the verse *Is it not to examine* [paros] *the hungry before giving him thy bread,*[131] [for so we may translate, since] the word *'paros'* is written with a *sin,* as much as to say "Examine and then give to him," whereas later it is written *When thou seest the naked, that thou cover him,*[132] that is to say, immediately. Rab Judah, however, said that applicants for clothes are to be examined, but not applicants for food. This rule can be based, if you like, on common sense; or, if you prefer on Scripture. If you like, on common sense because the one [without food] is actually suffering, but not the other; or, if you prefer, on Scripture because it says *Is it not to deal thy bread to the hungry,* that is, at once, whereas later it is written *When thou seest the naked,* that is to say, "When you shall have seen [that he is deserving]." It has been taught in agreement with Rab Judah: If a man says "Clothe me," he is examined; but if he says "Feed me," he is not examined.

We have learned in another place: The minimum to be given to a poor man who is on his way from one place to another is a loaf which costs a *pundion* where four *se'ahs* of wheat are sold for a *sela.* If he stays overnight, he is given his requirements for the night. What is meant by "requirements for the night?" R. Papa said, "A bed and a pillow. If he stays over Sabbath, he is given food for three meals."

A Tanna taught: "If he is a beggar who goes from door to door, we pay no attention to him." A certain man who used to beg from door to door came to R. Papa [for money], but he refused him. Said R. Samma, the son of R. Yeba, to R. Papa, "If you do not pay attention to him, no one else will pay attention to him; is he then to die of hunger?" "But," [replied R. Papa,] "has it not been taught, 'If he is a beggar who goes from door to door, we pay no attention to him?'" He replied, "We do not listen to his request for a large gift, but we do listen to his request for a small gift."

R. Assi said, "A man should never neglect to give the third of a shekel [for charity] in a year, as it says, *Also we made ordinances for us, to charge ourselves yearly with the third part of a shekel for the service of the house of our Lord.*" [133] R. Assi further said, "Charity is equivalent to all the other religious precepts combined, as it says, *Also we made ordinances;* it is not written 'an ordinance' but 'ordinances.'"

R. Eleazar said, "He who causes others to do good is greater than the doer, as it says, *And the work of righteousness (zedakah) shall be peace, and the effect of righteousness quiet and confidence forever.*[134] If a man is not deserving, then *shalt thou not deal thy bread to the hungry;*[135] but if he is deserving, then *thou shalt bring the poor that are cast out to thy house.*" [136] Raba said to the townsfolk of Mahuza, "I beg of you, hasten [to the assistance of] one another, so that you may be on good terms with the government." R. Eleazar further said, "When the Temple stood, a man used to bring his shekel, and so make atonement. Now that the Temple no longer stands, if they give for charity, well and good, and if not the heathens will come and take from them forcibly. And even so it will be reckoned to them as if they had given charity, as it is written: *[I will] make thine exactors righteousness (zedakah).*" [137]

Raba said, "The following was told me by the suckling who perverted the way of his mother, in the name of R. Eleazar. 'What is the meaning of the verse, *And he put on righteousness as a coat of mail?*[138] It tells us that just as in a coat of mail every small scale joins with the others to form one piece of armor, so every little sum given to charity combines with the rest to form a large sum.'" R. Ḥanina said, "The same lesson may be learned from here, *And all our righteousness is as a polluted garment.*[139] Just as in a garment every thread unites with the rest to form a whole garment, so every farthing given to charity unites with the rest to form a large sum."

Why was he [R. Shesheth] called "the suckling who perverted the way of his mother?" The reason is this. R. Aḥadboi b. Ammi asked R. Shesheth, "Whence do we infer that a leper, while he is counting his days [for purification], renders unclean a man [who touches him]?" He replied, "Since he renders garments unclean, he renders a man unclean." "But," he said, "perhaps this only applies to clothes which he actually wears, for similarly we have the case of the lifting of a carcass, which makes the garment unclean but not the man?" He replied, "And whence do we know that a creeping thing makes a man unclean? Is it not from the fact that it makes garments unclean?" He replied, "Of the creeping it is distinctly written: *Or whosoever toucheth any creeping thing whereby he may be made unclean.*" [140] "How then," he [R. Shesheth] said, "do we know that [human] semen makes a man unclean? Do we not say that because it makes garments unclean, therefore it makes a man unclean?" He replied, "The rule of semen is also distinctly stated, since it is written in connection with it, *Or a man whose seed goeth from him,* [141] where [the superfluous phrase 'or a man'] brings under the rule one who touches the seed." He (R. Aḥadboi] made his objection in a mocking manner which deeply wounded R. Shesheth, and soon after R. Aḥadboi b. Abba lost his speech and forgot his learning. His mother came and wept before him, but in spite of all her cries he paid no attention to her. At length she said, "Behold these breasts from which you have sucked." Then at last he prayed for him and he was healed.

But what is the answer to the question that has been raised? As it has been taught: R. Simeon b. Yoḥai says, "Washing of garments is mentioned in connection with the period of the leper's counting, and washing of garments is also mentioned in connection with the period of his definite uncleanness. Just as in the latter case he renders any man he touches unclean, so also in the former case."

R. Eleazar said, "A man who gives charity in secret is greater than Moses our Teacher, for of Moses it is written, *For I was afraid because of the anger and the wrath;* [142] and of one who gives charity [secretly] it is written, A gift *in secret subdues anger.*" [143] In this he [R. Eleazar] differs from R. Isaac, for R. Isaac said that it subdues 'anger' but not 'wrath,' since the verse continues, *And a present in the bosom fierce wrath,* [which we can interpret to mean] "Though a present is placed in the bosom, yet wrath is still fierce." According to others, R. Isaac said, "A judge who takes a bribe brings fierce wrath upon the world, as it says, *And a present etc.*"

R. Isaac also said, "He who gives a small coin to a poor man obtains six blessings, and he who addresses to him words of comfort obtains eleven blessings." "He who gives a small coin to a poor man obtains six blessings," as it is written, *Is it not to deal thy bread to the hungry and bring the poor to thy house etc., when thou seest the naked etc.* [144] "He who addresses to him comforting words obtains eleven blessings," as it is written, *If thou draw out thy soul to the hungry and satisfy the afflicted soul, then shall thy light rise in the darkness and thine obscurity be as the noonday; and the Lord shall guide thee continually and satisfy thy soul in drought . . . and they shall build from thee the old waste places and thou shalt raise up the foundations of many generations, etc.* [145]

R. Isaac further said, "What is the meaning of the verse, *He that followeth after righteousness and mercy findeth life, righteousness, and honor?* [146] Because a man has followed after righteousness, shall he find righteousness? The purpose of the verse, however, is to teach us that if a man is anxious to give charity, the Holy One, blessed be he, furnishes him money with which to give it." R. Naḥman b. Isaac says, "The Holy One, blessed be he, sends him men who are fitting recipients of charity, so that he may be rewarded for assisting them." Who, then, are unfit? Such as those mentioned in the exposition of Rabbah, when he said, "What is the meaning of the verse, *Let them be made to stumble before thee; in the time of thine anger deal thou with them*"? [147] Jeremiah said to the Holy One, blessed be he: "Sovereign of the Universe, even at the time when they conquer their evil inclination and seek to do charity before thee, cause them to stumble through men who are not fitting recipients, so that they should receive no reward for assisting them."

R. Joshua b. Levi said, "He who does charity habitually will have sons wise, wealthy, and versed in the Aggaddah. 'Wise,' as it is written, *He shall find life;* 'wealthy,' as it is written, *[He shall find] righteousness;* 'versed in the Aggaddah,' as it is written, *And [he shall find] honor.* And it is written elsewhere, *The wise shall inherit honor.*" [148]

It has been taught: R. Meir used to say, "The critic [of Judaism] may bring against you the argument, 'If your God loves the poor, why does he not support them?' If so, answer him, 'So that through them we may be saved from the punishment of Gehinnom.'" This question was actually put by Turnus Rufus to R. Akiba "If your God loves the poor, why does he not support them?" He replied, "So that we may be saved through them from the punishment of Gehinnom." "On the contrary," said the other, "it is this which condemns you to Gehinnom. I will illustrate by a parable. Suppose an earthly king was angry with his servant and put him in prison, and ordered that he should be given no food or drink, and a man went and gave him food and drink. If the king heard, would he not be angry with him? And you are called 'servants,' as it is written, *For unto me the children of Israel are servants.*" [149] R. Akiba answered him, "I will illustrate by another parable. Suppose an earthly king was angry with his son and put him in prison, and ordered that no food or drink should be given to him, and someone went and gave him food and drink. If the king heard of it, would he not send him a present? And we are called 'sons,' as it is written, *Sons are ye to the Lord your God.*" [150] He said to him, "You are called both sons and servants. When you carry out the desires of the Omnipresent you are called 'sons,' and when you do not carry out the desires of the Omnipresent, you are called 'servants.' At the present time you are not carrying out the desires of the Omnipresent." R. Akiba replied, "The Scriptures say, *Is it not to deal thy bread to the hungry and bring the poor that are cast out to thy house.* When 'dost thou bring the poor who are cast out to thy house?' Now; and it says [at the same time], 'Is it not to deal thy bread to the hungry?'"

R. Judah, son of R. Shalom, preached as follows, "In the same way as a man's earnings are determined for him from New Year, so his losses are determined for him from New Year. If he finds merit [in the sight of Heaven], then, 'deal out thy bread to the poor'; but if not then he will 'bring the poor that are outcast to his house.'" A case in point is that of the nephews of Rabban Johanan b. Zakkai. He saw in a dream that they were to lose seven hundred denars in that year. He accordingly forced them to give him money for charity until only seventeen denars were left [of the seven hundred]. On the eve of the Day of Atonement, the Government sent and seized them. R. Johanan b. Zakkai said to them, "Do not fear [that you will lose any more]; you had seventeen denars, and these they have taken." They said to him, "How did you know this was going to happen?" He replied, "I saw it in a dream." "Then why did you not tell us?" they asked. "Because," he said, "I wanted you to perform the religious precept [of giving charity] quite disinterestedly."

As R. Papa was climbing a ladder, his foot slipped and he narrowly escaped falling. "Had that happened," he said, "mine enemy had been punished like Sabbath breakers and idolaters." Hiyya b. Rab from Difti said to him, "Perhaps a beggar appealed to you and you did not assist him, for so it has been taught: R. Joshua b. Korhah says, 'Whoever turns away his eyes from [one who appeals for] charity is considered as if he were serving idols.'" It is written in one place, *Beware that there be not a base thought in thine heart;* [151] and in another place, *Certain base fellows are gone out.* [152] Just as in the second case the sin is that of idolatry, so in the first case the sin is equivalent to that of idolatry.

It has been taught: R. Eliezer, son of R. Jose, said, "All the charity and deeds of kindness which Israel perform in this world [help to promote] peace and good understanding between them and their Father in heaven; as it says, *Thus saith the Lord,*

Enter not into the house of mourning, neither go to lament, neither bemoan them, for I have taken away my peace from this people . . . even loving-kindness and tender mercies,[153] [where] 'loving-kindness' refers to acts of kindness, and 'tender mercies' to charity."

It has been taught: R. Judah says, "Great is charity, in that it brings the redemption nearer; as it says, *Thus saith the Lord, Keep ye judgment and do righteousness* [zedakah], *for my salvation is near to come and my righteousness to be revealed.*"[154] He also used to say, "Ten strong things have been created in the world. The rock is hard, but the iron cleaves it. The iron is hard, but the fire softens it. The fire is hard, but the water quenches it. The water is strong, but the clouds bear it. The clouds are strong, but the wind scatters them. The wind is strong, but the body bears it. The body is strong, but fright crushes it. Fright is strong, but wine banishes it. Wine is strong, but sleep works it off. Death is stronger than all, and charity saves from death; as it is written, *Righteousness* [zedakah] *delivereth from death.*"[155]

R. Dosthai, son of R. Jannai, preached [as follows], "Observe that the ways of God are not like the ways of flesh and blood. How does flesh and blood act? If a man brings a present to a king, it may be accepted or it may not be accepted; and even if it is accepted, it is still doubtful whether he will be admitted to the presence of the king or not. Not so God. If a man gives but a farthing to a beggar, he is deemed worthy to receive the Divine Presence, as it is written, *I shall behold thy face in righteousness* [zedakah], *I shall be satisfied when I awake with thy likeness.*"[156] R. Eleazar used to give a coin to a poor man and straightway say a prayer, "Because," he said, "it is written, *I in righteousness shall behold thy face.*" What is the meaning of the words, *I shall be satisfied when I awake with thy likeness?* R. Nahman b. Isaac said, "This refers to the students of the Torah who banish sleep from their eyes in this world, and whom the Holy One, blessed be he, feasts with the resplendence of the Divine Presence in the future world."

R. Johanan said, "What is the meaning of the verse, *He that hath pity on the poor lendeth unto the Lord?* [157] Were it not written in the Scripture, one would not dare to say it, as it were, *the borrower is a servant to the lender."* [158]

R. Ḥiyya b. Abin said, "R. Johanan pointed out that it is written, *Riches profit not in the day of wrath, but righteousness* [zedakah] *delivereth from death,* [159] and it is also written, *Treasures of wickedness profit nothing, but righteousness* [zedakah] *delivereth from death.* [160] Why this double mention of righteousness? One that delivers him from an unnatural death and one that delivers him from the punishment of Gehinnom." Which is the one that delivers him from the punishment of Gehinnom? The one in connection with which the word 'wrath' is used, as it is written, *A day of wrath is that day.* [161] What kind of charity is that which delivers a man from an unnatural death? When a man gives without knowing to whom he gives, and the beggar receives without knowing from whom he receives. "He gives without knowing to whom he gives"; this excludes the practice of Mar 'Ukba. "The beggar receives without knowing from whom he receives"; this excludes the practice of R. Abba. How is a man then to do? He should put his money into the charity box.

The following was adduced in objection to this, "What is a man to do in order that he may have male offspring? R. Eliezer says that he should give generously to the poor; R. Joshua says that he should make his wife glad to perform the marital office. R. Eliezer b. Jacob says, 'A man should not put a farthing into the charity box unless it is under the supervision of a man like R. Ḥanina b. Teradion.'" In saying [that a man should put his money into the charity box,] we mean when it is under the supervision of a man like R. Ḥanina b. Teradion.

R. Abbahu said, "Moses addressed himself to the Holy One, blessed be he, saying, 'Sovereign of the Universe, wherewith shall the horn of Israel be exalted?' He replied, 'Through taking their ransom.'" R. Abbahu also said, "Solomon, the son of David, was asked, 'How far does the power of charity extend?' He replied, 'Go and see what my father David has stated on the matter, *He hath dispersed, he hath given to the needy, his righteousness endureth forever.'* " [162] R. Abba said, "[The answer might be given] from here, *He shall dwell on high; his place of defense shall be the munitions of the rocks; his bread is given him, his waters are sure.*[163] Why shall he dwell on high and his place be with the munitions of the rocks? *Because his bread is given* [to the poor], *and his waters are sure.*"

R. Abbahu also said, "Solomon was asked, 'Who has a place in the future world?' He answered, 'He to whom are applied the words, *and before his elders shall be glory.*' " [164] A similar remark was made by Joseph, the son of R. Joshua. He had been ill and fell in a trance. [After he recovered,] his father said to him, "What vision did you have?" He replied, "I saw a world upside down, the upper below and the lower above." He said to him, "You saw a well-regulated world." [He asked further,] "In what condition did you see us [students]?" He replied, "As our esteem is here, so it is there. I also, "[he continued,]" heard them saying, 'Happy, he who comes here in full possession of his learning.' I also heard them saying, 'No creature can attain to the place [in heaven] assigned to the martyrs of the [Roman] Government.'" Who are these? Shall I say R. Akiba and his comrades? Had they no other merit but this? Obviously even without this [they would have attained this rank]. What is meant, therefore, must be the martyrs of Lud.[165]

Rabban Johanan b. Zakkai said to his disciples, "My sons, what is the meaning of the verse, *Righteousness exalteth a nation, but the kindness of the peoples is sin*"? [166] R. Eliezer answered and said, "*Righteousness exalteth a nation;* this refers to Israel, of whom it is written, *Who is like thy people Israel one nation in the earth?* [167] But *the kindness of the peoples is sin;* all the charity and kindness done by the heathen is counted to them as sin, because they only do it to magnify themselves; as it says, *That they may offer sacrifices of sweet savor unto the God of heaven, and pray for the life of the king and his sons.*" [168] But is not an act of this kind charity in the full sense of the word, seeing that it has been taught: If a man says, "I give this *sela* for charity in order that my sons may live and that I may be found worthy of the future world," he may all the same be a righteous man in the full sense of the word? There is no contradiction; in the one case we speak of an Israelite, in the other of a heathen.

R. Joshua answered and said, "*Righteousness exalteth a nation;* this refers to Israel, of whom it is written, *Who is like thy people Israel, one nation in the earth? The kindness of peoples is sin;* all the charity and kindness that the heathen do is counted sin to them, because they only do it in order that their dominion may be prolonged, as it says, *Wherefore, O king, let my counsel be acceptable to thee, and break off thy sins by righteousness, and thy iniquities by showing mercy to the poor, if there may be a lengthening of thy tranquility.*" [169] Rabban Gamaliel answered, saying, "*Righteousness exalteth a nation;* this refers to Israel, of whom it is written, *Who is like thy people Israel,* etc. *And the kindness of the peoples is sin;* all the charity and kindness that the heathen do is counted as sin to them, because they only do it to display haughtiness, and whoever displays haughtiness is cast into Gehinnom, as it says, *The proud and haughty man, scorner is his name, he worketh in the wrath* ['ebrah] *of pride,*[170] and 'wrath' connotes Gehinnom, as it is written, *A day of wrath is that day.*" [171] Said Rabban Gamaliel, We have still to hear the opinion of the Modiite. R. Eliezer the Modiite says "*Righteousness exalteth a nation;* this refers to Israel, of whom it is written, *Who is like thy people Israel, one nation in the earth. The kindness of the peoples is sin;* all the charity and kindness of the heathen is counted to them as sin, since they do it only to reproach us, as it says, *The Lord hath brought it and done according as he spake, because ye have sinned against the Lord and have not obeyed his voice, therefore this thing is come upon you.*" [172] R. Nehuniah b. ha-Kanah answered saying, "*Righteousness exalteth a nation,* and there is kindness for Israel and a sin offering for the peoples." Said R. Johanan b. Zakkai to his disciples, "The answer of R. Nehuniah b. ha-Kanah is superior to my answer and to yours, because he assigns charity and kindness to Israel and sin to the heathen." This seems to show that he also gave an answer; what was it? As it has been taught: R. Johanan b. Zakkai said to them, "Just as the sin offering makes atonement for Israel, so charity makes atonement for the heathen."

Ifra Hormiz, the mother of King Shapur, sent four hundred denars to R. Ammi, but he would not accept them. She then sent them to Raba, and he accepted them, in order not to offend the government. When R. Ammi heard, he was indignant and said, "Does he not hold with the verse, *When the boughs thereof are withered they shall be broken off, the women shall come and set them on fire?"* [173] Raba [defended himself] on the ground that he wished not to offend the government. Was not R. Ammi also anxious not to offend the government? [He was angry] because he ought to have distributed the money to the non-Jewish poor. But Raba did distribute it to the non-Jewish poor?—The reason R. Ammi was indignant was that he had not been fully informed.

It has been taught: The following incident is related of Benjamin the Righteous, who was a supervisor of the charity fund. One day a woman came to him in a year of scarcity and said to him, "Sir, assist me." He replied, "I swear, there is not a penny in the charity fund." She said, "Sire, if you do not assist me, a woman and her seven children will perish." He accordingly assisted her out of his own pocket. Some time afterward he became dangerously ill. The angels addressed the Holy One, blessed be he, saying, "Sovereign of the Universe, thou hast said that he who preserves one soul of Israel is considered as if he had preserved the whole world; shall then Benjamin the Righteous who has preserved a woman and her seven children die at so early an age?" Straightway his sentence was torn up. It has been taught that twenty-two years were added to his life.

Our Rabbis taught: It is related of King Monobaz [174] that he dissipated all his own hoards and the hoards of his fathers in years of scarcity. His brothers and his father's household came in a deputation to him and said to him, "Your father saved money and added to the treasures of his fathers, and you are squandering them." He replied, "My fathers stored up below and I am storing up above, as it says, *Truth springeth out of the earth and righteousness looketh down from heaven.*[175] My fathers stored in a place which can be tampered with, but I have stored in a place which cannot be tampered with, as it says, *Righteousness and judgment are the foundation of his throne.*[176] My fathers stored something which produces no fruits, but I have stored something which does produce fruits, as it is written, *Say ye of the righteous* [zaddik] *that it shall be well with them, for they shall eat of the fruit of their doings.*[177] My fathers gathered treasures of money, but I have gathered treasures of souls, as it is written. *The fruit of the righteous* [zaddik] *is a tree of life, and he that is wise winneth souls.*[178] My fathers gathered for others and I have gathered for myself, as it says, *And for thee it shall be righteousness* [zedakah].[179] My fathers gathered for this world, but I have gathered for the future world, as it says, *Thy righteousness* [zedakah] *shall go before thee, and the glory of the Lord shall be thy rearward."* [180]

ON EDUCATION [181]

MISHNAH. IF A MAN DESIRES TO OPEN A SHOP IN A COURT-YARD, HIS NEIGHBOR MAY PREVENT HIM ON THE GROUND THAT HE WILL NOT BE ABLE TO SLEEP THROUGH THE NOISE OF PEOPLE COMING AND GOING. A MAN, HOWEVER, MAY MAKE ARTICLES IN THE COURTYARD TO TAKE OUT AND SELL IN THE MARKET, AND HIS NEIGHBOR CANNOT PREVENT HIM ON THE GROUND THAT HE CANNOT SLEEP FROM THE NOISE OF THE HAM-MER OR OF THE MILLSTONES OR OF THE CHILDREN.

GEMARA. Why is the rule in the second case not the same as in the first? Abaye replied, "The second clause must refer to [a man in] another courtyard." Said Raba to him, "If that is so, the Mishnah should say: 'In another courtyard it is permissi-ble?'" "No," said Raba, "the concluding words refer to school children, from the time of the regulation of Joshua b. Gamala, of whom Rab Judah has told us in the name of Rab, 'Verily, the name of that man is to be blessed, to wit Joshua ben Gamala, for but for him the Torah would have been forgotten from Israel.' For at first if a child had a father, his father taught him; and if he had no father, he did not learn at all. By what [verse of the Scripture] did they guide themselves? By the verse, *And ye shall teach them to your children*,[182] laying the emphasis on the word 'ye.' They then made an ordinance that teachers of children should be appointed in Jerusalem. By what verse did they guide themselves? By the verse, *For from Zion shall the Torah go forth*.[183] Even so, however, if a child had a father, the father would take him up to Jerusalem and have him taught there; and if not, he would not go up to learn there. They therefore ordained that teachers should be appointed in each prefecture, and that boys should enter school at the age of sixteen or seventeen. [They did so,] and if the teacher punished them they used to rebel and leave school. At length Joshua b. Gamala came and ordained that teachers of young children should be appointed in each district and each town, and that children should enter school at the age of six or seven."

Rab said to R. Samuel b. Shilath, "Before the age of six do not accept pupils; from that age you can accept them, and stuff them with Torah like an ox." Rab also said to R. Samuel b. Shilath, "When you punish a pupil, only hit him with a shoe latchet. The attentive one will read [of himself]; and if one is inattentive, put him next to a diligent one."

An objection was raised [from the following answer of Raba], "If a resident in a courtyard desires to become a *Mohel*, a bloodletter, a tanner, or a teacher of children, the other residents can prevent him?" The reference here is to a teacher of non-Jewish children.

Come and hear: If two persons live in a courtyard and one of them desires to become a *Mohel*, a bloodletter, a tanner, or a teacher of children, the other can prevent him. Here, too, the reference is to a teacher of non-Jewish children.

Come and hear: If a man has a room in a courtyard which he shares with another, he must not let it either to a *Mohel*, or a bloodletter, or a tanner, or a Jewish teacher, or a non-Jewish teacher. The reference here is to the head teacher of the town [who superintends the others].

Raba said, "Under the ordinance of Joshua ben Gamala, children are not to be sent [every day to school] from one town to another, but they can be compelled to go from one synagogue to another [in the same town]. If, however, there is a river in between, we cannot compel them. But if again there is a bridge, we can compel them—not, however, if it is merely a plank."

Raba further said, "The number of pupils to be assigned to each teacher is twenty-five. If there are fifty, we appoint two teachers. If there are forty, we appoint an assistant, at the expense of the town."

Raba also said, "If we have a teacher who gets on with the children and there is another who can get on better, we do not replace the first by the second, for fear that the second when appointed will become indolent." R. Dimi from Nehardea, however, held that he would exert himself still more if appointed, "The jealousy of scribes increaseth wisdom."

Raba further said, "If there are two teachers of whom one gets on fast but with mistakes and the other slowly but without mistakes, we appoint the one who gets on fast and makes mistakes, since the mistakes correct themselves in time." R. Dimi from Nehardea, on the other hand, said that we appoint the one who goes slowly but makes no mistakes, for once a mistake is implanted it cannot be eradicated. This can be shown from the Scripture. It is written, *For Joab and all Israel remained there until he had cut off every male in Edom.*[184] When Joab came before David, the latter said to him, "Why have you acted thus [i.e., killed only the males]"? He replied, "Because it is written, *Thou shalt blot out the males* [zekar] *of Amalek.*"[185] Said David, "But *we* read, *the remembrance* [zeker] *of Amalek*"? He replied, "I was taught to read *zekar*." He [Joab] then went to his teacher and asked, "How didst thou teach me to read"? He replied: "*Zeker*." Thereupon he drew his sword and threatened to kill him. "Why do you do this"? asked the other. He replied, "Because it is written, *Cursed be he that doeth the work of the Lord negligently.*"[186] He said to him, "Be satisfied that I am cursed." To which Joab rejoined, "[It also says,] *Cursed be he that keepeth back his sword from blood.*"[187] According to one report he killed him; according to another, he did not kill him.

V

THE FUTURE LIFE

Jewish thought in the Maccabean era and after was more deeply concerned with the problems of the ultimate destinies of the people and of each individual than it had been in any other period of Jewish history. Elaborating on ideas that were briefly alluded to by the prophets, some apocalyptic and "rational" writers, both orthodox and sectarian, during the last two centuries of the Second Commonwealth, speculated deeply and intensely on the cosmic "end of days" and on the Hereafter facing the individual, whether Jew or Gentile. The rabbis accepted the principles of the Pharisaic religion and added to its formulations some relatively minor, though far from insignificant, ingredients. Rabbinic speculations are, therefore, continuous with the eschatological expectations expressed before the fall of Jerusalem.

The fact that most of the rabbinic speculations are concentrated in a single chapter of the Babylonian Talmud should not mislead the reader into the conclusion that they had been relegated to a small corner within the structure of talmudic thought. They required little detailed elaboration, as compared with the minutiae of ritual or civil law; yet they had a place at the very core of Jewish existence, and were prominent in the rabbinic homilies and in the daily thought and discussions of the people.

THE MESSIAH [188]

THE DISCIPLES OF R. JOSE B. KISMA asked him, "When will the Messiah come?" He answered, "I fear lest ye demand a sign of me [that my answer is correct]." They assured him, "We will demand no sign of you." So he answered them, "When this gate falls down, is rebuilt, falls again, and is again rebuilt, and then falls a third time; before it can be rebuilt, the son of David will come." They said to him, "Master, give us a sign." He protested. "Did ye not assure me that ye would not demand a sign?" They replied, "Even so [we desire one]." He said to them, "If so, let the waters of the grotto of Paneas turn into blood," and they turned into blood. When he lay dying, he said to them, "Place my coffin deep [in the earth], for there is not one palm tree in Babylon to which a Persian horse will not be tethered, nor one coffin in Palestine out of which a Median horse will not eat straw."

Rab said, "The son of David will not come until the [Roman] power enfolds Israel for nine months, as it is writen, *Therefore will he give them up, until the time that she which travaileth hath brought forth: then the remnant of his brethren shall return unto the children of Israel.*" [189]

'Ulla said, "Let him [the Messiah] come, but let me not see him."

Rabbah said likewise, "Let him come, but let me not see him."

R. Joseph said, "Let him come, and may I be worthy of sitting in the shadow of his ass' saddle." Abaye enquired of Rabbah, "What is your reason [for not wishing to see him]? Shall we say, because of the birth pangs [preceding the advent] of the Messiah? But it has been taught, R. Eleazar's disciples asked him: 'What must a man do to be spared the pangs of the Messiah?' [He answered,] 'Let him engage in study and benevolence,' and you, Master, do both." He replied, "[I fear] lest sin cause it, in accordance with [the teaching of] R. Jacob b. Idi, who opposed [two verses] [viz.,] It is written: *And, behold, I am with thee, and will guard thee in all places whither thou goest:* [190] but it is written: *Then Jacob was greatly afraid and distressed.*" [191] He was afraid that sin might cause [the nullification of God's promise]. Even as it was taught: *Till thy people pass over, O Lord;* [192] this refers to the first entry [into Palestine]. *Till thy people pass over, which thou has purchased;* [193] this refers to their second entry. Hence you may reason: The Israelites were as worthy of a miracle being wrought for them at the second entry as at the first, but that sin caused it [not to happen].

R. Johanan said likewise, "Let him come, and let me not see

him." Resh Lakish said to him, "Why so? Shall we say, because it is written, *As if a man did flee from a lion, and a bear met him; or went into the house and leaned his hand on the wall, and a serpent bit him?* [194] But come, and I will show you its like even in this world. When one goes out into the field and meets a bailiff, it is as though he had met a lion. When he enters the town and is accosted by a tax collector, it is as though he had met a bear. On entering his house and finding his sons and daughters in the throes of hunger, it is as though he were bitten by a serpent. But [his unwillingness to see the Messiah] is because it is written, *Ask ye now, and see whether a man doth travail with child? Wherefore do I see every man* [geber] *with his hands on his loins, as a woman in travail, and all faces are turned into paleness?* [195] What is meant by *wherefore do I see every* geber? Raba b. Isaac said in Rab's name, "It refers to him to whom all *geburah* [strength] belongs." And what is the meaning of *and all faces are turned into paleness?* R. Johanan said, "[This refers to God's] heavenly family [i.e., the angels] and his earthly family [i.e., Israel,] when God says, 'These [the Gentiles] are my handiwork, and so are these [the Jews]; how shall I destroy the former on account of the latter?'" R. Papa said: "Thus men say, 'When the ox runs and falls, the horse is put into his stall.'"

R. Giddal said in Rab's name, "The Jews are destined to eat [their fill] in the days of the Messiah." R. Joseph demurred, "Is this not obvious; who else then should eat—Hilek and Bilek?" [196] This was said in opposition to R. Hillel, who maintained that there will be no Messiah for Israel, since they have already enjoyed him during the reign of Hezekiah.

Rab said, "The world was created only on David's account." Samuel said, "On Moses' account." R. Johanan said, "For the sake of the Messiah." What is his [the Messiah's] name? The School of R. Shila said: "His name is Shiloh, for it is written, *until Shiloh come.*" [197] The School of R. Yannai said: His name is Yinnon, for it is written: *His name shall endure forever; e'er the sun was, his name is Yinnon.*" [198] The School of R. Haninah maintained, "His name is Haninah, as it is written, *Where I will not give you Ḥaninah."*[199] Others say, "His name is Menaḥem, the son of Hezekiah, for it is written, *Because Menahem* ['the comforter'] *that would relieve my soul is far."*[200] The Rabbis said, "His name is 'the leper scholar,' as it is written, *Surely he hath borne our griefs and carried our sorrows; yet we did esteem him a leper, smitten of God, and afflicted."*[201]

R. Naḥman said, "If he [the Messiah] is of those living [today], it might be one like myself, as it is written, *And their nobles shall be of themselves, and their governors shall proceed from the midst of them."*[202] Rab said, "If he is of the living, it would be our holy Master;[203] if of the dead, it would have been Daniel, the most desirable man." Rab Judah said in Rab's name: "The Holy One, blessed be he, will raise up another David for us, as it is written, *But they shall serve the Lord their God, and David their king, whom I will raise up unto them;*[204] not 'I raise up', but 'I will raise up' is said.' R. Papa said to Abaye, "But it is written, *And my servant David shall be their prince* [nasi] *forever?*[205] e.g., an emperor and a viceroy."

R. Simla expounded, "What is meant by, *Woe unto you, that desire the day of the Lord! to what end is for you? the day of the Lord is darkness, and not light?*[206] This may be compared to a cock and a bat who were hopefully waiting for the light [i.e., dawn]. The cock said to the bat, 'I look forward to the light because I have sight; but of what use is the light to thee?' " And thus a *Min*[207] said to R. Abbahu: "When will the Messiah come?" He replied, "When darkness covers those people." "You curse me," he exclaimed. He retorted, "It is but a verse, *For behold the darkness shall cover the earth, and gross darkness the people: but the Lord shall shine upon thee, and his glory shall be seen upon thee."*[208]

It has been taught: R. Eliezer said, "The days of the Messiah will last forty years, as it is written, *Forty years long shall I take hold of the generation."*[209] R. Eleazar b. Azariah said, "Seventy years, as it is written, *And it shall come to pass in that day, that Tyre shall be forgotten seventy years, according to the days of one king.*[210] Now, who is the one [uniquely distinguished] king? The Messiah, of course." Rabbi said, "Three generations; for it is written, *They shall fear thee with the sun, and before the moon* [they shall fear thee] *a generation and generations."* [211]

R. Hillel said, "There shall be no Messiah for Israel, because they have already enjoyed him in the days of Hezekiah." R. Joseph said, "May God forgive him [for saying so]. Now, when did Hezekiah flourish? During the first Temple. Yet Zechariah, prophesying in the days of the second, proclaimed, *Rejoice greatly, O daughter of Zion; shout, O daughter of Jerusalem; behold, thy king cometh unto thee! he is just, and having salvation; lowly, and riding upon an ass, and upon a colt the foal of an ass."* [212]

Another [Baraitha] taught: R. Eliezer said, "The days of the Messiah will be forty years. Here it is written, *And he afflicted thee, and suffered thee to hunger, and fed thee with manna;* [213] whilst elsewhere it is written, *Make us glad, according to the days wherein thou hast afflicted us."* [214] R. Dosa said, "Four hundred years. It is here written, *And they shall serve them; and they shall afflict them four hundred years;* [215] whilst elsewhere it is written, *Make us glad, according to the days wherein thou has afflicted us."* Rabbi said, "Three hundred and sixty-five years, even as the days of the solar year, as it is written, *For the day of vengeance is in mine heart, and the year of my redemption is come."* [216] What is meant by *the day of vengeance is in mine heart?* R. Johanan said, "I have [so to speak] revealed it to my heart, but not to my [outer] limbs." Abimi, the son of R. Abbahu, learned: The days of Israel's Messiah shall be seven thousand years, as it is written, *And as the bridegroom rejoiceth over the bride, so shall thy God rejoice over thee.* [217] Rab Judah said in Samuel's name, "The days of the Messiah shall endure as long as from the Creation until now, as it is written, *[That your days may be multiplied, and the days of your children, in the land which the Lord sware unto your fathers to give to them] as the days of heaven upon the earth."* [218] R. Nahman b. Isaac said, "As long as from Noah's days until our own, as it is written, *For this is as the waters of Noah, which are mine, so I have sworn,* etc." [219]

R. Hiyya b. Abba said in R. Johanan's name, "All the prophets prophesied [all the good things] only in respect of the Messianic era; but as for the world to come, *the eye hath not seen, O Lord, beside thee, what he hath prepared for him that waiteth for him.*" [220] Now he disagrees with Samuel, who said, "This world differs from [that of] the days of the Messiah only in respect of servitude to [foreign] powers."

DO THE DEAD KNOW WHAT HAPPENS ON EARTH?

R. Ḥiyya and R. Jonathan were once walking about in a cemetery, and the blue fringe of R. Jonathan was trailing on the ground. Said R. Ḥiyya to him: "Lift it up, so that they [the dead] should not say, 'Tomorrow they are coming to join us, and now they are insulting us!' " He said to him, "Do they know so much? Is it not written, But the dead know not anything?" [222] He replied to him, "If you have read once, you have not repeated; if you have repeated, you have not gone over a third time; if you have gone over a third time, you have not had it explained to you. *For the living know that they shall die;* [223] these are the righteous who in their death are called living, as it says, *And Benaiah the son of Jehoiada, the son of a living man from Kabzeel, who had done mighty deeds, he smote the two altar hearths of Moab; he went down and also slew a lion in the midst of a pit in the time of snow.* [224] *The son of a living man;* are all other people, then, the sons of dead men? Rather *the son of a living man* means that even in his death he was called living. *From Kabzeel, who had done mighty deeds;* this indicates that he gathered *[kibbez]* numerous workers for the Torah. *He smote two altar hearths of Moab;* this indicates that he did not leave his like either in the first Temple or in the second Temple. *He went down and also slew a lion in the midst of a pit in the time of snow;* some say that this indicates that he broke blocks of ice and went down and bathed; others say that he went through the Sifra of the School of Rab on a winter's day. *But the dead know nothing;* these are the wicked who in their lifetime are called dead, as it says, *And thou, O wicked one, that art slain, the prince of Israel.* [225] Or, if you prefer, I can derive it from here, *At the mouth of two witnesses shall the dead be put to death.*[226] He is still alive! What it means is, he is already counted as dead."

The sons of R. Ḥiyya went out to cultivate their property, and they began to forget their learning. They tried very hard to recall it. Said one to the other, "Does our father know of our trouble?" "How should he know," replied the other, "seeing that it is written, *His sons come to honor and he knoweth it not?"* [227] Said the other to him, "But does he not know? Is it not written, *But his flesh grieveth for him, and his soul mourneth over him?* [228] And R. Isaac said, [commenting on this], 'The worm is as painful to the dead as a needle in the flesh of the living?'" [He replied,] "It is explained that they know their own pain, they do not know the pain of others." Is that so? Has it not been taught: It is related that a certain pious man gave a *denar* to a poor man on the eve of New Year in a year of drought, and his wife scolded him, and he went and passed the night in the cemetery, and he heard two spirits conversing with one another. Said one to her companion, "My dear, come and let us wander about the world, and let us hear from behind the curtain what suffering is coming on the world." Said her companion to her, "I am not able, because I am buried in a matting of reeds. But do you go, and whatever you hear tell me." So the other went and wandered about, and returned. Said her companion to her, "My dear, what have you heard from behind the curtain?" She replied, "I heard that whoever sows after the first rainfall will have his crop smitten by hail." So the man went and did not sow till after the second rainfall, with the result that everyone else's crop was smitten and his was not smitten. The next year he again went and passed the night in the cemetery, and heard the two spirits conversing with one another. Said one to her companion, "Come and let us wander about the world and hear from behind the curtain what punishment is coming upon the world." Said the other to her, "My dear, did I not tell you that I am not able because I am buried in a matting of reeds? But do you go, and whatever you hear come and tell me." So the other went and wandered about the world, and returned. She said to her, "My dear, what have you heard from behind the curtain?" She replied, "I heard that whoever

sows after the later rain will have his crop smitten with blight."
So the man went and sowed after the first rain, with the result
that everyone else's crop was blighted and his was not blighted.
Said his wife to him, "How is it that last year everyone else's crop
was smitten and yours was not smitten, and this year everyone
else's crop is blighted and yours is not blighted?" So he related to
her all his experiences. The story goes that shortly afterwards a
quarrel broke out between the wife of that pious man and the
mother of the child, and the former said to the latter, "Come and
I will show you your daughter buried in a matting of reeds." The
next year the man again went and spent the night in the cemetery and heard those conversing together. One said, "My dear,
come and let us wander about the world and hear from behind
the curtain what suffering is coming upon the world." Said the
other, "My dear, leave me alone; our conversation has already
been heard among the living." This would prove that they know?
Perhaps some other man after his decease went and told them.
Come and hear; for Ze'iri deposited some money with his land-
lady, and while he was away visiting Rab she died. So he went
after her to the cemetery and said to her, "Where is my money?"
She replied to him: "Go and take it from under the ground, in
the hole of the doorpost, in such and such a place, and tell my
mother to send me my comb and my tube of eye-paint by the
hand of So-and-so who is coming here tomorrow." Does not this
show that they know? Perhaps Dumah announces to them beforehand. Come and hear: The father of Samuel had some money
belonging to orphans deposited with him. When he died, Samuel
was not with him, and they called him, "The son who consumes
the money of orphans." So he went after his father to the cemetery and said to them [the dead], "I am looking for Abba." They
said to him, "There are many Abbas here." "I want Abba b.
Abba," he said. They replied, "There are also several Abbas b.
Abba here." He then said to them, "I want Abba b. Abba,
the father of Samuel; where is he?" They replied, "He has gone
up to the Academy of the Sky." Meanwhile he saw Levi sitting
outside. He said to him, "Why are you sitting outside? Why
have you not gone up to heaven?" He replied, "Because they said

to me, 'For as many years as you did not go up to the academy of R. Efes and hurt his feelings, we will not let you go up to the Academy of the Sky.'" Meanwhile his father came. Samuel observed that he was both weeping and laughing. He said to him, "Why are you weeping?" He replied: "Because you are coming here soon." "And why are you laughing?" "Because you are highly esteemed in this world." He thereupon said to him, "If I am esteemed, let them take up Levi, and they did take up Levi. He then said to him, "Where is the money of the orphans?" He replied, "Go and you will find it in the case of the millstones. The money at the top and bottom is mine; that in the middle is the orphans'." He said to him, "Why did you do like that?" He replied, "So that if thieves came, they should take mine, and if the earth destroyed any, it should destroy mine." Does not this show that they know? Perhaps Samuel was exceptional; as he was esteemed, they proclaimed beforehand, "Make way [for him]!"

R. Jonathan also retracted his opinion. For R. Samuel b. Naḥmani said in the name of R. Jonathan, "Whence do we know that the dead converse with one another? Because it says, *And the Lord said unto him: This is the land which I swore unto Abraham, unto Isaac, and unto Jacob, saying.*[229] What is the meaning of 'saying?' The Holy One, blessed be he, said to Moses, 'Say to Abraham, Isaac, and Jacob: The oath which I swore to you I have already carried out for your descendants.' Now if you maintain that the dead do not know, what would be the use of his telling them?" You infer then that they do know. In that case, why should he need to tell them? So that they might be grateful to Moses.

ON THE RESURRECTION AND THE AFTERLIFE[230]

MISHNAH. ALL ISRAEL HAVE A PORTION IN THE WORLD TO COME, FOR IT IS WRITTEN, "THY PEOPLE ARE ALL RIGHTEOUS; THEY SHALL INHERIT THE LAND FOREVER, THE BRANCH OF MY PLANTING, THE WORK OF MY HANDS, THAT I MAY BE GLORIFIED."[231] BUT THE FOLLOWING HAVE NO PORTION THEREIN: HE WHO MAINTAINS

THAT RESURRECTION IS NOT A BIBLICAL DOCTRINE, THE TORAH WAS
NOT DIVINELY REVEALED, AND AN EPIḲOROS. R. AKIBA ADDED, "ONE
WHO READS UNCANONICAL BOOKS. ALSO ONE WHO WHISPERS [A
CHARM] OVER A WOUND AND SAYS, 'I WILL BRING NONE OF THESE
DISEASES UPON THEE WHICH I BROUGHT UPON THE EGYPTIANS:
FOR I AM THE LORD THAT HEALETH THEE.'"[232] ABBA SAUL SAYS,
"ALSO ONE WHO PRONOUNCES THE DIVINE NAME AS IT IS SPELLED."

THREE KINGS AND FOUR COMMONERS HAVE NO PORTION IN THE
WORLD TO COME: THE THREE KINGS ARE JEROBOAM, AHAB, AND
MANASSEH. R. JUDAH SAID, "MANASSEH HATH A PORTION THEREIN,
FOR IT IS WRITTEN, 'AND HE PRAYED UNTO HIM, AND WAS IN-
TREATED OF HIM, AND HE HEARKENED TO HIS SUPPLICATION AND
THEY RESTORED HIM TO HIS KINGDOM.'"[233] THEY [THE SAGES] AN-
SWERED HIM, "THEY RESTORED HIM TO HIS KINGDOM, BUT NOT TO
[HIS PORTION IN] THE WORLD TO COME." FOUR COMMONERS, VIZ.,
BALAAM, DOEG, AHITOPHEL, AND GEHAZI.

GEMARA. And why such [severity]? A Tanna taught, "Since
he denied the resurrection of the dead, therefore he shall not
share in that resurrection, for in all measures [of punishment or
reward] taken by the Holy One, blessed be he, the Divine act
befits the [human] deed."[234] As it is written, *Then Elisha said,
Hear ye the word of the Lord; Thus saith the Lord. Tomorrow
about this time shall a measure of fine flour be sold for a shekel,
and two measures of barley for a shekel, in the gates of
Samaria.*[235] And it is written, *Then a lord on whose hand the
king leaned answered the man of God, and said, Behold, if the
Lord made windows in heaven, might this thing be? And he
said, Behold, thou shalt see it with thine eyes, but shalt not eat
thereof.*[236] And it is [further] written, *And so it fell unto him,
for the people trod upon him in the gate, and he died.*[237] But
perhaps this was the result of Elisha's curse, for Rab Judah said
in Rab's name, "The curse of a Sage, even if unmerited, is fulfilled?" If so, Scripture should have written, *they trod upon him
and he died.* Why *trod upon him in the gate?* [To show that it
was] on account of matters pertaining to the gate.

How is resurrection derived from the Torah? As it is written,
And ye shall give thereof the Lord's heave offering to Aaron the

priest.[238] But would Aaron live forever; he did not even enter Palestine, that *terumah* should be given him? But it teaches that he would be resurrected and Israel give him *terumah.* Thus resurrection is derived from the Torah. The school of R. Ishmael taught *To Aaron* [means to one] like Aaron; just as Aaron was a *ḥaber,* so his sons must be *ḥaberim.* R. Samuel b. Naḥmani said in R. Jonathan's name, "Whence do we know that *terumah* must not be given to a priest and *'am ha-arez?* From the verse, *Moreover he commanded the people that dwelt in Jerusalem to give the portion of the Levites, that they might hold fast to the law of the Lord;* [239] [thus] whoever holds fast to the law of the Lord, has a portion; whoever does not, has no portion." R. Aḥa b. Adda said in Rab Judah's name, "One who gives *terumah* to an ignorant priest is as though he had placed it before a lion; just as a lion may possibly tear his prey and eat it, and possibly not, so is an ignorant priest: he may possibly eat it undefiled and possibly defiled." R. Joḥanan said, "He even causes his [the ignorant priest's] death, for it is written, *and die therefore, if they profane it.*" [240] The School of R. Eliezer b. Jacob taught: He also embroils him in a sin of general trespass, for it is written, *Or suffer them to bear the iniquity of trespass when they eat their holy things.*[241]

It has been taught: R. Simai said, "Whence do we learn resurrection from the Torah? From the verse, *And I also have established my covenant with them* [the Patriarchs], *to give them the land of Canaan.*[242]—'[to give] *you'* is not said, but 'to give them, [personally]; thus resurrection is proved from the Torah."

(Mnemonic: ZeDeK, GaM, GeSHeM, KaM.) Sectarians [*minim*] asked Rabban Gamaliel, "Whence do we know that the Holy One, blessed be he, will resurrect the dead?" He answered them from the Torah, the Prophets, and the Hagiographa, yet they did not accept it [as conclusive proof]. "From the Torah," For it is written, *And the Lord said unto Moses, Behold, thou shalt sleep with thy fathers and rise up [again].*[243] "But perhaps," said they to him, "[the verse reads] *and the people will rise up?*" "From the prophets," as it is written, *Thy dead men shall live, together with my dead body shall they*

*arise. Awake and sing, ye that dwell in the dust: for thy dew is
as the dew of herbs, and the earth shall cast out its dead.*[244] But
perhaps this refers to the dead whom Ezekiel resurrected? [245]
"From the Hagiographa," as it is written, *And the roof of thy
mouth, like the best wine of my beloved, that goeth down
sweetly, causing the lips of those that are asleep to speak.*[246] But
perhaps it means merely that their lips will move, even as R.
Johanan said, "If a *halakhah* is said in any person's name in
this world, his lips speak in the grave, as it is written, *causing
the lips of those that are asleep to speak?*" [Thus he did not
satisfy them] until he quoted this verse, *which the Lord sware
unto your fathers to give to them;*[247] not 'to *you*,' but 'to *them*'
is said; hence resurrection is derived from the Torah. Others say
that he proved it from this verse, *But ye that did cleave unto the
Lord your God are alive every one of you this day;* [248] just as
you are all alive today, so shall you all live again in the world
to come.

The Romans asked R. Joshua b. Ḥananiah, "Whence do we
know that the Holy One, blessed be he, will resurrect the dead
and knows the future?" He replied: "Both are deduced from
this verse, *And the Lord said unto Moses, Behold thou shalt
sleep with thy fathers and rise up again; and this people shall
go awhoring* etc." [249] But perhaps *will rise up and go awhoring?* He replied, "Then at least you have the answer to half,
viz., that he knows the future." It has been stated likewise: R.
Johanan said on the authority of R. Simeon b. Yoḥai, "Whence
do we know that the Holy One, blessed be he, will resurrect
the dead and knoweth the future? From *Behold, Thou shalt
sleep with thy fathers and . . . rise again*, etc."

It has been taught: R. Eliezer, son of R. Jose, said, "In this
matter I refuted the books of the sectarians, who maintained that
resurrection is not deducible from the Torah. I said to them,
'You have falsified your Torah; yet it has availed you nothing.
For ye maintain that resurrection is not a Biblical doctrine, but
it is written, *[Because he hath despised the word of the Lord,
and hath broken his commandment], that soul shall utterly be
cut off.* [Heb. *hikkareth tikkareth*]: *his iniquity shall be upon*

him.[250] Now, [seeing that] he shall *utterly be cut off* in this world, when shall *his iniquity be upon him?* Surely in the next world.'" R. Papa said to Abaye, "Could he not have deduced both [this world and the next] from *he shall be* utterly *cut off?*" They would have replied, "The Torah employed human phraseology."

This is disputed by Tannaim: *That soul shall utterly be cut off; [hikkareth]* he shall be cut off in this world and *[tikkareth]* in the next; this is R. Akiba's view. R. Ishmael said, "But the verse has previously stated, *he reproacheth the Lord, and that soul shall be cut off;* are there then three worlds?" But [interpret thus]: *and [that soul] shall be cut off*—in this world; *hikkareth, he is to be cut off*—in the next; whilst as for [the repetition] *tikkareth,* that is because the Torah employs human phraseology. How do both R. Ishmael and R. Akiba utilize *his iniquity shall be upon him?* For that which has been taught: I might think that [this is so] even if he repented; therefore Scripture saith, *his iniquity is upon him.* I decreed [that he shall be cut off] only if his iniquity is still in him.

Queen Cleopatra asked R. Meir, "I know that the dead will revive, for it is written, *And they* [the righteous] *shall* [in the distant future] *blossom forth out of the city* [Jerusalem] *like the grass of the earth.*[251] But when they arise, shall they arise nude or in their garments?" He replied, "Thou mayest deduce by an *a fortiori* argument [the answer] from a wheat grain: if a grain of wheat, which is buried naked, sprouteth forth in many robes, how much more so the righteous, who are buried in their raiment!"

An emperor said to Rabban Gamaliel, "Ye maintain that the dead will revive; but they turn to dust, and can dust come to life?" Thereupon his [the emperor's] daughter said to him [the Rabbi], "Let me answer him: In our town there are two potters, one fashions [his products] from water, and the other from clay: who is the more praiseworthy?" "He who fashions them from water," he replied. "If he can fashion [man] from water, surely he can do so from clay!"

The School of R. Ishmael taught: It can be deduced from

glassware: if glassware, which, though made by the breath of human beings, can yet be repaired when broken, then how much more so man, created by the breath of the Holy One, blessed be he.

A sectarian [*min*] said to R. Ammi, "Ye maintain that the dead will revive; but they turn to dust, and can dust come to life?" He replied: "I will tell thee a parable. This may be compared to a human king who commanded his servants to build him a great palace in a place where there was no water or earth [for making bricks]. So they went and built it. But after some time it collapsed, so he commanded them to rebuild it in a place where water and earth was to be found; but they replied, 'We cannot.' Thereupon he became angry with them and said, 'If ye could build in a place containing no water or earth, surely ye can where there is!' Yet," [continued R. Ammi,] "If thou dost not believe, go forth into the field and see a mouse, which today is but part flesh and part dust, and yet by tomorrow has developed and become all flesh. And shouldst thou say, 'That takes a long time,' go up to the mountains, where thou wilt see but one snail, whilst by tomorrow the rain has descended and it is covered with snails."

A sectarian [*min*] said to Gebiha b. Pesisa, "Woe to you, ye wicked, who maintain that the dead will revive; if even the living die, shall the dead live!" He replied, "Woe to you, ye wicked, who maintain that the dead will not revive, if what was not [now] lives, surely what has lived will live again!" "Thou has called me wicked," said he. "If I stood up I could kick thee and strip thee of thy hump!" "If thou couldst do that," he retorted, "thou wouldst be called a great doctor and command large fees."

RESURRECTION TAUGHT EVERYWHERE [252]

MISHNAH. A MAN MAY NOT TAKE THE DAM WITH THE YOUNG EVEN FOR THE SAKE OF CLEANSING THE LEPER. IF IN RESPECT OF SO LIGHT A PRECEPT, WHICH DEALS WITH THAT WHICH IS

BUT WORTH AN ISSAR, THE TORAH SAID, THAT IT MAY BE WELL
WITH THEE AND THAT THOU MAYEST PROLONG THY DAYS,[253]
HOW MUCH MORE [MUST BE THE REWARD] FOR THE OBSERVANCE
OF THE MORE DIFFICULT PRECEPTS OF THE TORAH!

GEMARA. It was taught: R. Jacob says, "There is no precept in the Torah, where reward is stated by its side, from which
you cannot infer the doctrine of the resurrection of the dead.
Thus, in connection with honoring parents, it is written, *That
thy days may be prolonged, and that it may go well with thee.*[254]
Again, in connection with the law of letting [the dam] go from
the nest, it is written, *That it may be well with thee, and that
thou mayest prolong thy days.* Now, in the case where a man's
father said to him, 'Go up to the top of the building and bring
me down some young birds,' and he went up to the top of the
building, let the dam go and took the young ones, and on his
return he fell and was killed—where is this man's length of
days, and where is this man's happiness? But *that thy days may
be prolonged* refers to the world that is wholly long, and *that
it may go well with thee* refers to the world that is wholly good."

But perhaps such a thing could not happen? R. Jacob actually
saw this occurrence. Then perhaps that person had conceived
in his mind a sinful thought? The Holy One, blessed be he,
does not reckon the sinful thought for the deed. Perhaps then
he had conceived in his mind idolatry, and it is written, *That I
may take the house of Israel in their own heart,*[255] which, according to R. Aḥa b. Jacob, refers to thoughts of idolatry? This
was what he [R. Jacob] meant to convey: if there is a reward
for precepts in this world, then surely that [reward] should
have stood him in good stead and guarded him from such
thoughts that he come not to any hurt; we must therefore say
that there is no reward for precepts in this world.

But did not R. Eleazar say that those engaged in [the performance of] a precept never come to harm? When returning
from the performance of a precept it is different. But did not
R. Eleazar say that those engaged in a precept never come to
harm, either when going [to perform it] or when returning
[from the performance thereof]? It must have been a broken

ladder [that was used], so that injury was likely; and where injury is likely it is different, as it is written, *And Samuel said, How can I go? If Saul hear it, he will kill me.*[256]

R. Joseph said, "Had Aḥer[257] interpreted this verse as R. Jacob, his daughter's son, did, he would not have sinned." What actually did he see? Some say, "He saw such an occurrence." Others say, "He saw the tongue of R. Ḥuzpith the interpreter lying on a dungheap, and he exclaimed, 'Shall the mouth that uttered pearls lick the dust!'" But he knew not that the verse *that it may go well with thee* refers to the world that is wholly good, and that the verse *that thy days may be prolonged* refers to the world that is wholly long.

VI

THE AGGADDIC MIDRASH

In addition to the nonlegal materials that were included in the Talmud, the sages of the Jewish people collected a large number of homilies and much other theological, ethical, and folkloristic material in the so-called *aggaddic midrashim*. Some of these collections were arranged in the sequence of the biblical books, especially the Pentateuch and the Five Scrolls (Ecclesiastes, Esther, Lamentations, Ruth, and Canticles), which were recited in the synagogue on certain stated occasions. The most comprehensive of these collections, known as *Midrash Rabbah*, was compiled during a period of half a millennium. The earliest section of this compilation was Genesis Rabbah, which was assembled in its present form late in the talmudic age. Even those sections that were brought together centuries later, however, contained some authentic older sayings reaching back to the beginning of the Christian era. The selections from Ecclesiastes Rabbah and Lamentations Rabbah that are included here belong to the later stratum of assembling of *Midrash Rabbah*. They illustrate very well the method of the rabbinical orator expounding scriptural material in public auditory. In general, the literary problems associated with the many collections of *aggaddic midrashim* are among the most difficult and the most heatedly debated questions in the history of Jewish literature; these questions have been discussed by scholars ever since the publication of Leopold Zunz's classical work, *Die gottesdienstlichen Vorträge der Juden, historisch entwickelt*, (Berlin, 1832), now available in a thoroughly revised and up-to-date Hebrew translation.

CAST THY BREAD UPON THE WATERS [258]

R. BIBI SAID, "If it is your desire to practice charity, bestow it upon those who labor in the Torah, because THE WATERS means nothing else than words of Torah, as it is said: *Ho, everyone that thirsteth, come ye for water.*" [259]

R. Akiba said, "When I was traveling at sea, I saw a ship which had been wrecked, and I was greatly concerned about a Rabbinical scholar who had been on board and went down with the ship. On arriving at the province of Cappadocia, however, I noticed him sitting before me and asking questions. I said to him, 'My son, how did you come up out of the sea?' He replied, 'Rabbi, through your prayer on my behalf one wave tossed me to another, and so on until they brought me ashore.' I asked him, 'My son, what good deeds do you possess [which rescued you from drowning]?' He answered, 'When I went aboard the ship, a poor man accosted me and cried, "Help me!" and I gave him a loaf. He then said to me, "As you have restored my life to me by your gift, so will your life be restored to you."' " [R. Akiba added,] "I applied to him the text, CAST THY BREAD UPON THE WATERS."

A large ship was once sailing on the ocean, when a gale caught it and drove it to a place where there was no flowing water. When [the passengers] saw that they were in dire straits, they said, "Come, let us share our provisions, so that if we die we all die, and if we live we all live." [As a reward for this] the Omnipresent enlightened their eyes [with a plan]. They took a kid, roasted it, and hung it up on the west side of the ship. A large animal, attracted by the odor, came and began to drag [the ship] until it drew it to where the water was flowing, and they continued their voyage. When they reached their destination and entered Rome, they narrated the incident to R. Eliezer and R. Joshua, who applied to them the text, CAST THY BREAD UPON THE WATERS.

Bar Kappara was walking up and down the cliffs by the sea at Caesarea, when he saw a ship which had been wrecked in the ocean and a proconsul emerging from it naked. On seeing him, [Bar Kappara] went to him, greeted him, and gave him two selas. What [else] did he do? He brought him to his house, gave him to eat and drink, handed him three more selas, and said, "On a great man like you one should expend three more selas." Some time later Jews were arrested in a riot. They asked, "Who will go and intercede for us?" and they said one to the other, "Bar Ḳappara [is the man to go] because he is highly esteemed by the government." He told them, "You know that this government does nothing without being paid." They said to him, "Here are five hundred *denars;* take them and go to intercede for us." He took the five hundred *denars* and went to the government. When the proconsul saw him, he stood up, greeted him, and asked, "Why has the Rabbi troubled to come here?" He answered, "I beg of you to have mercy upon these Jews." He said to him, "You know that this government does nothing without being paid." He told him, "I have with me five hundred *denars;* take them and intercede for us." He replied, "These *denars* are pledged to you in exchange for the five *selas* which you gave me; your people are spared in return for the food and drink which you provided for me in your house; and as for you, go in peace and great honor." They applied to him the text, CAST THY BREAD UPON THE WATERS.

R. Eleazar b. Shammua was walking on the rocks by the sea when he saw a ship which was tossed about in the water suddenly sink with all on board. He noticed a man sitting on a plank of the ship [carried] from wave to wave until he stepped ashore. Being naked he hid himself among the rocks by the sea. It happened to be the time for the Israelites to go up to Jerusalem for the Festival. He said to them, "I belong to the descendants of Esau, your brother; give me a little clothing wherewith to cover my nakedness, because the sea stripped me bare and nothing was saved with me." They retorted, "So may all your people be stripped bare!" He raised his eyes and saw R. Eleazar who was walking among them; he exclaimed, "I observe that you are an old and respected man of your people, and you know the respect due to your fellow creatures. So help me and give me a garment wherewith to cover my nakedness, because the sea stripped me bare." R. Eleazar b. Shammua was wearing seven robes; he took one off and gave it to him. He also led him to his house, provided him with food and drink, gave him two hundred *denars,* drove him fourteen Persian miles, and treated him with great honor until he brought him to his home. Some time later the wicked emperor died, and they elected this man king in his stead, and he decreed concerning that province that all the men were to be killed and all the women taken as spoil. They said to R. Eleazar b. Shammua, "Go and intercede for us." He told them, "You know that this government does nothing without being paid." They said to him, "Here are four thousand *denars*: take them and go and intercede for us." He took them and went and stood by the gate of the royal palace. He said to [the guards], "Go, tell the king that a Jew is standing at the gate and wishes to greet the king." The king ordered him to be brought in. On beholding him the king descended from his throne and prostrated himself before him. He asked him, "What is my master's business here, and why has my master troubled to come here?" He replied, "That you should have mercy upon this province and annul this decree." The king asked him, "Is there any falsehood written in the Torah?" "No," was the reply; and he said to him, "Is it not written in your Torah, *An Ammonite or a Moabite shall not enter into the assembly of the Lord?* [260] *What is the reason? Because they met you not with bread and with water in the way.* [261] It is also written, *Thou shalt not abhor an Edomite, for he is thy brother;* [262] and am I not a descendant of Esau, [263] your brother, but they did not treat me with kindness! And whoever transgresses the Torah incurs the penalty of death." R. Eleazar b. Shammua replied to him, "Although they are guilty toward you, forgive them and have mercy upon them." He said to him, "You know that this government does nothing without being paid." He told him, "I have with me four thousand *denars;* take them and have mercy upon the people." He said to him, "These four thousand *denars* are presented to you in exchange for the two hundred which you gave me, and the whole province will be spared for your sake in return for the food and drink with which you provided me. Go also into my treasury and take seventy robes of honor in return for the robe you gave me, and go in peace to your people I forgive for your sake." They applied to him the text, CAST THY BREAD UPON THE WATERS.

It is related of a certain man that every day he took a loaf and threw it into the great sea. One day he went and bought a fish; on cutting it open he found a valuable object in it. People said of him, "This is the man whose loaf stood him in good stead" and they applied to him the text, CAST THY BREAD UPON THE WATERS.

R. Isaac said, "It is related that a merchant was traveling with an officer, who in the course of the journey conceived a strong liking for him. When they entered the city, [the merchant] took him to his house and provided him with food and drink. Some time later the merchant was arrested for selling garments which were stained with blood. The officer, hearing of it, went to him [in prison] and asked, 'What are you doing here?' He narrated to him what had happened, and [the officer] said to him, 'When you appear for judgment, tell them, "So-and-so knows evidence in my favor."' When he appeared for judgment, he said, 'So-and-so knows evidence in my favor.' They asked the officer, 'What evidence do you know in his favor?' He replied, 'The brother of the murdered man was in my debt and had nothing to pay; so I took his garments and gave them to this man to sell for me.' [The judges] declared, 'A trustworthy man received [the garments] from a trustworthy man, so he goes free.' They applied to him the text, CAST THY BREAD UPON THE WATERS."

THEY HAVE FORSAKEN MY LAW [264]

R. Abba b. Kahana opened his discourse with the text, *Who is the wise man, that he may understand this?* [265] R. Simeon b. Yoḥai taught, "If you behold cities uprooted from their site in the land of Israel know that the inhabitants failed to pay the fees of the instructors in Bible and Mishnah; as it is said, *Wherefore is the land perished? . . . And the Lord saith: Because they have forsaken my law.*" [266]

Rabbi sent R. Assi and R. Ammi on a mission to organize [religious education in] the cities of the land of Israel. They came to a city and said to the people, "Bring us the guardians of the city." They fetched the captain of the guard and the magistrate. The Rabbis exclaimed, "These the guardians of the city! They are its destroyers!" The people inquired, "Who, then, are its guardians?" and they answered, "The instructors in Bible and Mishnah, who meditate upon, teach, and preserve the Torah day and night." This is in accordance with what is said, *Thou shalt meditate therein day and night;* [267] and it is similarly stated, *Except the Lord build the house, they labor in vain that build it.* [268]

R. Huna and R. Jeremiah said in the name of R. Ḥiyya b. R. Isaac, "We find that the Holy One, blessed be he, may overlook idolatry, immorality, or bloodshed, but he does not overlook rejection of the Torah; as it is said, *Wherefore is the land perished?* It is not written here *because of idolatry, immorality, or bloodshed,* but *because they have forsaken My law.*"

R. Huna and R. Jeremiah said in the name of R. Ḥiyya b. Abba, "It is written, *They have forsaken me and have not kept my law* [269]—i.e., would that they had forsaken me but kept my law; since, by occupying themselves therewith, the light which it contains would have led them back to the right path."

R. Huna said, "Study Torah even if it be not for its own sake; since even if not for its own sake at first, it will eventually be for its own sake." R. Joshua b. Levi said, "Every day a *Bath Kol* issues from Mount Horeb, declaring, 'Woe to mankind for slighting Torah!'"

Samuel taught in the name of R. Samuel b. Ammi, "When can the government enact an oppressive measure and render it effective? At the time that Israel casts words of Torah to the ground; and so it is written, *And the host was given over to it together with the continual burnt offering through transgression.* [270] *Host* signifies nothing else than the [non-Jewish] governments, as it is said: *The Lord will punish the host of the high heaven on high.* [271] *The continual burnt offering* is Israel; as it is written, *Thou shalt meditate therein day and night. Through transgression* means through neglect of Torah. Whenever Israel casts words of Torah to the ground, the government enacts an oppressive measure which proves effective, as it is said, *And it cast down truth to the ground,* [272] *Truth* signifies nothing else than Torah; as it is said, *Buy the truth, and sell it not.* [273] If you have cast words of Torah to the ground, the government is immediately successful [in its oppressive measures]; and so it is written, *And it wrought, and prospered.*[274]

R. Judah b. Pazzi said, "*Israel hath cast off that which is good.*[275] *Good* signifies nothing else than Torah; as it is said, *For I give you good doctrine.*"[276]

R. Abba b. Kahana said, "There arose not among the heathen peoples philosophers like Balaam, the son of Beor and Oenomaus of Gadara. They were once asked, 'Can we overcome this people [of Israel]?' They replied, 'Go round to their synagogues; if there is a hum of children's voices [there studying the Torah], you cannot prevail over them; otherwise you can. For thus their patriarch assured them, saying, *The voice is the voice of Jacob, but the hands are the hands of Esau.*[277]—i.e., so long as the voice of Jacob persists in the synagogues and houses of study, the hands are not Esau's hands; but whenever there is no hum of voices in the synagogues and houses of study, the hands are Esau's hands.' Similarly it declares, *Therefore as stubble devoureth the tongue of fire.*[278] Can stubble devour fire? Is is not the nature of fire to devour stubble, and yet you say *As stubble devoureth the tongue of fire!* In fact, *stubble* denotes the house of Esau; as it is said, *And the house of Jacob shall be a fire, and the house of Joseph a flame, and the house of Esau for stubble.*[279] *The tongue of fire* denotes the house of Jacob. *And as the chaff is consumed in the flame*[280] denotes the house of Joseph. *So their root shall be as rottenness*[281] denotes the patriarchs who are the roots of Israel. *And their blossom shall go up as dust* denotes the tribes who are the blossoms of Israel. Why [will this fate befall them]? *Because they have rejected the law of the Lord of Hosts.*"[282] R. Judan said, "*Because they have rejected the law of the Lord of Hosts* denotes the written Torah; *and contemned the word of the Holy One of Israel*[283] denotes the oral Torah. Since they cast the words of Torah to the ground, Jeremiah began to lament over them, *Ekah.*"

Thus saith the Lord of hosts: Consider ye, and call for the mourning women.[284] R. Johanan, R. Simeon b. Lakish, and the Rabbis [comment as follows]: R. Johanan said, "God may be likened to a king who had two sons. He became enraged against the first of them, took a stick, thrashed him, drove him into banishment, and exclaimed, 'Woe to him! From what comfort has he been banished!' He later became enraged against the second son, took a stick, thrashed him, drove him into banishment, and exclaimed, 'The fault is with me, since I must have brought them up badly.' Similarly the ten tribes were exiled, and the Holy One, blessed be he, began to proclaim this verse over them, *Woe unto them, for they have strayed from me.*[285] But when Judah and Benjamin were exiled, the Holy One, blessed be he—if it is possible to say so—declared, *Woe is me for my hurt.*" [286]

R. Simeon b. Laḳish said, "God may be likened to a king who had two sons. He became enraged against the first of them, took a stick, and thrashed him so that he writhed in agony and died; and the father then began to lament over him. He later became enraged against the second son, took a stick, and thrashed him so that he writhed in agony and died; and the father then exclaimed, 'No longer have I the strength to lament over them, so call for the mourning women and let them lament over them.' Similarly the ten tribes were exiled, and he began to lament of them, *Hear ye this word which I take up for a lamentation over you, O house of Israel.*[287] But when Judah and Benjamin were exiled, the Holy One, blessed be he—if it is possible to say so—declared, 'No longer have I the strength to lament over them.' Hence it is written, *Call for the mourning women . . . and let them make haste, and take up a wailing for us.*[288] It is not written here 'for them' but 'for us,' i.e., for me and them. *That our eyes may run down with tears*—it is not written here 'that *their* eyes may run down with tears,' but '*our* eyes,' i.e., mine and theirs. It is not written here, 'And *their* eyelids gush out with water,' but '*our* eyelids,' i.e., mine and theirs."

The Rabbis say, "God may be likened to a king who had twelve sons, of whom two died. He began to console himself with the ten. Two more died, and he began to console himself with the eight. Two more died, and he began to console himself with the six. Two more died, and he began to console himself with the four. Two more died, and he began to console himself with the two. But when they had all died, he began to lament over them, *How sitteth solitary.*" [289]

PART SIX

PRAYER

PRAYER

Prayer in the Jewish tradition goes back to immemorial antiquity. Even at the time when the main emphasis of congregational services was laid on sacrificial worship, individuals turned to God with personal supplications or words of thanksgiving. The prayer of Hannah, mother of Samuel, is a recorded instance of such early private devotions.[1] In time, too, liturgical chants by Levites were used in the Temple services to supplement the sacrifices. With the cessation of the sacrificial worship after the desecration of the altars in the Judean provinces and, still more, during the Babylonian Exile, the emphasis shifted completely to the synagogues and their prayerful assemblies. Before the second fall of Jerusalem, a standardized Jewish liturgy had already developed, centered around the recitation of the *Shema'* (the profession of the unity of God, consisting of excerpts from the Book of Deuteronomy) and the *Tefillah* or *'Amidah* (the silent prayer).

Considerable liturgical freedom remained, however, enabling individuals and congregations to supplement the required prayers by words coming from their own hearts. The rabbis encouraged such individual creativity, composed new prayers of their own, and even incorporated some of the new creations in their ever-growing regional collections. In this way the original silent prayer grew by numerous accessions into the comprehensive prayer recited at the additional (*Musaf*) services of the New Year's Day. At the same time, the rabbis elaborated the laws governing worship, as they did those governing every other facet of public and private life.

The following excerpts include (in addition to the *'Amidah*, as recited on New Year's Day) a passage concerning the laws of worship, taken from the Palestinian Talmud, some recorded prayers of the rabbis, and two prayers found in the recently discovered Dead Sea scrolls, evidently stemming from sectarian circles. Recent years have witnessed an increased appreciation of the Palestinian Talmud, as compared with the Babylonian. As to the much debated Dead Sea scrolls, there is a growing conviction in scholarly circles that we have in these scrolls authentic records of an ancient sect, in some way connected with the New Covenanters, known for some time as a result of an earlier find by Solomon Schechter.[2]

211

SOME REGULATIONS FOR PRAYER [3]

IT IS WRITTEN, *To love the Lord your God, and to serve him with all your heart and with all your soul.*[4] Is there service with the heart? There is: prayer. It is indeed said, *[O Daniel,] servant of the living God, is thy god whom thou servest continually able to deliver thee?*[5] Is there divine service in Babylonia? There is: prayer. One might think that one could pray the three [daily] prayers at once. But is is explained in Daniel, *He kneeled upon his knees three times a day and prayed.*[6] One might think that one could pray in any direction one wishes. But it is written, *His windows being open in his upper chamber toward Jerusalem.*[7] One might think [that this custom began only] after they went into exile. But it is written, *As he did aforetime.*[8] One might think that one can pray all three prayers any time one wishes. But David already explained this by saying, *Evening and morning and at noonday will I complain.*[9] One might think that one could raise one's voice and pray. But it is explained in connection with Hannah, *Now Hannah spoke in her heart.*[10] One might think that one could but meditate in his heart. But it is written, *Only her lips moved.*[11] This means that one should enunciate with one's lips. Said R. Jose bar Ḥanina, "From this verse we learn four things: *Now Hannah, she spoke in her heart,* from this we learn that prayer requires intention; *only her lips moved,* from this we learn that one must enunciate with one's lips; *but her voice was not heard,* from this we learn that a man should not raise his voice in prayer; *therefore Eli thought she had been drunken,* from this we learn that a drunken man is forbidden to pray."

PRAYERS AND APHORISMS OF THE RABBIS [12]

R. Eleazar, on concluding his prayer, used to say the following, "May it be thy will, O Lord our God, to cause to dwell in our lot love and brotherhood and peace and friendship, and mayest thou make our borders rich in disciples and prosper our latter end with good prospect and hope, and set our portion in Paradise, and confirm us with a good companion and a good impulse in thy world; and may we rise early and obtain the yearning of our heart to fear thy name, and mayest thou be pleased to grant the satisfaction of our desires!"

R. Johanan, on concluding his prayer, added the following, "May it be thy will, O Lord our God, to look upon our shame and behold our evil plight, and clothe thyself in thy mercies and cover thyself in thy strength, and wrap thyself in thy loving-kindness and gird thyself with thy graciousness, and may the attribute of thy kindness and gentleness come before thee!"

R. Zera, on concluding his prayer, added the following: "May it be thy will, O Lord our God, that we sin not nor bring upon ourselves shame or disgrace before our fathers!"

R. Ḥiyya, on concluding his prayer, added the following, "May it be thy will, O Lord our God, that our Torah may be our occupation, and that our heart may not be sick nor our eyes darkened!"

Rab, on concluding his prayer, added the following, "May it be thy will, O Lord our God, to grant us long life, a life of peace, a life of good, a life of blessing, a life of sustenance, a life of bodily vigor, a life in which there is fear of sin, a life free from shame and confusion, a life of riches and honor, a life in which we may be filled with the love of Torah and the fear of heaven, a life in which thou shalt fulfill all the desires of our heart for good!"

Rabbi, on concluding his prayer, added the following, "May it be thy will, O Lord our God and God of our fathers, to deliver us from the impudent and from impudence, from an evil man, from evil hap, from the evil impulse, from an evil companion, from an evil neighbor, and from the destructive Accuser, from a hard lawsuit and from a hard opponent, whether he is a son of the covenant or not a son of the covenant!" [Thus did he pray,] although guards were appointed to protect Rabbi.

R. Safra, on concluding his prayer, added the following, "May it be thy will, O Lord our God, to establish peace among the celestial family and among the earthly family, and among the disciples who occupy themselves with thy Torah, whether for its own sake of for other motives; and may it please thee that all who do so for other motives may come to study it for its own sake!"

R. Alexandri, on concluding his prayer, added the following, "May it be thy will, O Lord our God, to station us in an illumined corner; and do not station us in a darkened corner, and let not our heart be sick nor our eyes darkened!" According to some this was the prayer of R. Hamnuna; and R. Alexandri, on concluding his prayer, used to add the following, "Sovereign of the Universe, it is known full well to thee that our will is to perform thy will, and what prevents us? The yeast in the dough and the subjection to the foreign powers. May it be thy will to deliver us from their hand, so that we may return to perform the statutes of thy will with a perfect heart!"

Raba, on concluding his prayer, added the following, "My God, before I was formed I was not worthy [to be formed], and now that I have been formed I am as if I had not been formed. I am dust in my lifetime, all the more in my death. Behold I am before thee like a vessel full of shame and confusion. May it be thy will, O Lord my God, that I sin no more; and the sins I have committed before thee wipe out in thy great mercies, but not through evil chastisements and diseases!" This was the confession of R. Hamnuna Zuti on the Day of Atonement.

Mar the son of Rabina, on concluding his prayer, added the following, "My God, keep my tongue from evil and my lips from speaking guile. May my soul be silent to them that curse me, and may my soul be as the dust to all. Open thou my heart in thy Law, and may my soul pursue thy commandments; and deliver me from evil hap, from the evil impulse and from an evil woman, and from all evils that threaten to come upon the world. As for all that design evil against me, speedily annul their counsel and frustrate their designs. May the words of my mouth and the meditation of my heart be acceptable before thee, O Lord, my rock and my redeemer."

When R. Shesheth kept a fast, on concluding his prayer he added the following, "Sovereign of the universe, thou knowest full well that in the time when the Temple was standing, if a man sinned he used to bring a sacrifice, and though all that was offered of it was its fat and blood, atonement was made for him therewith. Now I have kept a fast, and my fat and blood have diminished. May it be thy will to account my fat and blood, which have been diminished, as if I had offered them before thee on the altar, and do thou favor me."

When R. Johanan finished the Book of Job, he used to say the following, "The end of man is to die, and the end of a beast is to be slaughtered, and all are doomed to die. Happy he who was brought up in the Torah and whose labor was in the Torah, and who has given pleasure to his Creator and who grew up with a good name and departed the world with a good name; and of him Solomon said, *A good name is better than precious oil, and the day of death than the day of one's birth.*" [13]

A favorite saying of R. Meir was, "Study with all thy heart and with all thy soul to know my ways and to watch at the doors of my Law. Keep my Law in thy heart, and let my fear be before thy eyes. Keep thy mouth from all sin, and purify and sanctify thyself from all trespass and iniquity, and I will be with thee in every place."

A favorite saying of the Rabbis of Jabneh was, "I am God's creature, and my fellow is God's creature. My work is in the town, and his work is in the country. I rise early for my work, and he rises early for his work. Just as he does not presume to do my work, so I do not presume to do his work. Will you say, 'I do much and he does little?' We have learned: One may do much or one may do little; it is all one, provided he directs his heart to heaven."

A favorite saying of Abaye was, "A man should always be subtle in the fear of heaven. *A soft answer turneth away wrath,*[14] and one should always strive to be on the best terms with his brethren and his relatives, and with all men and even with the heathen in the street, in order that he may be beloved above and well-liked below and be acceptable to his fellow creatures. It was related to R. Johanan b. Zakkai that no man ever gave him greeting first, even a heathen in the street."

A favorite saying of Raba was, "The goal of wisdom is repentance and good deeds, so that a man should not study Torah and

Mishnah, and then despise his father and mother and teacher, and his superior in wisdom and rank; as it says, *The fear of the Lord is the beginning of wisdom, a good understanding have all they that do thereafter.*[15] It does not say 'that do' but 'that do thereafter,' which implies that do them for their own sake and not for other motives. If one does them for other motives, it were better that he had not been created."

A favorite saying of Rab was, "[The future world is not like this world.] In the future world there is no eating or drinking, nor propagation nor business nor jealousy nor hatred nor competition, but the righteous sit with their crowns on their heads, feasting on the brightness of the divine presence; as it says, *And they beheld God, and did eat and drink.*"[16]

The 'AMIDAH FOR NEW YEAR'S DAY[17]

O Lord, open thou my lips, and my mouth shall declare thy praise.

Blessed art thou, O Lord our God and God of our fathers, God of Abraham, God of Isaac, and God of Jacob, the great, mighty and revered God, the most high God, who bestowest loving-kindnesses and possessest all things; who rememberest the pious deeds of the patriarchs, and in love wilt bring a redeemer to their children's children for thy name's sake.

Remember us unto life, O King, who delightest in life, and inscribe us in the book of life, for thine own sake, O living God.

O King, Helper, Savior, and Shield. Blessed art thou, O Lord, the Shield of Abraham.

Thou, O Lord, art mighty forever, thou quickenest the dead, thou art mighty to save.

Thou sustainest the living with loving-kindness, quickenest the dead with great mercy, supportest the falling, healest the sick, loosest the bound, and keepest thy faith to them that sleep in the dust. Who is like unto thee, Lord of mighty acts, and who resembleth thee, O King, who killest and quickenest, and causest salvation to spring forth?

Who is like unto thee, Father of mercy, who in mercy rememberest thy creatures unto life?

Yea, faithful are thou to quicken the dead. Blessed art thou, O Lord, who quickenest the dead.

Thou art holy, and thy name is holy, and holy beings praise thee daily. (Selah.)

Now, therefore, O Lord our God, impose thine awe upon all thy works and thy dread upon all that thou hast created, that all works may fear thee and all creatures prostrate themselves before thee, that they may all form a single band to do thy will with a perfect heart, even as we know, O Lord our God, that dominion is thine, strength is in thy hand, and might in thy right hand, and that thy name is to be feared above all that thou hast created.

Give then glory, O Lord, unto thy people, praise to them that fear thee, hope to them that seek thee, and free speech to them that wait for thee, joy to thy land, gladness to thy city, a flourishing horn unto David thy servant, and a clear shining light unto the son of Jesse, thine anointed, speedily in our days.

Thee shall the just also see and be glad, and the upright shall exult, and the pious triumphantly rejoice, while iniquity shall close her mouth, and all wickedness shall be wholly consumed like smoke, when thou makest the dominion of arrogance to pass away from the earth.

And thou, O Lord, shalt reign, thou alone over all thy works on Mount Zion, the dwelling place of thy glory, and in Jerusalem, thy holy city, as it is written in thy Holy Words, The Lord shall reign forever, thy God, O Zion, unto all generations. Praise ye the Lord.

Holy art thou, and dreaded is thy name, and there is no God beside thee, as it is written, And the Lord of Hosts is exalted in judgment, and the holy God is sanctified in righteousness. Blessed art thou, O Lord, the holy King.

Thou has chosen us from all peoples, thou hast loved us and taken pleasure in us and hast exalted us above all tongues, thou has sanctified us by thy commandments and brought us near unto thy services, O our King, and called us by thy great and holy name.

On Sabbath add the words in brackets.

And thou has given us in love, O Lord our God, [this Sabbath day and] this Day of Memorial, a day of blowing the Shofar [on Sabbaths substitute for the last phrase—a day of remembrance of blowing the Shofar, in love]; an holy convocation, as a memorial of the departure from Egypt.

But on account of our sins we were exiled from our land, and removed far from our country, and we are unable to fulfill our obligations in thy chosen house, that great and holy Temple which was called by thy name, because of the hand that hath been stretched out against thy sanctuary. May it be thy will, O Lord our God and God of our fathers, merciful King, that thou mayest again in thine abundant compassion have mercy upon us and upon thy sanctuary, and mayest speedily rebuild it and magnify its glory. Our Father, our King, do thou speedily make the glory of thy kingdom manifest upon us; shine forth and exalt thyself upon us in the sight of all living; bring our scattered ones among the nations near unto thee, and gather our dispersed from the ends of the earth. Lead us with exultation unto Zion, thy city, and unto Jerusalem, the place of thy sanctuary, with everlasting joy; and there we will prepare before thee the offerings that are obligatory for us, the continual offerings according to their order, and the additional offerings according to their enactment; and the additional offerings of this [Sabbath day and this] Day of Memorial we will prepare and offer unto thee in love according to the precept of thy will, as thou has prescribed for us in thy Law through the hand of Moses thy servant, by the mouth of thy glory, as it is said:

[And on the Sabbath day two he-lambs of the first year without blemish, and two-tenth parts of an ephah of fine flour for a meal offering, mingled with oil, and the drink offering thereof; this is the burnt offering of every Sabbath, beside the continual burnt offering and the drink offering thereof.]

And in the seventh month, on the first day of the month, ye shall have an holy convocation; ye shall do no servile work: it shall be a day of blowing the Shofar unto you. And ye shall offer a burnt offering for a sweet savor unto the Lord; one young bullock, one ram, seven he-lambs of the first year without blemish. And their meal offering and their drink offerings as hath been ordained; three-tenth parts of an ephah for each bullock, and two-tenth parts for the ram, and one-tenth part for each lamb, with wine according to the drink offering thereof, and two he-goats wherewith to make atonement, and the two continual offerings, according to their enactment; beside the burnt offering of the New Moon and the meal offering thereof, and the continual burnt offering and the meal offering thereof, and their drink offerings, according to their ordinance, for a sweet savor, an offering made by fire unto the Lord.

[They that keep the Sabbath and call it a delight shall rejoice in thy kingdom; the people that hallow the seventh day, even all of them, shall be satiated and delighted with thy goodness, seeing that thou didst find pleasure in the seventh day and didst hallow it; thou didst call it the desirable of days, in remembrance of the creation.]

It is our duty to praise the Lord of all things, to ascribe greatness to him who formed the world in the beginning, since he hath not made us like the nations of other lands and hath not placed us like other families of the earth, since he hath not assigned unto us a portion as unto them, nor a lot as unto all their multitude. For we bend the knee and offer worship and thanks before the supreme King of kings, the Holy One, blessed be he, who stretched forth the heavens and laid the foundations of the earth, the seat of whose glory is in the heavens above, and the abode of whose might is in the loftiest heights. He is our God; there is none else: in truth he is our King; there is none besides him; as it is written in his Law, And thou shalt know this day, and lay it to thine heart, that the Lord he is God in heaven above and upon the earth beneath: there is none else.

We therefore hope in thee, O Lord our God, that we may speedily behold the glory of thy might, when thou wilt remove the abominations from the earth and the idols will be utterly cut off, when the world will be perfected under the kingdom of the

Almighty and all the children of flesh will call upon thy name, when thou wilt turn unto thyself all the wicked of the earth. Let all the inhabitants of the world perceive and know that unto thee every knee must bow, every tongue must swear. Before thee, O Lord our God, let them bow and fall; and unto thy glorious name let them give honor; let them all accept the yoke of thy kingdom, and do thou reign over them speedily, and forever and ever. For the kingdom is thine, and to all eternity thou wilt reign in glory; as it is written in thy Law, The Lord shall reign forever and ever.

And it is said, He hath not beheld iniquity in Jacob, neither hath he seen perverseness in Israel: the Lord his God is with him, and the trumpet shout of a King is among them. And it is said, And he became King in Jeshurun, when the heads of the people were gathered, the tribes of Israel together. And in thy Holy Words it is written, saying, For the kingdom is the Lord's, and he is ruler over the nations. And it is said, The Lord reigneth; he hath robed him in majesty; the Lord hath robed him, yea, he hath girded himself with strength: the world also is set firm, that it cannot be moved. And it is said, Lift up your heads, O ye gates, and be ye lifted up, ye everlasting doors, that the King of Glory may come in. Who, then, is the King of Glory? The Lord, strong and mighty, the Lord mighty in battle. Lift up your heads, O ye gates; yea, lift them up, ye everlasting doors, that the King of Glory may come in. Who, then, is the King of Glory? The Lord of Hosts, he is the King of Glory. (Selah) And by the hands of thy servants, the prophets, it is written, saying, Thus saith the Lord, the King of Israel and his redeemer, the Lord of Hosts: I am the first, and I am the last; and beside me there is no God. And it is said, And saviors shall come up on Mount Zion to judge the Mount of Esau, and the kingdom shall be the Lord's. And it is said, And the Lord shall be king over all the earth; in that day shall the Lord be One and his name One. And in thy Law it is written saying, Hear, O Israel: the Lord our God, the Lord is One.

Our God and God of our fathers, reign thou in thy glory over the whole universe and be exalted above all the earth in thine

honor, and shine forth in the splendor and excellence of thy
might upon all the inhabitants of thy world, that whatsoever hath
been made may know that thou has made it, and whatsoever hath
been created may understand that thou has created it, and whatsoever hath breath in its nostrils may say, the Lord God of Israel
is King and his dominion ruleth over all. [Our God and God of
our fathers, accept our rest.] Sanctify us by thy commandments,
and grant us our portion in thy Law; satisfy us with thy goodness,
and gladden us with thy salvation: [and in thy love and favor,
O Lord our God, let us inherit thy holy Sabbath; and may Israel,
who hallow thy name, rest thereon]. O purify our hearts to serve
thee in truth, for thou art God in truth, and thy word is truth
and endureth forever. Blessed art thou, O Lord, King over all the
earth, who sanctifiest [the Sabbath and] Israel and the Day of
Memorial.

Thou rememberest what was wrought from eternity and art
mindful of all that hath been formed from of old: before thee all
secrets are revealed and the multitude of hidden things from the
beginning; for there is no forgetfulness before the throne of thy
glory; nor is there aught hidden from thine eyes. Thou rememberest every deed that hath been done: not a creature is concealed
from thee; all things are manifest and known unto thee, O Lord
our God, who lookest and seest to the end of all generations. For
thou wilt bring on the appointed time of memorial when every
spirit and soul shall be visited and the multitudinous works be
remembered with the innumerable throng of thy creatures. From
the beginning thou didst make this thy purpose known, and from
aforetime thou didst disclose it. This day, on which was the beginning of thy work, is a memorial of the first day; for it is a
statute for Israel, a decree of the God of Jacob. Thereon also
sentence is pronounced upon countries, which of them is destined
to the sword and which to peace, which to famine and which to
plenty; and each separate creature is visited thereon and recorded
for life or for death. Who is not visited on this day? For the remembrance of every creature cometh before thee, each man's
deeds and destiny, his works and ways, his thoughts and schemes,
his imaginings and achievements. Happy is the man who forgetteth

thee not, and the son of man who strengtheneth himself in thee; for they that seek thee shall never stumble, neither shall any be put to shame who trust in thee. Yea, the remembrance of all works cometh before thee, and thou enquirest into the doings of them all. Of Noah also thou wast mindful in thy love, and didst visit him with a promise of salvation and mercy, when thou broughtest the waters of the flood to destroy all flesh on account of their evil deeds. So his remembrance came before thee, O Lord our God, to increase his seed like the dust of the earth, and his offspring like the sand of the sea: as it is written in thy Law, And God remembered Noah, and every living thing, and all the cattle that were with him in the ark: and God made a wind to pass over the earth, and the waters subsided. And it is said, And God heard their groaning, and God remembered his covenant with Abraham, with Isaac and with Jacob. And it is said, Then will I remember my covenant with Jacob; and also my covenant with Isaac, and also my covenant with Abraham will I remember; and I will remember the land. And in thy Holy Words it is written saying, He hath made a memorial for his wondrous works: the Lord is gracious and full of compassion. And it is said, He hath given food unto them that fear him: he will ever be mindful of his covenant. And it is said, And he remembered for them his covenant and repented according to the multitude of his loving-kindnesses. And by the hands of thy servants, the prophets, it is written saying, Go and cry in the ears of Jerusalem, saying, Thus saith the Lord, I remember for thee the kindness of thy youth, the love of thy bridal state; how thou wentest after me in the wilderness, in a land that was not sown. And it is said, Nevertheless, I will remember my covenant with thee in the days of thy youth, and I will establish unto thee an everlasting covenant. And it is said, Is Ephraim a precious son unto me? Is he a caressed child? As often as I spake against him, I earnestly remembered him; therefore my heart yearneth for him; I will surely have mercy upon him, saith the Lord.

Our God and God of our fathers, let us be remembered by thee for good: grant us a visitation of salvation and mercy from thy heavens, the heavens of old; and remember unto us, O

Lord our God, the covenant and the loving-kindness and the oath which thou swarest unto Abraham our father on Mount Moriah; and may the binding with which Abraham our father bound his son Isaac on the altar appear before thee, how he overbore his compassion in order to perform thy will with a perfect heart. So may thy compassion overbear thine anger against us; in thy great goodness may the fierceness of thy wrath turn aside from thy people, thy city and thine inheritance. Fulfill unto us, O Lord our God, the word in which thou hast bidden us trust in thy Law through the hand of Moses thy servant, from the mouth of thy glory, as it is said, But I will remember unto them the covenant of their ancestors, whom I brought forth out of the land of Egypt in the sight of the nations, that I might be their God: I am the Lord. For thou art he who remembereth from eternity all forgotten things, and before the throne of whose glory there is no forgetfulness. O remember the binding of Isaac this day in mercy unto his seed. Blessed art thou, O Lord, who rememberest the covenant.

Thou didst reveal thyself in a cloud of glory unto thy holy people in order to speak with them. Out of heaven thou didst make them hear thy voice and wast revealed unto them in clouds of purity. The whole world trembled at thy presence, and the works of creation were in awe of thee, when thou didst thus reveal thyself, O our King, upon Mount Sinai to teach thy people the law and commandments, and didst make them hear thy majestic voice and thy holy utterances out of flames of fire. Amidst thunders and lightnings thou didst manifest thyself to them, and while the Shofar sounded thou didst shine forth upon them; as it is written in thy Law, And it came to pass on the third day, when it was morning, that there were thunders and lightnings, and a thick cloud upon the mount, and the sound of the Shofar exceeding loud; and all the people that were in the camp trembled. And it is said, And the sound of the Shofar waxed louder and louder; Moses spake, and God answered him by a voice. And it is said, And all the people perceived the thunderings and the lightnings, and the sound of the Shofar, and the mountain smoking: and when the people saw it, they were moved and stood afar off. And in thy Holy Words it is written, saying, God is gone up with a shout, the Lord with the sound of a Shofar. And it is said, With trumpets and sound of Shofar shout joyously before the King, the Lord. And it is said, Blow the Shofar on the new moon, at the beginning of the month, for our day of festival: for it is a statute for Israel, a decree of the God of Jacob. And it is said, Praise ye the Lord. Praise God in his sanctuary: praise him in the firmament of his power. Praise him for his mighty acts: praise him according to his abundant greatness. Praise him with the blast of the Shofar: praise him with the harp and the lyre. Praise him with timbrel and dance: praise him with stringed instruments and the pipe. Praise him with the clear-toned cymbals: praise him with the loud-sounding cymbals. Let everything that hath breath praise the Lord. Praise ye the Lord. And by the hands of thy servants, the prophets, it is written saying, All ye inhabitants of the world and ye dwellers on the earth, when an ensign is lifted up on the mountains, see ye; and when the Shofar is blown, hear ye. And it is said, And it shall come to pass on that day that a great Shofar shall be blown; and they shall come who were lost in the land of Assyria and they that were outcasts in the land of Egypt, and they shall worship the Lord in the holy mountain at Jerusalem. And it is said, And the Lord shall be seen over them, and his arrow shall go forth as the lightning; and the Lord God shall blow the Shofar and shall go with the whirlwinds of the south. The Lord of Hosts shall be a shield unto them. So be a shield unto thy people Israel with thy peace.

Our God and God of our fathers, sound the great Shofar for our freedom, lift up the ensign to gather our exiles; bring our scattered ones among the nations near unto thee and gather our dispersed from the ends of the earth. Lead us with exultation unto Zion, thy city, and unto Jerusalem the place of thy sanctuary with everlasting joy; and there we will prepare before thee the offerings that are obligatory for us, as is commanded us in thy Law through the hand of Moses thy servant, from the mouth of thy glory, as it is said, And in the day of your gladness, and in your set feats, and in the beginnings of your months, ye shall blow with the trumpets over your burnt offerings, and over the sacrifices of your peace offerings; and they shall be to you for a memorial before your God: I am the Lord your God. For thou hearest the sound of the Shofar and givest heed to the trumpet blast, and there is none like unto thee. Blessed art thou, O Lord, who in mercy hearest the sound of the trumpet blast of thy people Israel.

Accept, O Lord our God, thy people Israel and their prayer; restore the service to the oracle of thy house; receive in love and favor both the fire offerings of Israel and their prayer; and may the service of thy people Israel be ever acceptable unto thee.

And let our eyes behold thy return in mercy to Zion. Blessed art thou, O Lord, who restorest thy divine presence unto Zion.

We give thanks unto thee, for thou art the Lord our God and the God of our fathers forever and ever; thou art the rock of our lives, the shield of our salvation through every generation. We will give thanks unto thee and declare thy praise for our lives, which are committed unto thy hand; and for our souls, which are in thy charge; and for thy miracles, which are daily with us; and for thy wonders and thy benefits, which are wrought at all times, evening, morn and noon.

Congregation in an undertone:

We give thanks unto thee, for thou art the Lord our God and the God of our fathers, the God of all flesh, our Creator and the Creator of all things in the beginning. Blessings and thanksgivings be to thy great and holy name, because thou hast kept us in life and hast preserved us; so mayest thou continue to keep us in life and to preserve us. O gather our exiles to thy holy courts to observe thy statutes, to do thy will, and to serve thee with a perfect heart, seeing that we give thanks unto thee. Blessed be the God to whom thanksgivings are due.

O thou who art all-good, whose mercies fail not; thou, merciful Being, whose loving-kindnesses never cease, we have ever hoped in thee.

For all these things thy name, O our King, shall be continually blessed and exalted forever and ever.

O inscribe all the children of thy covenant for a happy life.

And everything that liveth shall give thanks unto thee forever, and shall praise thy name in truth, O God, our salvation and our help. Blessed art thou, O Lord, whose name is All-good, and unto whom it is becoming to give thanks.

At the repetition of the 'Amidah by the Reader, the following is introduced:

Our God and God of our fathers, bless us with the threefold blessing of thy Law written by the hand of Moses thy servant, which was spoken by Aaron and his sons, the priests, thy holy people, as it is said, The Lord bless thee, and keep thee: the Lord make his face to shine upon thee, and be gracious unto thee: the Lord turn his face unto thee, and give thee peace.

Grant peace, welfare, blessing, grace, loving-kindness, and mercy unto us and unto all Israel, thy people. Bless us, O our Father, even all of us together, with the light of thy countenance; for by the light of thy countenance thou has given us, O Lord our God, the Law of life, loving-kindness and righteousness, blessing, mercy, life and peace; and may it be good in thy sight to bless thy people Israel at all times and in every hour with thy peace.

In the Book of Life, blessing, peace, and good sustenance may we be remembered and inscribed before thee, we and all thy people, the House of Israel for a happy life and for peace. Blessed art thou, O Lord who makest peace.

O my God! guard my tongue from evil and my lips from speaking guile; and to such as curse me let my soul be dumb, yea, let my soul be unto all as the dust. Open my heart to thy Law, and let my soul pursue thy commandments. If any design evil against me, speedily make their counsel of none effect and frustrate their design. Do it for the sake of thy name, do it for the sake of thy right hand, do it for the sake of thy holiness, do it for the sake of thy Law. In order that thy beloved ones may be delivered, O save with thy right hand, and answer me. Let the words of my mouth and the meditation of my heart be acceptable before thee, O Lord, my rock and my redeemer. He who maketh peace in his high places, may he make peace for us and for all Israel, and say ye, Amen.

May it be thy will, O Lord our God and God of our fathers, that the Temple be speedily rebuilt in our days, and grant our portion in thy Law. And there we will serve thee with awe, as in the days of old and as in ancient years. Then shall the offering of Judah and Jerusalem be pleasant unto the Lord, as in the days of old and as in ancient years.

HYMNS FROM THE DEAD SEA SCROLLS [18]

I

I give thee thanks, Adonai!
For thou has placed my soul in the bundle of life,
and thou hast protected me from all the snares of the Pit.
And the violent sought my soul,
when I trusted in thy Covenant.
But they are an assembly of worthlessness
and a congregation of Belial;
they do not know that it is from thee that my existence comes
and that through thy mercies thou wilt save my soul.
For from thee proceed my steps,
and if they attack my soul, this also comes from thee,
that thou mayest be glorified when the wicked are judged
and thou mayest be strengthened in me in the presence of
    the sons of men.
For it is by thy mercy that I have my being,
and I said, "The valiant pitched their camp against me,
they surrounded me armed with all their weapons of war,
    and they let fly arrows for whose wounds there is no
    healing
and the flashing of the lances was like a fire which destroys
    the forest,
and like the tumult of mighty waters was the roaring of their
    voices:
an overwhelming hurricane, bringing destruction for many.
In their brooding they will hatch the asp and worthlessness!"
While their waves rose up,

and, as for me, while my heart melted like water
my soul laid hold on thy Covenant!
The net which they have spread for me entangles their feet;
into the snares which they have hidden for my soul, they
     have themselves fallen,
while my foot remains standing on solid ground!
In the assemblies, I will bless thy Name!

II

I give thee thanks, Adonai!
For thou hast redeemed my soul from the Pit
and from Sheol-Abaddon thou hast brought me up again to
     the top of the world.
Then I wandered on an endless plain;
and I knew that there was hope
for him whom thou hast formed from the dust and destined
     for the eternal Assembly.
Yea, the perverse spirit hast thou purified of a great sin
so that he might mount guard with the army of the Saints
and that he might enter into communion with the congrega-
     tion of the Sons of Heaven.
Yea, thou hast caused to fall on man an eternal Destiny
amongst the intelligent Spirits,
that he should praise thy Name in communion with them
and that he should tell of thy Wonders before all thy works.
But I, creature of clay, what am I?
Formed with water, for whom have I worth? And what
     strength can I have?
For I stood in the realm of malice
and amongst the wretched, through the working of Destiny.
Then thou didst stir the soul of the poor in the midst of
     many tribulations,
and overwhelming misfortune accompanied my steps:
while all the snares of the Pit opened up
and all the pitfalls of wickedness were spread out
and the net of the wretched stretched out on the surface of
     the waters;

while all the arrows of the Pit flew forth, straight to their
     target,
and were shot without leaving any hope;
while the rope of destruction descended on the damned,
and the Destiny of anger on the abandoned,
and the overflowing of wrath on the outcasts,
and it was the time of Fury for all Belial.
And the bonds of Death surrounded so that there was no
     escape,
and the torrents of Belial overflowed all their banks.
The fire consumes all beings who draw from it,
causing to disappear from their rivers every tree, both green
     and withered;
and it lashes with whirlwinds of flame
until there is no longer any creature who drinks there.
It consumes the foundations of asphalt
and the base of the earth;
the foundations of the mountains are the prey of burning,
and the roots of flint become torrents of pitch.
And it consumes even as far as the Great Abyss,
and the torrents of Belial break into Abaddon,
and the creatures of the Abyss endowed with reason make
     their din resound
amongst the tumult of the eddies of mud.
And the earth cries out because of the misfortune which has
     come upon the land,
and all the beings endowed with reason utter cries,
and all those who are thereon are in panic,
and they stagger in a great misfortune.
For God thunders in the tumult of his Strength,
and his holy Dwelling resounds with the truth of his Glory,
while the host of the heavens makes its voice to be heard.
The foundations of the world totter and tremble,
and the host of the Valiant of the heavens scourges the earth
and does not withdraw before executing the decree of ex-
     termination,
extermination final and unparalleled!

NOTES

APOCRYPHAL MATERIALS

[1] I Maccabees 4:36–61. English translation by Sidney Tedesche, *The First Book of Maccabees* (New York, Harper and Brothers, for the Dropsie College for Hebrew and Cognate Learning, 1950).

[2] Of the Seleucid era, equivalent to 165 B.C.

[3] A border town in the south of Palestine.

[4] II Maccabees 1:1–10. English translation by James Moffatt, in R. H. Charles, *Apocrypha and Pseudepigrapha of the Old Testament* (Oxford, Oxford University Press, 1913).

[5] 145 B.C.

[6] 126 B.C.

[7] II Maccabees 7. English translation by James Moffatt, in Charles, *op. cit.*

[8] III Maccabees 2:1–20. English translation by Cyril W. Emmet, in *ibid.*

[9] Simon II, high priest 219 to 199 B.C.

[10] IV Maccabees 1:13–3:18. English translation by Moses Hadas, in *The Third and Fourth Books of Maccabees* (New York, Harper and Brothers, for the Dropsie College for Hebrew and Cognate Learning, 1953).

[11] Numbers 16:12–30.

[12] Genesis 34:30.

[13] II Samuel 23:15–17, where *three* of the warriors risked their lives to satisfy David's whim.

[14] Wisdom of Solomon 9–10. English translation by Samuel Holmes, in Charles, *op. cit.*

[15] Adam.

[16] Cain.

[17] Noah.

[18] Abraham.

[19] Lot.

[20] The biblical five cities of the plain: Sodom, Gomorrah, Admah, Zeboim, and Zoar.

[21] Lot's wife; cf. Genesis 19:26.

[22] Jacob; cf. Genesis 27:41 and subsequent chapters.

[23] Joseph; cf. Genesis 37:26 and subsequent chapters.

[24] Moses; cf. Exodus 7 and subsequent chapters

[25] An echo of Exodus 13:19.

[26] Exodus 14.

[27] Exodus 15.

[28] II Baruch 27–30. English translation by R. H. Charles, in Charles, *op. cit.*

[29] Job 40:15–24.

[30] Job 41.

[31] About 120 gallons.

[32] Tobit 4. English translation by D. C. Simpson, in Charles, *op. cit.*

[33] Tobit 13. English translation by D. C. Simpson, in Charles, *op. cit.*

[34] The Prayer of Manasses. English translation by the Right Reverend Bishop Herbert E. Ryle, in Charles, *op. cit.*

[35] II Chronicles 33:12–13, 18.

HELLENISTIC MATERIALS

[1] Philo Judaeus, *The Special Laws*, I, 32–50. English translation by F. H. Colson, in *Philo*, Vol. VII (Loeb Classical Library; Cambridge, Massachusetts, Harvard University Press, 1937).

[2] The Socratic dictum, with which Philo was familiar because of his Platonic studies, takes on a new dimension in the religious context.

[3] The reference to the Platonic doctrine of ideas is clear.

[4] Philo Judaeus, *On the Creation of the World*, 53–57; 69–71. English translation by F. H. Colson and G. H. Whitaker, in *Philo*, Vol. I (Loeb Classical Library; London, William Heinemann, Ltd., 1929).

[5] Genesis 1:26.

[6] Philo Judaeus, *Hypothetica*, in Eusebius, *Praeparatio Evangelica*, VII, 6–19. English translation by F. H. Colson, in *Philo*, Vol. IX (Loeb Classical Library; Cambridge, Massachusetts, Harvard University Press, 1941).

[7] Philo Judaeus, *The Life of Moses*, I, 65–71. English translation by F. H. Colson, in *Philo*, Vol. VI (1935).

[8] Moses; cf. Exodus 3.

[9] Philo Judaeus, *The Life of Moses*, I, 147–159.

[10] *Ibid.*, I, 210–213.

[11] Exodus 17:1–6.

[12] Exodus 15:22–25.

[13] Philo Judaeus, *op. cit.*, II, 25–40.

[14] See Josephus, "The Jewish Theocracy," pp. 54–63.

[15] A fuller but essentially identical account of the Septuagint translation of the Bible is to be found in *Aristeas to Philocrates (Letter of Aristeas)*, edited and translated by Moses Hadas (New York, Harper and Brothers, for the Dropsie College of Hebrew and Cognate Learning, 1951).

[16] Philo Judaeus, *The Special Laws*, III, 33–34. English translation by F. H. Colson, in *Philo*, Vol. VII (1937).

[17] Moses.

[18] Editors' correction.

[19] Philo Judaeus, *In Flaccum*, VII, 45–52. English translation by F. H. Colson, in *Philo*, Vol. IX (1941).

[20] Josephus, *Against Apion*, II, 16–19, 33–38. English translation by William Whiston, *The Works of Flavius Josephus* (London, George Routledge and Sons, n.d.).

[21] Moses.

[22] He was, however, well known as a rhetorician in his day, although his works have not survived. In 81 B.C. Molon served the people of Rhodes as their envoy; he is known also to have taught both Julius Caesar and Cicero.

SECTARIAN MOVEMENTS

[1] Tractate Kutim, 1, 2, English translation by Michael Higger, in *Seven Minor Treatises* (New York, Bloch Publishing Company, 1930).

[2] Deuteronomy 14:21.

[3] That is, with the pagan priests of Baal.

[4] Josephus, *Antiquities of the Jews*, XVIII, 1, §§ 2–6. English translation by William Whiston, *The Works of Flavius Josephus* (London, George Routledge and Sons, n.d.).

[5] 'Dwellers in cities.'

[6] Gessius Florus, a Roman officer, became Procurator (Governor) of Judea in 64 A.D. His cruel and rapacious administration was one of the factors that provoked the revolt of the Jews, leading to the destruction of the Temple in 70 A.D.

[7] Josephus, *The Wars of the Jews,* Book II, 8, §§ 2–13. English translation by Whiston, *op. cit.*

[8] Moses.

[9] Philo Judaeus, *On the Contemplative Life.* English translation by F. H. Colson, in *Philo,* Vol. IX (Loeb Classical Library; Cambridge, Massachusetts, Harvard University Press, 1941).

[10] The Feast of Pentecost.

[11] Exodus 15.

[12] Fragments of a Zadokite work, selections from Chs. 2, 3, 6, 8, and 9. English translation by R. H. Charles, in Charles, *op. cit.*

[13] Isaiah 24:17. The JPS translation reads: "Terror, and the pit, and the trap are upon thee, O inhabitant of the earth."

[14] Isaiah 54:16. The JPS translation reads: "He bringeth forth a weapon for his work."

[15] Amos 5:26–27. The JPS translation reads: "So shall ye take up Siccuth your King and Chiun your images, the star of your God, which ye made to yourselves. Therefore will I cause you to go into captivity beyond Damascus. . . ."

[16] Amos 9:11.

[17] Numbers 24:17. The JPS translation reads: "There shall step forth . . . ."

[18] Fragments from A. Dupont-Sommer, *The Dead Sea Scrolls: A Preliminary Survey.* Translated from the French by E. Margaret Rowley (Oxford, Basil Blackwell, 1952).

TANNAITIC COLLECTIONS

[1] *Pirke Aboth.* English translation by R. Travers Herford (New York, The Jewish Institute of Religion Press, 1930), Chs. I–II.

[2] Gamaliel, the Elder.

[3] Zechariah 8:16. The JPS translation reads: "Execute the judgment of peace and truth in your gates."

[4] Judah ha-Nasi (the Prince) is referred to by this honorary title without the addition of his name.

[5] Psalms 37:21. The JPS translation reads: ". . . the righteous dealeth graciously. . . ."

[6] Joel 2:13. The JPS translation reads: "For he is gracious and compassionate, long-suffering, and abundant in mercy. . . ."

[7] This term is used to denote a person who denies God and rejects the Torah.

[8] "Baraitha d' R. Ishmael." English translation by the Reverend S. Singer, in *The Standard Prayer Book,* enlarged American edition (New York, Bloch Publishing Company, 1935).

[9] *The Mishnah,* Tractate Shabbath, VII, 1–2; I–II. English translation by Herbert Danby (Oxford, Clarendon Press, 1933).

[10] *The Mishnah,* Tractate Baba Metzia, V. English translation by Danby, *op. cit.*

[11] Leviticus 25:37. The JPS translation reads: "Thou shalt not give him thy money upon interest."

[12] Leviticus 25:36. The JPS translation reads: "Take thou no interest of him."

[13] Leviticus 22:24. The JPS translation reads: ". . . Neither shall ye lay upon him interest."

[14] Leviticus 19:14.

[15] *The Mishnah,* Tractate Kelim. I, 6–9, English translation by Danby, *op. cit.*

[16] Cf. Leviticus 23:10 ff.

[17] *The Mishnah,* Tractate Berakoth, IX. English translation by Danby, *op. cit.*

[18] The Mediterranean Sea.

[19] Deuteronomy 6:5.

[20] Ruth 2:4.

[21] Judges 6:12.

[22] Proverbs 23:22. The point of using this text here is that it is used to mean: "Do not abandon ancient customs."

[23] Psalms 119:126.

[24] Philo Judaeus, cited above, p. 39.

[25] *Mekhilta,* Tractate Bahodesh, 5 (on Exodus 20:2). English translation by Jacob Z. Lauterbach (Philadelphia, Jewish Publication Society of America, 1933).

[26] Deuteronomy 29:28.

[27] Exodus 15:3.

[28] Exodus 24:10.

[29] *Ibid.*

[30] Daniel 7:9.

[31] Daniel 7:10.

[32] Deuteronomy 32:39.

[33] Isaiah 46:4.

[34] Isaiah 44:6.

[35] Isaiah 41:4.

[36] Isaiah 45:19.

[37] *Ibid.*

[38] *Ibid.* The JPS translation reads: "Seek ye me in vain."

[39] *Ibid.*

[40] Jeremiah 46:18.

[41] Judges 5:4.

[42] Judges 5:5.

[43] Psalms 29: 4–9.

[44] Isaiah 54:9.

[45] Psalms 29:11.

[46] Deuteronomy 33:2.

[47] Deuteronomy 5:17.

[48] Genesis 27:40.

[49] Deuteronomy 5:17.

[50] Genesis 19:36.

[51] Deuteronomy 5:17.

[52] Genesis 16:12.

[53] Genesis 40:15.

[54] Deuteronomy 33:2.

[55] Exodus 24:7.

[56] Habakkuk 3:6.

[57] 'Scoundrel.'

[58] Inference from a minor to a major; *cf.* above, p. 107.

[59] Deuteronomy 7:8.

[60] *Mekhilta,* Tractate Nezikin, 18 (on Exodus 22:20–23). English translation by Jacob Z. Lauterbach (Philadelphia, Jewish Publication Society of America, 1935).

[61] The word *Ger* used here refers to a proselyte.

[62] Deuteronomy 10:19.

[63] Exodus 23:9.

[64] Judges 3:31.

[65] Deuteronomy 10:18.

[66] Leviticus 25:55.

[67] Isaiah 56:6.

[68] Isaiah 61:6.

[69] Isaiah 56:6.

[70] Isaiah 41:8.

[71] Deuteronomy 10:18.

[72] Genesis 17:13.

[73] Isaiah 56:6.

[74] Exodus 28:38.

[75] Isaiah 56:7.

[76] Psalms 121:4.

[77] Psalms 146:9.

[78] Genesis 23:4.

[79] Psalms 119:19.

[80] I Chronicles 29:15.

[81] Psalms 39:13.

[82] Isaiah 42:21.

[83] Isaiah 44:5.

[84] Isaiah 57:1.

[85] Isaiah 57:2.

[86] Isaiah 57:3.

[87] Deuteronomy 11:17.

[88] II Samuel 20:3.

[89] Zechariah 7:9.

[90] Zechariah 8:16.

[91] Isaiah 56:1.

[92] Deuteronomy 6:2.

[93] Deuteronomy 11:19–21.

[94] Isaiah 65:22.

[95] Isaiah 65:23.

[96] Isaiah 48:19.

[97] Deuteronomy 5:26.

[98] Isaiah 66:22.

[99] Isaiah 59:20–21.

[100] *Midrash Sifre on Numbers, Selections from Early Rabbinic Scriptural Interpretations,* § 42 (on Numbers 6:26). English translation by Paul P. Levertoff (London, A. Golub, 1926), revised by the editors.

[101] Isaiah 9:6. The JPS translation reads: ". . . that the government may be increased, and of peace there be no end."

[102] Psalms 29:11. 'Strength' is frequently interpreted to mean the Torah.

[103] Genesis 18:12, 13.

[104] Cf. I Samuel 15:1–2.

[105] Cf. Judges 13:3.

[106] Psalms 20:11.

[107] Hosea 4:17. The JPS translation reads: ". . . joined to idols . . ."

[108] Deuteronomy 20:10. The interpretation is that the first act of war is a demand for peace. The JPS translation reads: ". . . to fight against it, then proclaim peace unto it." Cf. Deuteronomy 2:26, Judges 11:12.

[109] Genesis 15:15.

[110] Jeremiah 34:5.

[111] Isaiah 57:19. The JPS translation reads: ". . . to him that is far off and to him that is near."

[112] Isaiah 57:2. The JPS translation reads: "He entereth into peace. . . ."

[113] Isaiah 57:21.

[114] Psalms 119:165. The JPS translation reads: "Great peace have they that love thy Law.' '

[115] Isaiah 54:13.

[116] Psalms 37:11. The JPS translation reads: "And the humble shall inherit. . . ."

[117] Isaiah 32:17.

[118] Judges 6:24. The JPS translation reads: ". . . called it Adonai-shalom."

[119] Isaiah 45:7. The JPS translation reads: "I form light and create darkness; I make peace."

[120] Job 25:2. The JPS translation reads: "He maketh peace in his high places."

[121] Job 25:3.

[122] Daniel 7:10. The JPS translation reads: "Thousand thousands ministered unto him, and ten thousand times ten thousand stood before him."

AMORAIC COLLECTIONS

[1] *The Babylonian Talmud,* Tractate Makkoth, 23b–24a. English translation by H. M. Lazarus. Edited by I. Epstein (London, Soncino Press, 1935).

[2] Deuteronomy 33:4.

[3] The Hebrew letters, like those of other ancient languages, were used to represent numbers. Every Hebrew word, therefore, has a numerical equivalent.

[4] Psalms 15.

[5] Genesis 17:1.

[6] Genesis 27:12.

[7] Leviticus 18:24.

[8] Isaiah 33:15–16.

[9] Genesis 18:19.

[10] Micah 6:8.

[11] Isaiah 56:1.

[12] Amos 5:4.

[13] Habakkuk 2:4.

[14] The Babylonian Talmud, Tractate Pesahim, 50b–51b. English translation by H. Freedman, in Epstein, op cit. (1938).

[15] Proverbs 1:8.

[16] 'Cake.' Cf. Numbers 15:20.

[17] Leviticus 25:20.

[18] The Babylonian Talmud, Tractate Makkoth, 7a. English translation by H. M. Lazarus, in Epstein, op. cit. (1935).

[19] Numbers 35:29.

[20] Deuteronomy 16:18.

[21] The juridical point involved in asking such intimate questions is this—that if the witnesses could not be absolutely certain on any material point in the evidence, they could not be expected to take a lead in the actual execution of the offender, as required by law (Deuteronomy 17:6–7).

[22] The Babylonian Talmud, Tractate Yoma, 85b–87b. English translation by Leo Jung, in Epstein, op. cit. (1938).

[23] Leviticus 16:30.

[24] Ezekiel 36:25.

[25] Jeremiah 17:13.

[26] Exodus 20:7.

[27] Ibid.

[28] Exodus 34:7.

[29] This passage has been emended by the editors to agree with the original.

[30] Jeremiah 3:14.

[31] Leviticus 16:30.

[32] Psalms 89:33.

[33] Isaiah 22:14.

[34] Deuteronomy 6:5.

[35] Isaiah 49:3.

[36] Ezekiel 36:20.

[37] Hosea 14:5.

[38] Jeremiah 3:22.

[39] Jeremiah 3:14.

[40] Hosea 14:2.

[41] Jeremiah 3:1.

[42] Isaiah 59:20.

[43] Hosea 14:2.

[44] Ezekiel 33:19.

[45] Hosea 14:3.

[46] Ibid.

[47] Ibid.

[48] Hosea 14:5.

[49] Psalms 32:1.

[50] Proverbs 28:13.

[51] Amos 2:6.

[52] Job 33:29.

[53] Proverbs 26:11.

[54] Psalms 51:5.

[55] Exodus 32:31.

[56] Psalms 32:1.

[57] Numbers 21:12.

[58] Ezekiel 3:20.

[59] Job 20:6–7.

[60] Proverbs 27:24.

[61] Proverbs 18:5.

[62] I Kings 21:29.

[63] Proverbs 18:5.

[64] Leviticus 10:12.

[65] Psalms 16:9.

[66] Proverbs 28:17.

[67] II Samuel 2:25.

[68] Proverbs 6:1–3.

[69] Job 33:27.

[70] Genesis 50:17.

[71] I Samuel 2:8.

[72] This was Rab's real name.

[73] The 'Amidah, the central prayer of the Jewish service. See below, pp. 220–231.

[74] The phrases quoted from here to the end of this selection all are from the Prayer Book.

[75] *The Babylonian Talmud,* Tractate Zebahim, 88b. English translation by H. Freedman, in Epstein, *op. cit.* (1948).

[76] Leviticus 7 and 8:1 ff.

[77] Genesis 37:31.

[78] Exodus 28:42.

[79] Exodus 28:15.

[80] Hosea 3:4.

[81] Exodus 28:38.

[82] Jeremiah 3:3.

[83] Cf. Deuteronomy 21:1–9.

[84] Numbers 17:12.

[85] *Babylonian Talmud,* Tractate Sanhedrin, 107 b.

[86] Tractate *Gerim,* 1, 3, 4. English translation by Michael Higger, *Seven Minor Treatises* (New York, Bloch Publishing Company, 1930).

[87] Esther 8:17.

[88] Leviticus 19:33.

[89] Deuteronomy 24:14.

[90] Leviticus 19:13.

[91] Deuteronomy 23:17.

[92] Exodus 22:20.

[93] Isaiah 41:8.

[94] Malachi 1:2.

[95] Deuteronomy 10:18.

[96] Leviticus 25:55.

[97] Isaiah 56:6.

[98] Exodus 28:38.

[99] Isaiah 56:7.

[100] Psalms 121:5.

[101] Psalms 146:9.

[102] Isaiah 61:6.

[103] Isaiah 56:6.

[104] *The Babylonian Talmud,* Tractate Yebamoth, 46b–47b. English translation by Israel W. Slotki, in Epstein, *op. cit.* (1936).

[105] Leviticus 19:33.

[106] *Ibid.*

[107] Leviticus 19:34.

[108] Deuteronomy 1:16.

[109] The firstborn; Deuteronomy 21:17.

[110] Isaiah 14:1.

[111] Ruth 1:18.

[112] Ruth 1:16.

[113] *The Babylonian Talmud,* Tractate Yebamoth, 79a. English translation by Israel W. Slotki, in Epstein, *op. cit.* (1936).

[114] *The Babylonian Talmud,* Tractate Sukkah, 49b. English translation by Israel W. Slotki, in Epstein, *op. cit.* (1938).

[115] Canticles 7:2.

[116] Micah 6:8.

[117] Proverbs 21:3.

[118] Hosea 10:12.

[119] Psalms 33:5.

[120] Psalms 36:8.

[121] Psalms 103:17.

[122] Proverbs 31:26.

[123] *The Babylonian Talmud,* Tractate Baba Bathra, 8b–11a. English translation by Maurice Simon and Israel W. Slotki, in Epstein, *op. cit.* (1935).

[124] Exodus 28:5.

[125] Jeremiah 30:20.

[126] Daniel 12:3.

[127] *Ibid.*

[128] Judges 5:31.

[129] II Kings 12:16.

[130] *Ibid.*
[131] Isaiah 58:7.
[132] *Ibid.*
[133] Nehemiah 10:33.
[134] Isaiah 32:17.
[135] Isaiah 58:7.
[136] *Ibid.*
[137] Isaiah 60:17.
[138] Isaiah 59:17.
[139] Isaiah 64:5.
[140] Leviticus 22:5.
[141] Leviticus 22:4.
[142] Deuteronomy 9:19.
[143] Proverbs 21:14.
[144] Isaiah 58:7.
[145] Isaiah 58:10–12.
[146] Proverbs 21:21.
[147] Jeremiah 18:23.
[148] Proverbs 3:35.
[149] Leviticus 25:55.
[150] Deuteronomy 14:1.
[151] Deuteronomy 15:9.
[152] Deuteronomy 13:14.
[153] Jeremiah 16:5.
[154] Isaiah 56:1.
[155] Proverbs 10:2.
[156] Psalms 17:15.
[157] Proverbs 19:17.
[158] Proverbs 22:7.
[159] Proverbs 11:4.
[160] Proverbs 10:2.
[161] Zephaniah 1:15.
[162] Psalms 112:9.
[163] Isaiah 33:16.
[164] Isaiah 24:23.
[165] Martyrs of 352 A.D., as contrasted with the martyrs of the Bar Kokheba revolt.
[166] Proverbs 14:34.
[167] II Samuel 7:23.
[168] Ezra 6:10.
[169] Daniel 4:27.
[170] Proverbs 21:24.
[171] Zephaniah 1:15.

[172] Jeremiah 40:3.
[173] Isaiah 27:11.
[174] King of Adiabene, in the first century A.D., who became a convert to Judaism.
[175] Psalms 85:11.
[176] Psalms 97:2.
[177] Isaiah 3:10.
[178] Proverbs 11:30.
[179] Deuteronomy 24:13.
[180] Isaiah 58:8.
[181] *The Babylonian Talmud*, Tractate Baba Bathra, 20b-21b. English translation by Maurice Simon and Israel W. Slotki, in Epstein, *op. cit.* (1935).
[182] Deuteronomy 11:19.
[183] Isaiah 2:3.
[184] I Kings 11:16.
[185] Deuteronomy 25:19.
[186] Jeremiah 48:10.
[187] *Ibid.*
[188] *The Babylonian Talmud*, Tractate Sanhedrin, 98a–99a. English translation by H. Freedman, in Epstein, *op. cit.* (1935).
[189] Micah 5:2.
[190] Genesis 28:15.
[191] Genesis 32:8.
[192] Exodus 15:16.
[193] *Ibid.*
[194] Amos 5:19.
[195] Jeremiah 30:6.
[196] That is, as we might put it, any 'Tom, Dick, or Harry.'
[197] Genesis 49:10.
[198] Psalms 72:17.
[199] Jeremiah 16:13.
[200] Lamentations 1:16.
[201] Isaiah 53:4.
[202] Jeremiah 31:21.
[203] That is, R. Judah the Prince.
[204] Jeremiah 30:9.
[205] Ezekiel 37:25.

[206] Amos 5:18.

[207] 'A heretic.'

[208] Isaiah 60:2.

[209] Psalms 95:10.

[210] Isaiah 23:15.

[211] Psalms 72:5.

[212] Zechariah 9:9.

[213] Deuteronomy 8:3.

[214] Psalms 90:15.

[215] Genesis 15:13.

[216] Isaiah 63:4.

[217] Isaiah 62:5.

[218] Deuteronomy 11:21.

[219] Isaiah 54:9.

[220] Isaiah 64:3.

[221] *The Babylonian Talmud,* Tractate Berakoth, 18a–19a. English translation by Maurice Simon, in Epstein, *op. cit.* (1948).

[222] Ecclesiastes 9:5.

[223] *Ibid.*

[224] II Samuel 23:20.

[225] Ezekiel 21:30.

[226] Deuteronomy 17:6.

[227] Job 14:21.

[228] Job 14:22.

[229] Deuteronomy 34:4.

[230] *The Babylonian Talmud,* Tractate Sanhedrin, 90a–91a. English translation by H. Freedman, in Epstein, *op. cit.* (1935).

[231] Isaiah 60:22.

[232] Exodus 15:26.

[233] II Chronicles 33:13.

[234] See, above, Philo Judaeus, pp. 48–51.

[235] II Kings 7:1.

[236] II Kings 7:2.

[237] II Kings 7:30.

[238] Numbers 18:28.

[239] II Chronicles 31:4.

[240] Leviticus 22:9.

[241] Leviticus 22:16.

[242] Exodus 6:4.

[243] Deuteronomy 31:16.

[244] Isaiah 26:19.

[245] Ezekiel 27.

[246] Canticles 7:9.

[247] Deuteronomy 11:21.

[248] Deuteronomy 4:4.

[249] Deuteronomy 31:16.

[250] Numbers 15:31.

[251] Psalms 72:16.

[252] *The Babylonian Talmud,* Tractate Hullin, 142a. English translation by Eli Cashdan, in Epstein, *op. cit.,* (1948).

[253] Deuteronomy 22:7.

[254] Deuteronomy 5:16.

[255] Ezekiel 14:5.

[256] I Samuel 16:2.

[257] This word, which means 'another,' is the way in which Elisha b. Abuyah, the great scholar who became an apostate, is referred to. While his name is thus blotted out, his teachings are still repeated with respect.

[258] *Midrash Rabbah,* Ecclesiastes, 11:1. Edited by H. Freedman and Maurice Simon. English translation by A. Cohen (London, Soncino Press, 1939).

[259] Isaiah 55:1.

[260] Deuteronomy 23:4.

[261] Deuteronomy 23:5.

[262] Deuteronomy 23:8.

[263] In rabbinic legend, Rome, both pagan and Christian, was identified with the Jews' hereditary enemy, Edom, or the descendants of Esau.

[264] *Midrash Rabbah,* Lamentations, Proem II. English translation by A. Cohen, in Freedman and Simon, *op. cit.*

[265] Jeremiah 9:11.

[266] Jeremiah 9:11 f.

[267] Joshua 1:8.
[268] Psalms 127:1.
[269] Jeremiah 16:11.
[270] Daniel 8:12.
[271] Isaiah 24:21.
[272] Daniel 8:12.
[273] Proverbs 23:23.
[274] Daniel 8:12.
[275] Hosea 8:3.
[276] Proverbs 4:2.
[277] Genesis 27:22.
[278] Isaiah 5:24. The JPS translation reads: ". . . the tongue of fire devoureth the stubble"
[279] Obadiah 18.
[280] Isaiah 5:24.
[281] *Ibid.*
[282] *Ibid.*
[283] *Ibid.*
[284] Jeremiah 9:16.
[285] Hosea 7:13.
[286] Jeremiah 10:19.
[287] Amos 5:1.
[288] Jeremiah 9:16 f.
[289] Lamentations 1:1.

PRAYER

[1] I Samuel 2:1–10.
[2] *Cf.* selections on pp. 91–94.
[3] *Palestinian Talmud,* Tractate Berakhot, 7a. English translation by the editors.
[4] Deuteronomy 11:13.
[5] Daniel 6:21.
[6] Daniel 6:11.
[7] *Ibid.*
[8] *Ibid.*
[9] Psalms 55:18.
[10] I Samuel 1:13.
[11] *Ibid.*
[12] *The Babylonian Talmud,* Tractate Berakoth, 16b–17b. English translation by Maurice Simon, in Epstein, *op. cit.* (1948).
[13] Ecclesiastes 7:1.
[14] Proverbs 15:1.
[15] Psalms 111:10.
[16] Exodus 24:11.
[17] Additional Service for the New Year.
[18] From A. Dupont-Sommer, *The Dead Sea Scrolls: A Preliminary Survey.* Translated from the French by E. Margaret Rowley (Oxford, Basil Blackwell, 1952). Another translation from the Scrolls, with full scholarly and textual notes, has been made by Meir Wallenstein, *Hymns from the Judean Scrolls* (Manchester, Manchester University Press, 1950).

GLOSSARY

Ab: The fifth month of the Jewish calendar, corresponding to July-August

Abaddon: One of the words used for the abode of the dead

Academy of the Sky: The pious dead, who are thought to continue their studies and discussions in an assembly over which God presides

Accuser: Satan

Adonai: My Lord—one of the names of God

Aggaddah: The non-legal part of the old rabbinical literature

Altar: The brazen altar for burnt-offerings that stood in the court of the priests outside the Sanctuary

Am ha-arez: Literally "people of the land." Originally used to mean the Israelite people, as opposed to the special classes of nobility or priesthood, it came later to mean "the unlearned," as opposed to the Rabbis and students

Amora (**pl.,** *Amoraim*); **Amoraic Age:** A teacher whose name is mentioned in the Gemara of either Talmud (q.v.), as distinguished from a Tanna (q.v.). These teachers lived between 200 and 500 A.D.

Baraitha: Any Tannaitic tradition not included in the Mishnah

Bath Kol: A heavenly or divine voice which proclaims God's will or judgments; hence, an inspiration or revelation

Beth Din: Any rabbinical court; especially the "Beth Din ha-Gadol" or Great Sanhedrin which existed at the time of the Temple. It constituted the highest religious and civil authority after the destruction of the Temple to about the end of the third century A.D.

Court of the Israelites: The western part of the inner forecourt of the Temple

Court of the Priests: The inner area of the Temple court, containing the brazen altar for burnt-offerings

Court of the Women: The eastern part of the inner forecourt of the Temple

Day of Atonement (*Yom Kippur*): The holiest day of the Jewish year, on the 10th of Tishre, corresponding to mid-September-beginning of October

Demai: Products of the soil on which it is uncertain whether the

241

appropriate tithes have been paid; hence produce of uncertain status

Dumah: Name of the angel who has charge of the souls in the nether world (Rabbinical)

Elders: Distinguished men of each tribe, who took part in the government of the Hebrew commonwealth. Although the Bible nowhere defines their function, later writings speak of them as the forerunners of the Sanhedrin (q.v.) and as recipients of the Oral Law from Joshua

Ephod: An image placed in the sanctuary, apparently like the teraphim (q.v.)

Erub: The technical casuistic device whereby adjacent properties were amalgamated as one on the eve of Sabbath or Holy Days in order to mitigate the severity of the restrictions for the observance of these days

Gehinnom: The Hebrew name for hell; Gehenna is a corrupt form

Gemiluth Hasadim: Deeds of charity, the sympathetic sharing not only of material goods, but also of joy, sorrows, and even ideas

Great Abyss: The abode of the dead

Great Synagogue: The legislative body supposed to have been brought into being by Nehemiah immediately after the return from the Babylonian exile. The spiritual heirs of the Prophets

Haber (pl., *haberim*): A Hebrew word meaning "associate" or "companion." The term is used to refer to a member of a Pharisaic or other special cultic group, such as the Essenes

Hagiographa: The third major division of the O.T. in the Hebrew canon, containing the miscellaneous writings—Ruth, Psalms, Job, Proverbs, Canticles, Lamentations, Ecclesiastes, Daniel, Esther, Ezra-Nehemiah, Chronicles. See *Torah, Nebiim*

Halakhah: Legal sections of the rabbinical commentaries in contrast to *Aggaddah* (q.v.)

Halizah: The ceremony that releases a widow and her brother-in-law from the obligation of contracting a levirate marriage

Hanukkah: The Jewish Feast of Lights, or Feast of Dedication, celebrated for eight days beginning on the 25th of Kislev (usually mid-December)

Holy of Holies: The innermost room of the Sanctuary, in the Temple of Solomon, containing the Ark of the Covenant. The Holy of Holies was entered only once each year, by the High Priest on the Day of Atonement

Jeshurun: A poetic name for Israel

Kislev: The ninth month of the Jewish calendar, corresponding to November-December

Law: See Torah

Levirate: The obligation incumbent upon a brother-in-law or nearest of kin to marry his brother's childless widow. See Deuteronomy 25: 5–10

Mar (mari): Aramaic noun meaning "lord," used in Palestinian schools and later in Babylonia as equivalent of Rabbi

Midrash (pl., *Midrashim*): Homiletic interpretation of the Bible, in contrast to the codified legal interpretations of the *Mishnah* (q.v.)

Mishnah: The codified collections of laws made by Judah the Prince and his colleagues at the beginning of the third century A.D.

Mohel: The ritual surgeon who performs circumcision

Musaf: The "additional" offering, besides the regular morning and afternoon sacrifices, offered in the Temple, on Sabbaths, New Moons, the 3 major festivals, New Year and the Day of Atonement. After the destruction of the Temple, when prayer replaced sacrifice, the term *Musaf* was used for the additional prayer on these occasions

Nebiim: The prophets; the second major division of the Hebrew scriptural canon. See *Torah,* Hagiographa

New Year (*Rosh Hashanah*): The festival of the New Year celebrated on the 1st (in traditional circles, also the 2nd) of Tishre, corresponding to mid-September. New Year opens the most important period of the Jewish Year, the ten-day period of religious and moral rededication which closes with the Day of Atonement (q.v.)

Noahide: Any non-Israelite; the "noahide laws" (i.e., moral laws for the whole human race) were seven negative commandments: against (1) idolatry (2) adultery and incest (3) bloodshed (4) blasphemy (5) robbery (6) social injustice and (7) the eating of flesh cut from a living animal

Passover (*Pesach*): Jewish festival lasting 7 days from the 14th of Nisan (corresponding to the latter part of March and the first part of April). Originally probably an agricultural festival, it has become the festival reminiscent of the departure from Egypt

Pit: The abode of the dead

Porch: The portico of the Sanctuary (q.v.)

Rabbi: An expert in the Torah, a teacher

Rampart: The barrier surrounding the Temple area that non-Jews and those who were ritually unclean might not pass

Sages: A term used in general reference to the Rabbis and more specifically to the ancient Rabbis

Sanctuary: The actual temple building itself, the house of God, as distinguished from the surrounding courts and additional buildings. It contained an outer room (*hechal*) and the inner shrine (Holy of Holies, q.v.)

Sanhedrin: A rabbinical court, which had jurisdiction in civil as well as religious matters whenever the Jewish community was allowed self-government

Second Tithe: The tithe, ordained in Deuteronomy 14: 22–29, that was to be taken to Jerusalem and consumed there by the landowner and his family

Shedim: Demons

Shekinah: A term used to express the immanent aspect of God

Shema': The prayer recited as the confession of Jewish faith; originally only the one verse, Deuteronomy 6:4, the confession has been expanded in the liturgy to include Deuteronomy 6: 4–9; 11: 13–21 and Numbers 15: 37–41

Sheol-Abaddon: A combination of two of the words used for the abode of the dead

Shofar: A curved wind instrument made of ram's horn, used ritually on several occasions in the Jewish year, notably on New Year's Day

Sifra: The Halakhic Midrash to Leviticus

Sons of Heaven: The angels

Stripes, the punishment of: Corporal punishment imposed by Jewish law for offenses too mild for capital punishment, used instead of imprisonment or fines

Tabernacle: The shrine in which the Ark of the Covenant was kept prior to the building of the Temple

Talmud (pl., *Talmudim*): Two commentaries on the Mishnah (q.v.); each reprints the text of the Mishnah with the commentary, called *Gemara*. The Mishnah with the Palestinian Gemara, known as the Palestinian Talmud (sometimes Jerusalem Talmud), was compiled about the middle of the fourth century A.D. The Mishnah with the Babylonian Gemara was compiled during the fifth century A.D.

Tanna (pl., *Tannaim*); **Tannaitic age:** Teacher, applied to the scholars who lived in the period from about 10 A.D. to about 220 A.D.

Tefillah, 'Amida, Shemoneh Esreh: Various names for the central prayer of the Jewish liturgy

Temple Mount: The site of the Temple, Mount Moriah (Mount Zion), a hill about 2470 feet high

Teraphim: Images used in primitive Semetic worship, possibly continued into the biblical period

Terumah: The heave-offering prescribed for the support of the priests in Numbers 18: 8–11

Tishre: The seventh month of the calendar, corresponding to September-October

Torah: The Law, *par excellence.* The first division of the Hebrew scriptural canon, comprising the Pentateuch. See *Nebiim,* Hagiographa. By extension, the term, which means "teaching" is used to cover all later interpretations of the religious code—the oral Torah supplementing the written Torah

Tosefta: A collection of teachings and traditions of the Tannaim (q.v.) supplementary to the Mishnah (q.v.)

Waving: A ceremony through which certain sacrificial offerings had to pass before being placed on the altar.

Weights, Measures, and Coinage

Cubit: Equals 6 handbreadths; the length of the forearm to the elbow

Denar: Originally a weight of 3.585 grams; later a coin containing this weight of silver

Ephah: A Hebrew dry measure equivalent to 36.44 liters

Issar: A small copper coin of the Talmudic period worth 1/24 of a silver denar

Kor: A Hebrew measure equal to 364.4 liters

Mina: A Hebrew measure of weight equal to 573.6 grams

Omer: A biblical dry measure equal to 3.644 liters

Perutah: A small coin of the Talmudic period worth 1/192 of a silver denar

Seah: A Hebrew dry measure equal to 13,184.44 cubic centimeters

Sela: A weight equal to 4 denars, or about 14.34 grams

Shekel: A Hebrew weight (also coin) whose equivalent at different periods varied from 11.95 grams to 14.34 grams

Talent: A Hebrew weight equal to 21,510 grams

Zuz: A Hebrew measure of weight equal to 3.585 grams.